THE PATH YOU MAKE

*A woman's search for purpose
walking the Via Francigena
from Canterbury to Rome*

Kym Wilson

Cover design and interior layout by Euan Monaghan
Map of the route by Dijana Vilic

THE ART OF PILGRIMAGE © 1998, 2012 by Phil
Cousineau used with permission from Red Wheel Weiser,
LLC Newburyport, MA www.redwheelweiser.com.

PILGRIM'S BLESSING by Macrina Wiederkehr
used with permission from Macrina Wiederkehr
http://www.macrinawiederkehr.com.

Epub ISBN 978-0-6482864-1-7
Print ISBN 978-0-6482864-0-0

www.kymwilson.com.au

For pilgrims, seekers, and anyone on the path of healing. May this book inspire and encourage your journey.

For Mum, there was pain and suffering, but there was also love.

Contents

Map of the Via Francigena

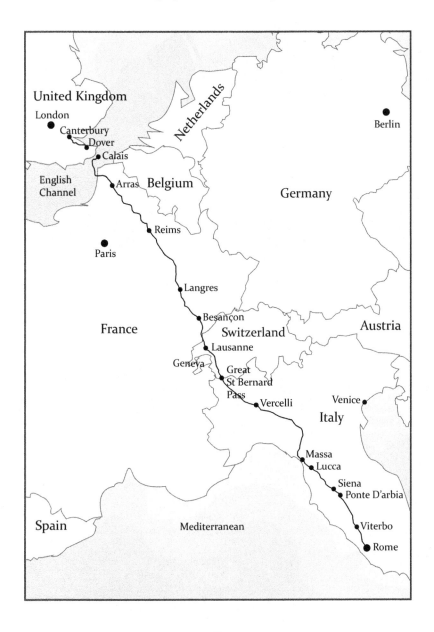

The route day by day

Day	Date	Town	Country	Distance (km)
0	31-Aug	Canterbury	England	0
1	1-Sep	Barham	England	12
2	2-Sep	Dover	England	22
3	3-Sep	Wissant via Calais	France	22
4	4-Sep	Guînes	France	21
5	5-Sep	Licques	France	21
6	6-Sep	Wisques	France	23.5
7	7-Sep	Auchy-au-Bois	France	29.5
8	8-Sep	Bruay-la-Buissiere	France	24
9	9-Sep	Arras	France	38.5
10	10-Sep	Bapaume	France	26
11	11-Sep	Peronne	France	28.5
12	12-Sep	Trefcon	France	22
13	13-Sep	Tergnier	France	34.5

14	14-Sep	Laon	France	32
15	15-Sep	Corbeny	France	27
16	16-Sep	Reims	France	30
17	17-Sep	Rest day in Reims	France	0
18	18-Sep	Conde-sur-Marne	France	33
19	19-Sep	Chalons-en-Champagne	France	20.5
20	20-Sep	le-meix-Tiercelin	France	38
21	21-Sep	Brienne-le-Château	France	31.5
22	22-Sep	Bar-sur-Aube	France	28
23	23-Sep	Châteauvillain	France	38
24	24-Sep	Mormant	France	22.5
25	25-Sep	Langres	France	28
26	26-Sep	Champlitte	France	41
27	27-Sep	Dampierre-sur-Salon	France	17.5
28	28-Sep	Choye via Gy	France	34
29	29-Sep	Besançon	France	36
30	30-Sep	Nods	France	36.5
31	1-Oct	Pontarlier	France	28.5
32	2-Oct	Orbe via Jougne	Switzerland	39.5
33	3-Oct	Lausanne	Switzerland	33
34	4-Oct	Vevey	Switzerland	25.5

35	5-Oct	Rest day in Vevey	Switzerland	0
36	6-Oct	Aigle	Switzerland	24
37	7-Oct	Saint Maurice	Switzerland	14
38	8-Oct	Martigny	Switzerland	16
39	9-Oct	Orsières	Switzerland	21
40	10-Oct	Bourg-Saint-Pierre	Switzerland	14
41	11-Oct	Aosta via Étroubles	Italy	16
42	12-Oct	Châtillon	Italy	29
43	13-Oct	Ponte-Saint-Martin	Italy	31
44	14-Oct	Ivrea	Italy	22.5
45	15-Oct	Viverone	Italy	22
46	16-Oct	Santhià	Italy	16
47	17-Oct	Vercelli	Italy	28
48	18-Oct	Mortara via Robbio	Italy	34.5
49	19-Oct	Garlasco	Italy	23.5
50	20-Oct	Pavia	Italy	26
51	21-Oct	Rest day in Pavia	Italy	0
52	22-Oct	Santa Cristina	Italy	29.5
53	23-Oct	Orio Litta	Italy	16.5
54	24-Oct	Piacenza	Italy	21.5
55	25-Oct	Fiorenzuola d'Arda	Italy	36

56	26-Oct	Fidenza	Italy	24
57	27-Oct	Fornovo di Taro	Italy	36
58	28-Oct	Berceto via Cassio	Italy	30
59	29-Oct	Pontremoli via Cisa Pass	Italy	29
60	30-Oct	Aulla	Italy	24.5
61	31-Oct	Sarzana	Italy	16.5
62	1-Nov	Rest day in Cinque Terre	Italy	0
63	2-Nov	Rest day in Cinque Terre	Italy	0
64	3-Nov	Sarzana to Marina di Massa	Italy	27
65	4-Nov	Pietrasanta	Italy	12.5
66	5-Nov	San Donato (Lucca)	Italy	32
67	6-Nov	Rest day in Lucca	Italy	0
68	7-Nov	Altopascio	Italy	18
69	8-Nov	San Miniato	Italy	26.5
70	9-Nov	Gambassi Terme	Italy	24
71	10-Nov	San Gimignano	Italy	12.5
72	11-Nov	Monteriggioni	Italy	31.5
73	12-Nov	Siena	Italy	16
74	13-Nov	Rest day in Siena	Italy	0
75	14-Nov	Ponte d'Arbia	Italy	28
76	15-Nov	San Quirico d'Orcia	Italy	27.5

77	16-Nov	Radicofani	Italy	33
78	17-Nov	Acquapendente	Italy	32
79	18-Nov	Montefiascone via Bolsena	Italy	37
80	19-Nov	Viterbo	Italy	18
81	20-Nov	Vetralla	Italy	18
82	21-Nov	Sutri via Capranica	Italy	19.5
83	22-Nov	Campagnano di Roma	Italy	25.5
84	23-Nov	La Storta	Italy	19
85	24-Nov	Rome	Italy	17
			Total	*2020*

One—The call

"Oh no! I'm not interested in walking that far. Ever!"

That was my response several years ago when my employer asked me to join a team that would walk 50 kilometres to raise money for the Leprosy Mission. I can't help but laugh kindly at that younger version of myself who scoffed at the idea and was adamant that she would never walk that far. I don't believe everything in our lives is predetermined, but there are some things that life wants us to experience. If at first we turn our backs on those things or head in a different direction, life has a miraculous way of finding an alternative way in or choosing another way to speak to us so that we hear and understand. It calls us forward again and again to come down the path it wants us to follow, until finally we say yes and take those steps.

At the time, I had been heading down a career path that I didn't want to pursue. I had entered the financial planning industry with the intention of becoming a financial planner to help people by using what I thought were my strongest gifts, my problem-solving and analytical skills. I joined the industry just as a period of prolonged market downturn commenced, and my romantic notion of helping people reach their financial goals was quashed, to be replaced by the commercial reality of sales targets and what happens if you don't meet them. I decided that I didn't want to be a financial planner. Instead,

I went down the management path. I worked hard and was handed responsibility and opportunity. I built what I thought was the perfect life. I was an executive manager in an ASX-listed financial services company and had amazing career potential. I earned a six-figure salary, lived in a trendy suburb of Melbourne with my partner of five years, and used all of my annual leave to travel to tropical destinations so I could pursue my love of scuba diving. Then slowly, my life started unravelling and I didn't know why.

My personal relationship was failing. The pressure at work was high and I was struggling to stay on top of my workload and the politics. I cried on the way to work, on the way home and often in bed at night after my partner had fallen asleep. I isolated myself from friends in an effort to hide how imperfect my 'perfect' life was. A restructure at work gave me the opportunity to relocate to Sydney for a six-month project before returning to Melbourne in a new role. I jumped at the idea of a change of scenery, the chance to have my own space again and the opportunity to try something new. The role was not yet defined, but my manager promised me that if I didn't like it, he would find me something else. I trusted him. The risk was hedged, and it felt like a safe move. As the project progressed and I wrote the position description for my new role based on what the company needed, I realised I really didn't like the job. It was heavily focused on investment products, which were my least favourite aspect of financial planning.

I became increasingly anxious about returning to Melbourne to do work that I really disliked, so I had a meeting with my manager to hold him to his promise and ask for something else. He told me there was nothing else for now, but he asked me a question that turned out to be an unexpected gift.

"What do you want to do?"

I looked at him blankly. Dumbfounded. I hadn't thought about that for years.

What *did* I want to do?

My mind raced through blankness, looking for something to settle on. It was like a slot machine with reels that kept spinning. My tongue was silent. No words came. I had no answer. I didn't know what I wanted to do. Panicked, I sought the advice of a careers coach. I rushed the four coaching sessions into the three weeks before I was due to move back to Melbourne. We worked through psychometric tests and questionnaires, only for her to tell me in the final session that I should be a business analyst. I walked away feeling hopeless. Business analysis was already a component of my work, and although I enjoyed it and was good at it, I knew it wasn't the answer. I resigned myself to returning to Melbourne and dreading going to work in a job I really didn't want to do, without having any escape route in mind.

We don't always make our best decisions when we are panicked. I was desperate, and as I couldn't answer the question for myself about what I wanted to do, I hoped someone else would answer it for me. The thing was that I didn't want anyone else to tell me what I was good at; I wanted to know what my heart wanted to do. What could I do that would bring me alive every day, using my gifts and abilities to make a real difference in the world? Although I had a sense of it at the time, it would take me a few years to learn that life isn't about other people's answers. It's about finding and following our own, without needing to be validated externally.

Back in Melbourne, my relationship unravelled completely and I moved out to start a new life on my own. I grieved over the ending of that relationship but also started dreaming about what I wanted uniquely for me. I looked for the answer in books but I didn't find it, so I tried to make one up within the framework of what I knew. With the help of a colleague, I identified a new role that we thought the business needed and that I would love to do. I wrote a proposal and submitted it to the executive committee two weeks before I went on a post break-up holiday to India and the Similan Islands. I felt confident that the committee would love the idea, so I was surprised when they didn't give me an indicative answer before I started my leave. I had just passed through immigration at the airport and was walking towards the boarding gate when one of the executives phoned me.

"Your proposal was great, but..."

How many dreams and apologies have been let down by that one small word 'but'? I was angry and upset, although it only lasted until I boarded the plane. I was going on an amazing adventure, so I decided to leave my worries at the airport and only collect them when I returned.

After I recovered from the initial culture shock of New Delhi—the crowds, the intense staring, the dirt, the rubbish, the beggars and the poverty—I fell in love with India. I enjoyed sailing down the Ganges River with children running along the banks, laughing and giggling and calling for us to take their photos, and seeing the villagers who washed themselves and their clothes in the shallows, waving and smiling at us as we passed. I discovered a feeling I had not experienced in a long time—not through my relationship breakdown, nor in my career crisis or the lingering grief from my mum's death ten years ago. I felt a lightness of being, free and alive. I felt joy. My heart was overflowing with pure and abundant happiness.

From India I went to Thailand to scuba dive in the Andaman Sea around the Similan Islands. On my last night on the boat before I commenced the transit back home, I sat on the top deck beneath the star-filled sky. A warm breeze brushed my hair and made the boat bob gently on the calm sea. As I drank beer with the tour leader and one of the divemasters, all I could think over and over was how cool their lives were, getting to do something they loved every day. On the plane back to Melbourne, I stared out the window at the same star-filled sky, aware of this deep yearning within me to follow my love of scuba diving, to travel and be free for a while.

Once I disembarked from the plane in Melbourne, I picked up the worries I had left behind, but I returned to work still hopeful of a resolution to my job dilemma. My manager had promised me he would find me something else. I was sure he would stay true to his word and that we could work this situation out, except we didn't, or at least not in the way I hoped. Once more, I was told there was nothing else in the company for me right now, but they valued me and wanted me to stay. I cried. I got angry. The way I saw it, my manager had broken his promise. As I started to accept the reality of my situation, I realised I had three choices: accept the situation and stay, resign and leave immediately, or resign after I found another job. I was scared. I had never left a job without having another one to go to, but I didn't want to spend the next few months job-hunting while hating my time at work and counting down the hours until I could escape the drudgery.

I decided to resign, declaring this was my Year of Change. One week later, I was unemployed with no job to go to but the intention of finding a six-month contract position and then travelling for a year. My mind tried to tell me it was a bad idea, a waste of money, having worked hard to save for something more practical with investment growth potential, like a house, and this was a career-sabotaging move. But the fire of longing was now simmering inside me and it wasn't going to be extinguished easily. I was unemployed for two enjoyable months then I received two phone calls on the same day about the same six-month contract position with some ex-colleagues in a new business, working on a project that was perfectly suited to my skills. I was reluctant to return to work and an office, but the opportunity seemed to have been divinely offered. It was the perfect role and perfect timing. I took the job.

Outside of work, I tried to plan my twelve-month sabbatical. I knew I wanted to complete my rescue diver course and maybe a divemaster course as well. I also wanted to see the temples of Angkor Wat and definitely to return to India, as she had gotten under my skin. But no matter how hard I tried or how creative I was, I couldn't formulate a plan that seemed to work. I knew what I wanted to do first, but not what I wanted to do in three months' time, and I didn't understand why I couldn't figure this out. My career had been all about planning. I had written hundreds of financial plans, showing clients how to reach their goals. I had been involved in many projects, all of which required planning, for without a good plan a project risks failure. I knew all of this, but I was unable to plan my own life. Frustrated and scared that I didn't know what the hell I was doing, I cried. In the end, I did the only thing I could do. I gave up planning. I decided just to begin at my starting point, my rescue diver course in Phuket. I booked a one-way plane ticket and two weeks' accommodation, but I was still chasing that question of what I wanted to do with my life.

On the plane, I devoured *Thirty-something and Over It* by Kasey Edwards, who woke up one day and realised that she never wanted to go to work again. I was sure that this book held the answer for me, and if I found it I could just have a nice three-month holiday and go back to Melbourne and live a normal life again. Reading the book, I discovered that Kasey found her answer. She wanted to be a writer. To be honest, I was disappointed that she didn't want to dedicate her life to achieving world peace, finding the cure for cancer or being the next Mother Teresa. A life-changing purpose should be grand, shouldn't it? I put the book away and decided to let go of my searching, to have fun and follow my heart for a while.

Once in Thailand, I started swinging through the jungle of my life, following my intuition about where to go and what to do next. I trained in Muay Thai while undertaking my rescue diver and divemaster courses. I met interesting people from all over the world and made new friends. We shared dinners and beers and sometimes joined the crazy party that happens every night in Soi Bangla in Patong. My German friend, Ina, taught me how to ride a motorbike and patiently followed me as I rode at only 20 kilometres per hour, scared and wobbling, until I gained confidence and speed. I took a Portuguese lover. It was a relationship that I knew wouldn't last but I was intrigued by his free spirit and he was too attractive for me to say no, despite the fact that he openly told me he was seeing someone else and wanted the experience of being in love with two women at the same time.

On a whim, I jumped over to Koh Phi Phi in search of manta rays and whale sharks, and then went on to Koh Phagnan for a ten-day fasting detox, where I met Viv, a vivacious Irish woman with a wicked sense of humour and joy for life. To this day, both Viv and Ina are two of my dearest friends. When my dive courses were completed, I spent three months travelling around the rest of Thailand, as well as through Malaysia, Cambodia and Indonesia. I returned to Phuket to apply for a visa for India and spend time with Ina. I was tired after months of moving from place to place, and thinking about travelling around India made me feel even more tired. I was surprised to realise that I didn't want to go. It was such a change of heart, given that I had longed to return there ever since I left. Instead, I decided to stay in Phuket. I completed my open water scuba instructor certification and met my Italian love, David. I didn't know it at the time, but this relationship would later lead me to discover the pilgrimage path.

At the end of the scuba diving high season, I returned to Australia to work through Melbourne's autumn and winter, and top up my savings so I could go back to Phuket again in the next high season, to dive and be with David. Returning to Melbourne in winter, resuming standard working hours in an office in a glass and concrete city tower, and commuting by train, surrounded by the tired and despondent energy of those around me, was an unexpected shock to my system. I felt caged and my spirit felt contained. I missed being outdoors. I missed riding my motorbike to the pier and being on the boat on the way out to my underwater playground. I missed paying attention to the cycles of the moon and the weather to know what effect it would have on the sea and diving conditions. I missed the warmth. I missed being barefoot with wild and tangled hair. I missed lying on the sand, swimming in the sea and my spirit merging with the tangerine sunsets that I watched almost every day.

On my lunch breaks, I walked to the Flagstaff Gardens near the office so I could lie on the earth beneath the trees, feeling protected and nurtured by this small oasis in the city. I moved in with some friends in Richmond, only four kilometres from my office, and began to walk to and from work through Yarra Park, past the iconic Melbourne Cricket Ground, through Fitzroy Gardens with its avenue of elm trees losing their golden leaves, through Treasury Gardens, and down along the 'Paris end' of Collins Street, which shimmered silver and purple on damp winter nights. At first I walked to escape the depressing energy of the train and for some exercise. Soon I was walking because I loved going through the parks and gardens, taking step after step on the earth, and observing how the trees and the light changed as the seasons progressed. I would arrive at work feeling energised and happy. Walking saved my spirit from withering as I discovered the wonder of my hometown on foot.

I returned to Thailand and at the end of the next high season, I followed David to Italy to spend the summer with him. He wanted to spend the first week catching up with his friends, so I started exploring different options for how I could spend that time alone. I wanted to visit the Cinque Terre, the five clifftop towns on the Italian Riviera in the north-west of Italy. With its clusters of colourful buildings surrounded by wine terraces on the rugged cliffs overlooking the turquoise and sapphire Ligurian Sea, it held a mystical appeal. I also wanted to visit the hilltop villages of Tuscany that I had seen between fields of sunflowers, olive groves and grapevines as I travelled from Florence to Siena on a bus tour of Europe in my twenties, but I didn't want to do the typical tourist bus tour from village to village. Now that I liked walking, I considered completing part of the Camino Francés, the most popular of the pilgrimage routes to Santiago de Compostela in Spain, except it was in the wrong direction, heading away from Italy, and it was far too long. However, in exploring this idea, I stumbled across a different pilgrimage trail I had never heard of: the Via Francigena.

This was an ancient pilgrim trail, spanning 2000 kilometres, that started in Canterbury in England and ended at St Peter's Square in the Vatican City in Italy. Curious, I investigated it and discovered that it not only passed through Tuscany, but there was a perfect section of it that started in San Miniato, just outside Florence, and ended in San Quirico d'Orcia, covering 120 kilometres over six days. A specialist travel company could book my accommodation and transport my main bag from town to town, so I would only have to walk with a daypack. I buzzed with nervous excitement. I could walk through Tuscany. Except the idea was crazy. I had never walked long-distance before. I had never really wanted to until then. I sat with the idea for a week to be sure. When the week passed and I still felt excited, I booked.

I really had no idea what I was getting myself into. It was only after I arrived in London and had received and flicked through the guidebook that I realised this might be a little more challenging than a pleasant stroll through the Tuscan countryside between hilltop villages. The guidebook contained instructions like "ford the stream", as well as stating compass headings. I bought a tiny compass from a sailing shop in Greenwich at the last minute, just in case, and tied it to my dive computer watch with a hairband. It was a wise decision, because I got lost—a lot. I cried—a lot. On the first day, I walked in circles for forty minutes trying to find the next sign. I used my tiny compass to navigate my way down south from the wrong hilltop village. I climbed through a construction site under the yellow steel arm of a massive earthmover and squeezed through the locked wire gate on the other side to get out. I ran around the blind bends of roads heavy with traffic and non-existent edges, squealing and praying that I didn't die that day. My trail runners were too small for my feet. My toes throbbed painfully, and my feet and knees ached constantly. The nail bed of the big toe on my right foot turned black. Three months later, the nail fell off. I learned that walking through a city is not the same thing as walking through countryside and woodlands. Turns out it was more like hiking. While I had been told it was a popular time of year to do this walk, I saw only four other hikers and spent my days walking alone. Despite the challenges, I loved it: making my own way slowly from place to place through Tuscany, connecting with the earth beneath my feet and the ever-changing sky above me, and experiencing the landscape in a way I never could have if I were in a bus or train or car.

I didn't make it all the way. By the time I arrived in Murlo, my feet were so swollen that I couldn't get them back in my trail runners. David drove all the way from his hometown near Ancona to pick me up, and together we drove to San Quirico d'Orcia, where my accommodation had been booked and paid. Although my trek was over, this was only the beginning. The seed of a new dream had been planted in me. I wanted to walk the whole trail one day, all the way from Canterbury to St Peter's Square in Rome. One day I would do it. Sometime in the future, whenever that may be. It came to greet me sooner than I expected.

After my relationship with David ended, I returned to Australia. I loved living in Phuket but I didn't want to work in diving and I couldn't stay in Thailand without working. I felt I was meant to be doing something more with my life. I just didn't know what it was. The question that led me away also brought me back. I returned to work in financial planning. This time it was just a fill-in position, working three days per week to give me enough income to live while I wrote a book and figured out what to do next. Fifteen months later I finished the first draft of my book but was still figuring out what else I was going to do when I was made redundant. It was swift and severe. Half of our small organisation was let go instantly on the instruction of the new owners. Suddenly, I was swimming in a world of new possibilities, with time and space to contemplate the future, thanks to my small redundancy payment. And I had a back catalogue of experiences to remind me that everything always turns out okay, often better than okay, in ways I never imagined. There was the contract opportunity that was delivered to me by two ex-colleagues for the exact six-month period I'd hoped for, paying me exactly what I wanted, and perfectly suited to my skills and experience while also offering me a new challenge. And although I was scared that my sabbaticals would send me broke and negatively impact on my future employability, I was offered contracts every time I returned to Australia during the diving low season in Phuket that coincided with my return date and the length of time I was available to work.

After being made redundant, there were days when I was so happy to be free that even without a job I felt there was great purpose to my life and reason to get out of bed in the morning. Then there were days when I had no commitments and no idea of what I was going to do next. On those days, anxiety took over and my bed held me tight. I was at a crossroads again. I didn't want to stay working in financial planning, but I still didn't know what else I wanted to do. Two weeks after my redundancy, I had brunch with my friend, Holly. She had resigned and left her job the same day as I had, to try and make her living from trading foreign exchange. She told me she hoped to be retired by November, which was only five months away. *Retired by November.* That was a dream. A big, out there, unconventional, clearly stated dream. Although I knew nothing about her personal financial circumstances, I wondered if she was being realistic, as she was only in her early thirties, but it made me think about my own dreams. I hid them away out of sight when I returned from my holiday.

Practical Me, the part that wanted to keep me safe and secure and wished I were a little more conventional than I'd turned out to be, put my dreams in the wardrobe on the grounds of de-cluttering. I retrieved my vision board from the top shelf, unrolled it and laid it out on my bed. In the top left corner of the board were images of the ocean, her creatures and scuba diving. The pictures included a female scuba diver hovering in the water in a meditation posture, a whale shark, a manta ray, a turtle, a black-tip reef shark, a frogfish, pygmy seahorses, ghost pipefish and my favourite little goby, guarding the hole of a digging shrimp.

There were words there too: *to be one with the sea, voice of the ocean, discover the wonders, immerse.* All of this represented my love of the sea and diving and expressed my desire to maintain this as a regular part of my life. I had just returned from diving in Komodo, where I had seen almost all of these creatures and experienced the wonder of the sea.

As I looked at the vision board, it was the bottom left-hand corner that drew my attention. It showed two hikers walking along a trail down the side of a hill, a Tuscan farmhouse surrounded by conifers and mist at sunrise, a picture of Manarola (one of the colourful cliff-top villages of the Cinque Terre in Italy), and the words *pilgrim trail, adventure, live with soul.* I had created the board months ago and conveniently forgotten what I had glued on there. Seeing it again, I felt excited and teary. I knew this was it. This is what I wanted to do next. I had stuck it on there as an out-there-maybe-one-day-a-long-time-away-maybe-never kind of dream, and now all the reasons I shouldn't do it started racing through my mind.

You didn't save any money this year, and you didn't save for this.

It's expensive.

It's a long walk.

It is summer, so it will be too hot.

Everyone goes on holidays in August. You won't be able to find any accommodation.

What if something happens to you?

You don't know anything about hiking. What if you can't finish it? What a waste of money that would be.

But the loudest objection I heard was the question of why on earth would I want to walk 2000 kilometres. What was the point of that? The truth was that I didn't know what the point was yet. Walking 2000 kilometres didn't make any sense, but there was also another voice in my head, reminding me that I had no job and I had to move house soon. In some ways, this was the perfect timing. What if I never had this freedom again?

Another thought entered my mind. *Where there's a will, there's a way.* These words found their way into my life when I was eight years old. They were the motto of the Australian team for the 1984 Summer Olympics in Los Angeles and were on a sticker that was given to me at school in the lead-up to the Games, along with a picture of mascot Willy the Koala, dressed in a green and gold tracksuit. I had stuck it on my wardrobe amid many other stickers, much to my mum's dismay, for they never peeled off cleanly, always leaving a sticky layer of paper. I loved that sticker more for Willy than the words on it, but they had affected me more than I realised, carried as dormant seeds that only sprouted now when I needed to know their meaning. *Where there's a will, there's a way.* If we want the dream enough, then we find a way to make it happen. Our authentic desires are more powerful than we realise. Then I heard the words of my friend and yoga teacher, Joey. Whenever I hesitated to go into a yoga pose I didn't particularly love, such as boat pose, or when I hesitated to go a little deeper, Joey always said, "If not now, when?" These words began repeating over and over in my head. *If not now, when? If not now, when?* If I didn't do it now, I may never do it.

The heart wants what the heart wants. There was no logical reason for me to even consider walking so far, but as I sat with my longing for adventure, my mind soon accepted that my heart wanted to go on a very long walk. Within a week, I stopped fighting the urge to go halfway around the world to walk this long and unknown path. Instead, I started making preparations.

Two—First steps

Canterbury to Barham

Canterbury Cathedral glowed a soft cream in the mid-afternoon sun on the last day of August. Its three belltowers soared towards the cloudless sky. Scaffolding covered the south wall of the transept, as part of the ongoing restoration works to the pale creamy French stones. The seven, high-arched stained glass windows built into the nave appeared black rather than colourful. Founded by St Augustine after his arrival in England in AD 597, the cathedral is one of the oldest churches in England and also one of the most important, as it is the seat of the Archbishop of Canterbury, the worldwide leader of Anglican churches. While Canterbury was an important spiritual centre ever since St Augustine arrived, it became a major pilgrimage destination after Archbishop Thomas Becket was murdered in the cathedral in 1170 and was later venerated as a saint.[1]

Before I left Australia, I emailed the cathedral to arrange for a pilgrim blessing, and now I stood outside the information office within the cathedral grounds, waiting for the Canon Clare. She was instantly recognisable as she strolled towards me wearing her long black religious robes. After exchanging greetings, she stamped the first box in my pilgrim passport. Also called a credential, it proved I was a bona fide pilgrim and not just a tourist trying to find a cheap place to stay. I could have the passport stamped at each of the towns I stayed in, and upon arrival in Rome, I could present it at a special office inside the Vatican to receive a testimonium to certify my pilgrim journey. The stamp was just an oval of black ink with the cathedral's name and insignia in it, but it was my first credential and signified that my journey really was beginning.

Canon Clare led me to a private chapel within the cathedral. I stood next to her, facing the small altar with my head bowed, as she prayed for me and for my protection. Next, she pulled out a bright yellow laminated card the same size as my pilgrim passport and read a poem called 'Pilgrim's Blessing' by Macrina Wiederkehr.

"May the feet that walked before you bless your every step.

May the weather that's important be the weather of your heart...

May the broken world ride upon your shoulders.

May you carry your joy and your grief in the backpack of your soul."

These were the words of the poem that resonated most deeply with me. For so many years, my world had felt broken. I had carried more grief than joy within my heart that I tried to lock down to stop myself from drowning in sorrow. My mum died when I was twenty years old. She was only fifty-three and had a muscular dystrophy, which caused the muscles in her face, shoulders and arms, along with other skeletal muscles, to progressively weaken and die. The illness affected her severely. She was confined to bed from the time I was eleven years old and was only able to leave the house in a wheelchair. Although she could still walk, her legs might give way without any notice and she would crash to the floor. Her knees were constantly covered in deep and painful carpet burns, and she was in constant pain as the muscle weakness put strain on her joints. Many nights, my brother and I took it in turns to pummel her lower legs with our fists, which either lessened her pain or distracted from it.

Mum knew that she would die younger than most. Intuitively, she started making preparations in the twelve months prior to her death: talking to my brother and I regularly about her dying, writing goodbye letters, buying final gifts, knitting a box full of booties for the grandchildren she knew she would never hold. But none of this prepared me for the pain of losing her. When she died, I ran for my life, first to get away from the place where she died and later by not talking about her. Whenever someone mentioned her, I said little or changed the topic to keep the tidal wave of grief inside where it couldn't be seen. To talk about her and her passing, and to fully feel the grief of her loss was so overwhelming that I felt like I would be swamped and drowned by a thirty foot wave. It was only in the previous twelve months that I finally faced my grief and pain.

I started working with Myree, a counsellor, coach and healer, to figure out what I was going to do with my life, only to discover my grief from Mum's death and unresolved childhood wounds standing right in front of me, blocking my path, and begging for my love and attention. Hurt people hurt other people. My mum was a hurt woman who sometimes lashed out with words and silence that hurt me. Mum inherited some of her hurt from her mother, my nana. When Nana was a young girl, around thirteen years old, her mother died, and she was sent to live with an uncle where something so bad happened to her that she never spoke about it, not even with my grandfather. All we know is that she pleaded with her children and grandchildren to never drink alcohol. The grief, trauma and relational wounds that Nana experienced but was never able to heal were passed onto my mum and Mum passed hers onto me. I had always described my relationship with Mum as difficult, but I didn't realise that my most frightening and painful interactions with her were emotionally abusive, and my experience of it was trauma. Myree named it for me and helped me to reintegrate the parts of myself that had become lost or stuck back in time. A cycle of this healing had just come to a natural completion when I was made redundant. To honour the healing that had taken place between us, I intended to light candles for Mum in the churches I stopped at along the way.

This pilgrimage was to be a sacred journey, one of love and remembrance, while I was also seeking the answer to my purpose in life and the next step I should take. Although I would walk alone, I hoped my path would be blessed by those pilgrims who had walked before me, as the words of Macrina Wiederkehr's poem said, but also that my steps would bless those that would follow mine, as a return offering. Having felt broken and now healed, I wanted to consciously carry compassion as a blessing for a world in pain. I hoped I could receive with grace all the challenges that the path and nature would throw at me along the way.

After Canon Clare and I recited the Lord's Prayer together, the blessing was complete and I felt the sanctity of the journey I was about to begin. Canon Clare led me back to the main part of the cathedral. I stood staring into the nave, where tourists wandered around snapping photos. I wanted to be alone to let the blessing sink in, so I walked out the main entrance and into the cloisters and cathedral grounds where there were fewer tourists. Later, on my way back to the hotel, I passed by the information centre to see if Canon Clare had left a copy of the poem for me as she had promised. The office was already closed for the day, but there was an envelope jutting out from beneath the window. I picked it up and could see the yellow laminated card through the envelope's clear window face. My name was written on the envelope in blue ink, and with it was a short note: "We pray for pilgrims every day, so you will be amongst them. Go well!" I clutched the envelope to my chest for a moment, touched by the kind words it contained, then slipped it inside the back cover of my pilgrim credential and into my waist bag to keep it close.

I woke early on that first day of September and got out of bed to write in my journal. I sat in the old leather-padded chair at the round wooden table next to the window, through which I could see the cathedral as the bells tolled, calling Christians to Holy Mass. In just over six hours, the walking part of my pilgrimage would commence. The bells echoed my solemn excitement. Writing down my thoughts, feelings and experiences was important to me, not only as a way of fully capturing, exploring and deepening my pilgrimage experience, but also so I could share it with others through the blog I had been writing since I had left on my initial yearlong sabbatical. I hoped that my blog would enable those who may never have the chance to go on pilgrimage or walk this particular route to experience it through my words and photos, and that it may also help and bless the steps of other pilgrims who walked behind me. I had brought my iPad mini with me in a keyboard case so I could write and post on my blog every night if I had wi-fi access. I would also use it to access email and Facebook to stay in touch with family and friends, and in addition, it held the three Lightfoot guidebooks that provided directions for the whole route, as well as Pocket Earth, an offline digital map that showed roads and off-road walking tracks.

After breakfast, I visited the cathedral again. Sitting in a wooden pew, I closed my eyes and spoke silently to the God I knew from when I was a little girl, asking for guidance and support as I walked. Then I joined the throng of tourists admiring the cathedral and taking photos. At the back of the cathedral, a lone candle sat on the stone floor, marking the place where St Thomas Becket, once Archbishop of Canterbury, was murdered. In a small enclave, I found an altar of candles and lit the first candle of this journey for my mum. I watched the flame flicker and felt like she was there with me in that moment, blessing my journey. I ate lunch, and then it was time to leave. With my backpack on, I stood for a few minutes in front of the Via Francigena stone marker that was laid on the grass to the left of the cathedral's main entrance, hesitating before I took my first step. I had made the decision to embark on this walk only ten weeks earlier, and it felt surreal that I was really here and about to begin. There was no fanfare, no cheering crowd, no one to see me off. It was just me, alone, taking that first step and then the next and the next until I walked out through the cathedral gate for the last time.

My first destination was not directly on the Via Francigena trail. I wanted to ease into the journey, and this did not include walking 30 kilometres to Dover on day one. I had found a lady in Barham, only 12 kilometres from Canterbury, who offered bed and breakfast free of charge to pilgrims. I liked the idea of being welcomed into the home of a stranger on my first night, of accepting help and support, which is something I sometimes struggled to do. I walked out of Canterbury along the North Downs Way, a long-distance walking route, then onto a bitumen road through the town of Patrixbourne. Walking along the edge of the road, I squealed as a large truck passed by too close. This was to be a common reaction whenever I walked along roads heavy with traffic, but soon I was walking along quiet country roads and on grassy public footpaths, finding my own way to Barham.

My backpack weighed at least fourteen kilograms with water and snacks. After only two hours, I desperately wanted to get it off my back. I couldn't get it to sit comfortably on my hips and shoulders, and the straps rubbed my skin, leaving red welts and pale blueberry bruises. It was hot, and without the sunscreen I had left behind, I was burning. I daydreamed of dragging the bag along behind me in a cart, and then about meeting my hostess for the night, and how we would exchange how do you dos and she would offer me a cup of English tea, served in a dainty china teacup covered in pink roses with a matching saucer, accompanied by jam-drop biscuits that I would accept with smiling delight. A twinge in my back jolted me back to reality, and I found myself trudging along a footpath in the south-east of England with my heavy pack on my aching back.

I lost my way for the first time an hour away from Barham. Coincidentally, or maybe miraculously, a lady with short white hair strolled towards me just after I had wandered onto a bitumen road, hoping I was heading the right way. We greeted each other and I almost continued walking, except I felt the impulse to confirm that I was walking in the right direction to Barham.

"Yes, but it's a long way," she answered.

I was puzzled by her response. Barham should have been only a few kilometres away from where I was.

"Do you know the name of this road? I think it is this one here." I held out my iPad to the lady, pointing to Covet Lane on the Pocket Earth map.

"Yes, that's the one."

"Do you know which way I am walking along it?"

"This way," she ran her finger along the map in a south-westerly direction. She was right. It was the long way to Barham. I had been walking the wrong way.

"There is a footpath just down there through the woods that you can take." She pointed in the opposite direction, and at the same time I noticed a round icon on my map that looked like a target. I pressed it and it zoomed in to reveal a pulsing triangular arrow that showed me exactly where I was standing. I grinned. It was an in-built offline GPS. I would never be lost.

I asked the lady where she was from, assuming she lived in a nearby village. It turned out that she was from Melbourne and was in England visiting her sister. Of all the people to save me from getting lost in the middle of the English countryside, it turned out to be another Melbournian. We said our goodbyes and walked away in opposite directions. I turned onto the path through the woods as she had directed, looking excitedly at the pulsing arrow on my map that showed me exactly where I was and which way I was going.

It took me three and a half hours to walk the twelve kilometres to Barham. I knew that my average hiking pace was four kilometres per hour, so this was a bit longer than I expected, but I had stopped frequently to take photos of the golden countryside. I didn't want to rush my journey, but I didn't have time to dawdle either. Once I set foot on French soil, my visa only allowed me 90 days to arrive in Rome then I had to leave the Schengen area countries for 90 days before I could return. When I first started planning the trip, I estimated that it would take me 93 days to walk the whole trail if I followed all the stages set out in the guidebook, with 91 of those days in Schengen countries. That was one day too many. I considered riding a bicycle for the first two weeks to save time, except I didn't want to ride, I wanted to walk. Many pilgrims break the walk into smaller sections to complete it over a longer period of time, often years, but I didn't want to do that either. I wanted to walk it from start to finish in one go. After I found the itineraries of a few pilgrims who had completed the journey between 69 and 84 days, I gave up on the bike idea. All I could do was try. If I couldn't make the whole trail within the visa, then I would have to find short cuts or take a train or bus to skip sections.

True to my guiding mantra, I trusted that where there's a will, there's a way.

Although my backpack was still giving me grief, the terrain was flat and easy to walk across, except for the stiles that I had to climb over. I finally arrived feeling hot and tired but triumphant. I had navigated my way to my first destination without using the guidebook and without becoming completely lost. While I felt a little uncomfortable about staying in the home of a stranger, it also felt like an authentic way to start my pilgrimage, accepting help like many pilgrims of old had done. My discomfort vanished once my hostess welcomed me inside and immediately ushered me straight up two flights of stairs to an attic room with a sloping roof. On the double bed, she had placed dusk blue towels and a hairdryer. As I was soon to discover, this was one of the few times I would have access to one. Just outside the room was the bathroom with a claw-foot bathtub and she showed me up one more flight of stairs to the other bathroom in case I preferred to have a shower. There was no offer of tea and jam-drop biscuits, but instead we had salmon and vegetable soup with crusty white bread for supper, followed by chocolates, as we watched television in her lounge room. I went to bed early and fell asleep quickly.

Three—Opting out of easy
Barham to Wissant

I woke early to soft light gently streaming in through the sky-light on the slanting roof. It was almost six o'clock, too early to be awake. I rolled onto my left side so my back was to the window and willed myself back to sleep, but my mind had already slipped into first gear, thinking about the day ahead and beyond. *Which way would I walk to Dover? Where would I find coffee and lunch? When I arrive in Calais, will I follow the official route west to Wissant or save myself a day and walk the alternative route directly south to the next town,* Guînes? *I have to start speaking French tomorrow. What French words do I remember?* Bonjour, merci, oui, non, excusez-moi. *How do I ask for a room? How do I say I am a pilgrim?* Je suis un perregrini? *Or is* perregrini *a bird, like a falcon? How do I say 'help me I am lost'? Surely I will need to say that sooner than later.* In between waves of thoughts, I rolled onto my stomach and asked my mind to switch off, but sleep didn't return.

I dressed in my hiking clothes from the day before without any excitement about the day ahead. It wasn't that I didn't want to walk, but I didn't feel enthusiastic about it the way I thought I should have, given it was only my second day of walking. Despite yesterday's short distance and flat terrain, the journey had taken longer than expected and was hard on my body. My face and arms were sunburned. During the night, I had woken a few times from a nerve twinging painfully near my coccyx and there was a shooting pain into my hip. It still hurt. Before going downstairs for breakfast, I gathered and began packing my belongings. During my preparations for this journey, I read Cheryl Strayed's book, *Wild*, about her three-month-long trek along the Pacific Crest Trail. Amused by how she named her backpack Monster, I jokingly nicknamed my bag too. I had called it the Devil, because it felt like such a heavy burden to carry. The name stuck and then names started appearing for everything else. My red hiking boots became the Red Beasts. My bright green rain poncho was Kermit Cloak, which I abbreviated to Kermit. My hiking poles were the Two Rodneys, and my one-person hiking tent was unimaginatively called Tent. It felt right to name them so, as they would provide essential support to me, just like close friends.

I had spent a lot of time figuring out what was essential for the journey, what was nice to have, and how I could pack as lightly as possible. I took my time in choosing the most comfortable and best-fitting hiking boots I could find for my large feet, with enough room in the boots that I wouldn't bang my toes and bruise them like last time. After buying and returning three pairs that weren't quite right for my feet, I ended up with the Red Beasts. I researched the weight of everything and weighed items on the kitchen scales to help me decide if they should be packed or left behind. In the world of hiking, the lighter something is, the more expensive it is, so I compromised. I left out the handheld GPS that I couldn't figure out how to use, along with the three-quarter sleeping mat and air pillow, the emergency external battery to recharge electronics, and small bottle of sunscreen that someone in a forum said I wouldn't need if I were walking in autumn and winter. Despite this, the backpack still weighed eleven and a half kilograms without water or snacks. That made it five kilos heavier than the '10% of your bodyweight' rule that many hikers adopt.

I started packing by filling my hydration bladder with just enough water to last the day, so I didn't carry any extra weight. It had to be put inside the Devil first, as it was impossible to add it after the pack was loaded with my other belongings. My sleeping bag and synthetic-fill jacket were already in the bottom of the waterproof liner inside the bag. I had bought the soft-fill warm jacket only the day before I left Melbourne because I was worried that my other layers would be insufficient to keep my sensitive bones warm as I walked towards winter, and I hated feeling cold. On top of them, I shoved my clothing: lightweight pants and wrap top for evening, one spare set of hiking clothes, my leggings and a singlet to sleep in and to layer for warmth, underwear, followed by electrical cords and chargers, toiletries, first-aid kit, journal, and my Kindle inside my iPad keyboard case. Many pilgrims would consider these last two as non-essential items, but the keyboard would make blogging easier and the Kindle held a backup guidebook in case I broke the iPad, so their usefulness surpassed their weight. Between the waterproof liner and the bag, I shoved my canvas ballet shoes and lightweight polar fleece jacket. On the outside, I attached the Rodneys and a mini camera tripod on the left and put the tent on the right. The tent was my heaviest item, weighing 1.7 kilograms, but I refused to pay hundreds of dollars extra to halve the weight, and I didn't want to risk a night alone beneath the stars in the non-tourist parts of France, where accommodation could be limited or non-existent. I would be scared to death and probably end up frozen as well. The whole packing process took me around forty minutes, but it wasn't a chore. I was taking care of the limited belongings I had with me to help me along the way, and as I packed I prepared my mind to leave.

I had breakfast and then followed my hostess's directions back over the busy A2 motorway with morning peak hour traffic speeding past in both directions. I walked on the edge of the road beside a constant stream of cars and trucks, stepping aside onto the grass at times as they rushed passed. I was relieved when after five minutes I rejoined the North Downs Way and found myself walking past fields of golden wheat being harvested by distant tractors. Outside Woolage Village, I walked along a narrow bitumen road for a short distance and once again jumped, squealing, onto the embankment between the road and a paddock as cars sped past in both directions.

The sky was blue except for the occasional train of cloud drifting above the horizon. I walked along country paths and between fields of waist-high wheat that was ready for harvest where there was little shade. My black clothing, chosen to hide the dirt, also absorbed the sun. I was hot and burning again without sunscreen, and I regretted packing my sunhat down at the bottom of my pack where I couldn't reach it. Within a couple of hours, an old case of runner's knee flared up and my left knee ached painfully. I tried to ignore it and keep walking. I had found my walking rhythm and managed to get the Devil into a comfortable position on my back, but the pain in my knee increased. I sat down on some bench seats on the public footpath just outside of Shepherdswell and ate donut-shaped peaches, savouring their warm sweetness. I then stretched to release some of the tightness in my hips.

I continued towards Dover along my first old Roman road, which looked like an ordinary track of dirt and grass. I thought of pilgrims who had walked before me, their footprints turning to dust, and of the Pilgrim Blessing: "May the feet that walked before you bless your every step." I hoped my steps would bless those that followed behind me too. I hadn't seen any pilgrims yet and had passed only a handful of locals out walking their dogs. The Via Francigena wasn't a popular pilgrimage route then, with only a few thousand people walking or even cycling sections of the route each year, so I knew that encounters with fellow pilgrims could be rare. I felt open to meeting people along the way, but I didn't mind if I walked alone. Walking in silence, I felt more connected to the world around me, while also being present in my own body and aware of my thoughts and feelings. I was listening for that quiet voice of wisdom within that would guide me onto my future path. The silence, solitude and inner listening I needed were important and easier to find without the distraction of company.

On the outskirts of Dover, I rested in the old cemetery. I had three hours before I could check into my bed and breakfast, so there was no need to rush. I sat on the lush, manicured grass with the Devil still on my back, hoping that I was sitting in an aisle and not on an unmarked grave. It was quiet and serene there, among the sleeping and the peaceful. When I arrived into Dover an hour later, there was nothing I would have loved more than to dump the Devil from my back, remove the Red Beasts from my hot and aching feet, have a shower and then lie down, but I still had an hour and a half until my check-in time. I walked down to the sea, a choppy expanse of cloudy jade. Small waves licked the shore covered in tiny tan pebbles, its length broken up by brick retaining walls. Buildings obscured the base of the famous white cliffs. I strolled along the promenade, looking for somewhere to eat but found nothing appealing, so I walked back into the town to a pub where I had fish and chips and a pint of beer for my last meal in England.

Finally in my room, I removed the Red Beasts and inspected my tender feet. I had three blisters: one on the bottom of each of my fourth toes and one on the bottom of my right small toe. The blisters were unbroken with little fluid and they weren't too pain-ful. After showering, I massaged the complimentary moisturis-ing lotion I had found in the bathroom into the hot, sunburnt skin on my face and arms then double-dressed each blistered toe with adhesive gauze followed by a porous adhesive outer ban-dage. I wanted to rest and stay off my feet, but as I intended to catch the ferry over to France before the breakfast service start-ed, I walked to the supermarket 500 metres away to buy supplies. Even without the Devil on my back, my knees were so painful that I wasn't sure I would be able to walk the next day.

Back in my room, I lay down on the bed and planned the next day's journey. I discovered the earliest ferry I could take as a foot passenger departed at 9.25 a.m., arriving in Calais at 10.55 a.m. That was much later than I had hoped. Although the Via Francigena is not a single path, and historically there were several routes for it that have changed over the years, the gen-erally accepted route passed through the towns documented by Archbishop Sigeric of Canterbury around 990AD on his return journey from Rome, where he had travelled to collect his palli-um, a woollen cloak that represented his status as archbishop.[2] From Calais, the route heads west along the beach to Wissant, the original port where pilgrims and Sigeric himself landed, before it silted up and the new port was established in Calais. However, there was an alternative route directly south to Guînes that could reduce the length of the walk by one day and 30 kilo-metres. I wasn't convinced it was necessary to walk to Wissant just because Sigeric landed there, and with my knees painful and my body still adapting to the exertion, I decided to take the path to Guînes. I was in this walk for the long haul and didn't want to threaten my chance of making it all the way to Rome by going too hard too soon. Even so, I went to sleep with a niggling feeling that I was choosing the easier option because I was scared of discomfort, although this pilgrimage was not about taking the easy way out.

On the ferry to Calais the next day, I sat by the window, sipping a too hot and too strong cappuccino. Out to sea, I could see the white cliffs of Dover untarnished by the buildings at their base. Eventually they merged with the horizon, and all I could see was a long puff of cloud stretching over England. I had woken that morning still intending to walk the shorter, more direct route to Guînes, but as I watched the cliffs fade in the distance, the gently rolling sea soothed my water-loving soul and I changed my mind. Although I had explained this journey to many people simply as walking from Canterbury to Rome, it wasn't just a walk for me, and nor was it something that I was doing merely as a personal challenge or for some sense of achievement. This journey was a pilgrimage, a symbolic trek that I felt called to undertake and to undertake alone. As I packed and planned and prepared to leave to undertake the journey, I contemplated my intentions for the walk and decided that they were to clarify my life purpose and to make a decision about what I wanted to do, but I also knew there was a deeper meaning still unfolding that I may not fully understand until well after the physical journey had ended. While I didn't need to punish myself or make the journey unnecessarily hard, I am not one to take the easy way out because I am scared of pain or discomfort. If I walked directly to Guînes from Calais, I would miss out on walking in the footsteps of pilgrims of old between Wissant and Guînes. I decided to walk to Wissant.

In the heart of Calais, I called into a large convenience store in search of sunscreen but they were out of stock. Instead, I bought a pre-packaged ham and cheese sandwich for lunch. I walked on the sidewalk out of town then turned towards the sea, climbing over a sand dune and down onto a beach void of people.

After Dover, it was unexpectedly beautiful, with a wide expanse of golden sand, rippled from where the tide had retreated. I had expected soft grey sand or pebbles that would swallow my steps, but instead I walked on hard, damp sand and was surprised that it felt easier on my body than walking on bitumen or dirt and gravel tracks. My knees ached less than they had over the last two days, although I still struggled with the Devil. I fantasised briefly about dancing around a bonfire that was fuelled by my tent and sleeping bag so as to lighten my load, but I needed to carry the tent for another thirty days until I arrived in Switzerland and was sure I wouldn't have any trouble finding accommodation. I traded its weight for the peace of mind it provided.

I ate my ham and cheese sandwich sitting on the edge of a boardwalk with my bootless feet dangling above the sand. On the horizon, the white cliffs were dwarfed by distance, and a long row of lavender cloud hovered above the English continent. The ferries sailed parallel to the shore towards the port of Calais and back to Dover. Black seabirds rested on the cragged side of France's own chalky white cliffs, the Cap Blanc Nez. At the end of the cliffs, the sand was replaced by many small rocks and large boulders that were covered with moss-like seagrass. If the tide had been in, I would have been forced to walk up and over the white cliffs. Instead I was able to scramble over the exposed rocks and boulders, using my hands to keep my balance. On the other side, the beach was busy with day-walkers, some with packs and cameras. Five riders on horseback cantered along the water's edge and came right up to me as I took their photo.

I walked up a ramp onto an esplanade into Wissant and headed straight for the first hotel I saw. On the accommodation list I received as part of my membership to the Confraternity of Pilgrims to Rome, another pilgrim had rated it with zero stars, but right then I didn't care. It was quarter past five and I just wanted to secure a room for the night with as little effort as possible, and to shower and get off my feet. I used my high school French only to ask the owner if he spoke English, which he did a little, and paid for a simple, single-bed room.

I soothed my tired, aching body beneath the hot shower, then handwashed my socks and underwear in the bathroom basin and hung them on the window shutter to dry in the last of the day's sunlight. I had no new blisters on my toes, but the three existing ones were bursting with fluid. Despite my careful packing, I had forgotten that I might need to drain blisters and didn't pack any fine sewing needles. All I had were a few safety pins of varying sizes in case I needed to hold something together, like my pants if I lost a button. I undid the smallest of the pins. Its needle was much thicker and blunter than a sewing needle but it was all I had. I wiped it with disinfectant then started with the largest blister on my right fourth toe. Pressing my thumb down near the bottom of blister so the fluid bulged at the top, I pushed the pin into it slowly, being careful not to push too hard in case I slipped and jabbed the raw flesh beneath. It didn't break. The skin was too thick and needle too blunt. I applied extra pressure but it still didn't pierce. Finally, I swivelled the needle back and forth as I applied pressure, and after several turns the skin finally broke and clear fluid began to seep out. I pressed on the blister with a tissue until it was empty. After repeating this process with the blisters on each of my small toes, I double-bandaged them again then lay down on the bed, raising my feet above my head and resting them against the wall in an effort to help reduce the swelling.

It may have been a zero-star hotel but it was not a zero-star restaurant. I ate dinner outside on the decking with its railing covered in red and pink geraniums, next to a small pond containing a few resident ducks. I had beetroot mousse with dill mayonnaise, and strips of juicy beef with potatoes and green beans, all washed down with red wine and a lemon tart for dessert. It was simple but delicious. I left the restaurant as the sun was setting and walked through the sweet and compact town, down to the seaside. Day three of my pilgrimage ended with the sky glowing in tones of soft pastel pink, apricot and mauve that were mirrored on the damp sand below.

Four—Cold comfort

Wissant to Licques

In the morning, I woke and launched straight into my new routine. I dressed, filled the hydration bladder with just enough water to last the day, packed the Devil, ate breakfast then harnessed myself into my bags. It was nine o'clock when I checked out of the hotel and started walking out of town. The morning market was in full swing. The streets were lined with stalls selling summer fruits and vegetables, local cheese, cold cuts and clothes. I bought six ripe apricots and an apple from a fruit stall then a ham and cheese baguette from the *boulangerie*. It was too big to fit inside the Devil, so I tied it to the left side and tucked the bottom of it into the pocket that held my walking poles.

The market obscured the landmarks. I couldn't see the *mairie*, the town hall, to get my bearings. After a few false starts, I used the GPS to find my way out of town. I didn't bother with the guidebook at all for the rest of the day. The trail was well signposted and I had the map and GPS that I referred to more often than was necessary. As I went to check it again, I heard a firm but kind voice that I recognised as my own, coming from within but also beyond.

"You are so worried about getting lost, but can you afford not to?"

I stopped. I knew from my time in Tuscany that getting lost could mean miles of extra walking, physical pain and tiredness. It meant having to ask strangers for help and trying to communicate ineloquently in a foreign language then trying to interpret the reply. But I also knew that it was through getting lost that I discovered the most treasure. When I had lost my way in my career, taking on a role that I discovered I didn't like, it provided me with the opportunity to take a risk and leap into the unknown by quitting without another job lined up. In taking that leap, I found that I could live with uncertainty and I experienced the joy of slowing down and living one day at a time. When I lost my way walking through Tuscany, I discovered that I could navigate my own way back to the route or the next town, and that getting lost helped to sharpen my intuition. And once, after I was kicked out of a taxi in a part of Bangkok I didn't know because of horrendous traffic jams, I stumbled into the middle of a festival with bands and food stalls and streets jammed with tens of thousands of people wearing white. It was the Thai queen's birthday celebration, something I will always remember because of the unexpected delight of chancing upon it. What would I miss out on if I didn't get lost? What would my life be like if I had never lost my way in my career and decided as a result to step off that path in an unknown direction?

In *The Art of Pilgrimage,* Phil Cousineau writes that "what every traveller confronts sooner or later is that the way we spend each day of our travel ... is the way we spend our lives." I no longer wanted to live being so worried about not knowing what the hell I was doing or where I was going in my life. I didn't want to spend my life trying to keep myself on a safe and known path. I wanted to trust that if I followed my heart and my intuition, I would always find my way. I knew that if I kept hoping to find answers outside myself in books or from other people then I would never fine-tune my inner compass, and I would forever look outside myself when I needed to trust what was within. I promised myself that from then on I would only turn the GPS on if I really needed it.

The trail led through more farmland. Around me were fields of dry, yellow hay, some of it cut and bundled into giant circular bales. I climbed my first hills, the double humps of Mont de Couple, which gave a 360 degree vista over the countryside back to Wissant. It was another hot day and although I checked a couple of stores in Wissant, I didn't find any sunscreen. I wore my sunhat but my bare arms were burning on top of my last two days of sunburn. Of everything I had left behind to reduce the Devil's weight, that small travel-sized bottle of sunscreen was the only thing I regretted. By one o'clock, I was hungry but still walking between open fields with no trees to provide any shade, just some shrubs that occasionally lined the dirt road. I continued on, hoping to discover a small patch of woodland or even just a solitary tree. Thirty minutes later I gave up. I sat on the edge of the dirt road next to a freshly ploughed field and ate my baguette under the full blaze of the sun.

Guînes had few accommodation options, just a camping ground and two pricey *auberges* (restaurants that provide basic accommodation) so I planned to camp and use my tent. If I was going to carry it all that way then I may as well use it at least once. When I couldn't locate the camping ground on the map I asked the universe for a sign to show me where it was. Fifteen minutes later, I was given a large sign, a white and black metal one on the side of the road with an arrow pointing straight ahead to the town centre and an arrow to the right pointing towards the camping ground. I was allowed to camp for free because I was a pilgrim. As an added bonus, the receptionist at the camping ground drove me on a golf buggy to my site, showing me the facilities as we went: the toilets and showers, the pool, the kiosk and café. The camping area was at the back of the grounds, far away from the campervans, and I had it all to myself. I set up the tent beneath a tree where the grass looked plush. Without a sleeping mat, I would be lying on my spare clothing on the ground and needed all the padding I could get. This was the first time I had erected the tent fully, and although I wasn't sure that I had pegged it correctly, it stood up and was stable.

After a hot shower, in which I had to keep pumping the tap every two minutes to keep the water flowing, I dressed in clean clothes and walked to the café next to the pool, where I ate a simple dinner of spaghetti bolognaise then went to bed at half past nine. The campsite had no power to it, and although I had a headtorch, I had no other source of light and needed to conserve my iPad and phone charge for the next day and possibly the day after that if I camped again. I rolled over and tried to sleep. Although I was physically tired, I tossed and turned for hours. It felt good to have the hard earth beneath me as I stretched out my tight and aching muscles, but as the night grew deeper it also grew colder. I put on each layer of my spare clothing piece by piece until I was lying on the cold hard earth wearing all my clothing and still shivering. Finally my exhaustion outweighed my coldness and I drifted off to sleep, only to dream that someone was trying to pull me out of the tent by my feet. I woke up gasping with my legs drawn up towards my body. I pushed myself up onto my elbows, expecting to see the tent flap open but it was fully closed. I curled up for warmth and comfort and eventually fell asleep again, but I had more nightmares and slept fitfully.

My alarm went off at seven o'clock but I turned it off and unintentionally fell into a deep sleep. It was eight o'clock when I woke again and emerged from the tent to discover everything was damp from dew and cold: the ground, the tent even the Red

Beasts and my socks that I had left outside the tent beneath the rain-stop. I let out a tired and frustrated sigh. This was not a great start to my day. I left on the socks I slept in and hung the damp ones on the outside of the Devil to dry during the day. The Red Beasts were mostly damp on the outside and only a little on the inside. They still felt uncomfortably cold as I put them on my feet. Packing up the tent and the Devil took much longer than I expected, as I tried to shake off the dew and even waited in vain for the tent to dry a little in a patch of weak morning sun. I cursed at my stupid idea of camping to save money, but the cursing turned into unexpected laughter that bubbled up from deep within. The situation really wasn't as bad as it seemed. Yes, I had been cold, I'd had nightmares, I was exhausted and everything was damp and taking longer to pack, but I was about to walk into a sunny day to discover the wonders of another unknown landscape. I was in France. I was walking free. I was doing this by choice. And I had used my tent so at least it was not a wasted weight.

I detoured into the town centre to buy breakfast and supplies for my day: a *pain-au-chocolat* from a *boulangerie*, peaches and apricots from the épic*erie*, another ham and cheese baguette from the supermarket, and finally some sunscreen, a large 250ml bottle of clear SPF50. I didn't care that it was ten times heavier than the travel bottle I had left behind. I was now willing to carry the additional weight so I didn't burn anymore. On my way out of town, I visited the church and stood alone before a large statue of Mary in a grey stone grotto with fake pink and yellow carnations at her feet. The morning light streamed through the stained glass window, splashing elongated circles of blue, yellow and pink on the stone floor. The light, stillness and simplicity of the church felt sacred. I slipped some coins into the donation box then lit a single tealight candle and watched its small flame flicker as I remembered my mum. She had kept a small collection of Swarovski crystal animals that reflected the sunlight in streams of rainbow colour. She would have loved the light in this church too.

It was half past ten by the time I started walking towards Licques, first along a dirt country road and then over a railway line and towards a forest. I walked slowly and stopped often to take photos. Bees and wasps and butterflies flittered amongst the pale pink wildflowers growing beside the dirt and gravel path. In the woodlands, lush green trees more than 30 metres high surrounded me and shaded the path. I was grateful for the coolness and respite they provided from the blazing sun on my skin and black clothing. Deeper in the woods, I met a young man with a daypack on his back and a traditional paper map in his hands.

"*Bonjour*," I greeted him, and he responded in rapid French. I told him I didn't speak the language.

"English?" he asked.

"Yes."

"Is this the way to Licques?" he asked running his hand over the light stubble on his face.

"I am walking to Licques too but I am walking this way." I pointed in the direction I was facing.

"I am following the GR. Here." He showed me a trail on his map that marked the Grande Randonnée, a series of long-distance footpaths in Europe. I was following one too but a different one.

"Are you a pilgrim?" I asked as I looked at his map.

"No, I am walking a few days along this path."

"I saw a sign just a little farther back heading that way." I gestured to his left. "That might be the trail you are after."

He thanked me and we walked off in opposite directions.

The path narrowed and became overgrown with groundcover.

The guidebook stopped making sense to me again, and although I was in the middle of the woods I decided to back my instincts and didn't use the GPS. The small track wound its way back onto a wider track and seemed to be heading the right way. The forest was quiet. There was no wind and few birds chirped. My mind drifted ahead of me, thinking about my arrival in Licques, where I would stay and whether I would camp again. Suddenly I sensed that something large was just behind me to my right and was snapped out of my reverie by my racing heart. Before I left Australia, friends and acquaintances had often asked me if I was scared to walk alone, especially as a female. I didn't feel that I had any reason to be afraid. I was walking through safe countries, I was fit and strong, I trained regularly in boxing and had previously had training in self-defence, kickboxing and Muay Thai that I could call on if needed. Moreover, I practiced walking mindfully, being fully present in the moment and remaining aware of my surroundings. Except right then, I wasn't present. My mind had wandered out of the forest and into the future. I turned to face the threat as my body tensed, prepared to fight or run for my life. Instead I gasped and put my hand to my chest in surprise.

"Oh, you startled me! I didn't hear you coming."

It was the guy I'd seen earlier. Somehow he ended up on the same path as me and walked so quietly that I didn't hear his footsteps on the dirt track as he approached. He nodded to acknowledge me as he passed by but didn't speak and continued walking swiftly out of the woods. I reached the end of the woods a few minutes later. Beyond them lay open countryside littered with huge round hay bales. There was no shade to be seen, so I sat down on the side of the dirt road under the trees and ate my baguette.

Thirty minutes after my lunch break, I approached a farmhouse and was greeted by the barking of two dogs. In the driveway, a sheepdog was chained to a tree and a smaller black dog, no taller than my knees, stood nearby off its leash. They both growled and bared their teeth as I passed. I ignored them and kept walking until the black dog chased after me. I turned and stood my ground, pointing Right Rodney, my walking pole, directly at her.

"No!" I shouted. "Go on! Go home!"

She was unperturbed and kept coming towards me, barking. I backed away slowly while facing her, still pointing Rodney directly at her to keep space between us.

"Go on! Get! Go home!" I shouted again.

After a few minutes she gave up and walked back towards the farmhouse, only to turn around and start barking again.

"Oh, piss off!" I yelled.

She stood there, still barking, but she was now too far away to be of any concern. I walked on and she didn't follow.

As I rounded a bend in the gravel road, I saw the French walker only 100 metres ahead of me, standing in a field, facing a hedge. I guessed he must have just stopped for lunch and was now relieving himself before he continued on. I slowed down to a stroll, not wanting to catch up to him. As he had overtaken me in the woods without speaking, I suspected he wasn't keen for company and neither was I. I was enjoying my solitude and silence and I didn't feel like company or even speaking right now. I continued strolling until he was out of sight then returned to my normal walking pace. I never saw him again.

I passed through Licques and out the other side to the caravan and camping ground. Although the previous night's camping experience had been cold and miserable, and my tent and clothes were still damp from the dew and condensation, I was prepared to camp another night. However, I was offered a chalet at a reasonable pilgrim price and I accepted without second thought. The chalet was a portable cabin with its own small verandah. Inside there was a lounge, kitchen, bathroom and bedroom with a double bed. I draped everything that was damp, including the tent, over the verandah rails to dry in what was left of the afternoon sun then I grabbed my toiletry bag and went into the bathroom. I was looking forward to having hot water running down my body, washing away the dirt, sweat and aches. I turned on the hot water tap and waited for the water to run warm. After a few minutes, it was still freezing cold. I waited a few minutes more but it was still cold. Reluctantly I accepted that there was no hot water. I counted to ten then jumped under. My body recoiled and I held my breath as I spun around then jumped out of the stream and turned it off while I lathered my goosebumped skin with soap. When I was ready to rinse, I turned the water back on, counted to three then jumped under again. My body started to adjust to the temperature but I didn't linger longer than necessary.

After my shower, I removed the bandages from my toes and inspected my blisters. The one on my fourth right toe was painful and even deeper than yesterday. I re-pierced all of them using the safety pin, drained the fluid then dressed them in fresh bandages and rested with my feet up on the lounge. Fortunately there was a small café next to reception so I didn't have to walk far for dinner. It wasn't fancy. I had a steak sandwich with fries and a beer, but my stomach was full. I walked back to my chalet to study the next day's journey, reflecting that today I had a bed and a cold shower, while yesterday I had the ground and a hot shower. Strangely, the latter almost seemed like the better option.

Five—In the right place

Licques to Wisques

I hobbled around the chalet as I packed, taking one slow step after the other, easing my weight down on each foot to reduce the intensity of the pain. It took at least ten minutes of walking like this before my body started to loosen up and the pain subsided. This was only my sixth day of walking. My body was not adjusting well to the kilometres I was travelling or the weight I carried. I wondered how many more days of this I would have to endure before I was pain-free. I was fit from my boxing training, and after I decided to do the pilgrimage, I started walking up to 20 kilometres every second or third day and had even completed consecutive days carrying the Devil, but this appeared to do little to condition my body. This walking was the training. I realised that no matter how much you prepare yourself for a challenge, nothing really compares to doing it.

The next destination according to the guidebook was Tournehem-sur-la-Hem, only 14 kilometres away and the destination after that was Wisques, another 17 kilometres further on. My body was too sore to walk 31 kilometres that day, so I examined my map and found a shorter, more direct route, following country roads to Wisques. As Tournehem-sur-la-Hem was not on the list of towns Sigeric passed through, I decided to walk to Wisques my own way. The country roads were quiet but narrow with little shoulder to walk on. Although I preferred to be off-road on trails and tracks, it was nice to walk through the quiet little towns with their colourful gardens of geraniums, marigolds, pansies and petunias. The fresh morning greeted me with soft sunshine, but as the day grew older I watched grey clouds carpet the sky and wondered when it would start raining. I made it to a bus shelter in the town of Boisdinghem just as the first drops fell. When I had finished eating my ham and cheese baguette, I put on Kermit, my bright green nylon poncho, and kept walking. The poncho constantly moved out of place, so I kept picking it up at the shoulders and dropping it back into position. The capped hood slipped forward and obscured my vision, while rain penetrated the gaps between the press-studs that held it together on the right-hand side. From my right hip to knee, my pants were damp and cold. I walked in the rain for two hours, taking only a five-minute break beneath the rudimentary shelter of a tree. Kermit wasn't perfect but it kept me mostly dry.

It didn't matter that it was raining or that my blistered toe was screaming or that my hips and knees were silently groaning their aches and pains from the hard slap of the bitumen under foot. To my surprise, I felt completely and utterly happy. As I walked through the rain along the hard road, I felt the meaning of the words "May the weather that's important be the weather of your heart." I was walking through France, passing through villages and a landscape I had never seen before, with immense freedom within. I could not feel anything but happy. I arrived in Wisques tired and sore but content. It was a small town without a bar or *boulangerie*. Although there were two large convents that offered accommodation for pilgrims, I intended to stay at the cheap hotel that had a restaurant so I could eat dinner and breakfast there. When I finally found the hotel after walking down the main road out of town for ten minutes then back again after realising I had missed it, I was shocked to discover the price of a room was more than double what I expected. Add on half-board for breakfast and dinner and that pushed the cost into the ridiculous category. I hesitated. As much as I wanted to get a roof over my head, get off my feet and not have to walk anywhere for dinner, I couldn't justify paying that much. I walked back to the closest convent.

The Abbaye Notre Dame was filled with the sweet melody of nuns singing vespers, their evening prayers. I wasn't sure if I should wait in the foyer until I found someone or they found me, or if I should wait at the back of the chapel and approach a nun when the service was over. I was about to enter the chapel but was worried that the door might creak and interrupt the service, so I let go of the handle. As I was about to leave, the door opened and out walked a nun wearing a traditional black and white habit and chatting to two middle-aged ladies in French who walked on either side of her. They stopped and looked at me while I recited the sentence I had practiced on my way, to announce that I was a pilgrim needing somewhere to sleep. I knew what I said and how I said it wasn't quite right, but I spoke slowly and hoped they understood enough, except they looked at me without responding. This was going to be harder than I expected.

"How do you say 'pilgrim'? *Pèlerin*? *Je marche...*" I imitated a walking movement with my two right fingers. "I walk ... camino... Via Francigena. Canterbury to Roma."

Finally, the two ladies smiled and nodded.

"Oh!" the shorter of the two exclaimed, her blue eyes widening.

The other lady, taller and slim, wearing stylish gold-framed glasses nodded also. "*Oui. Pèlerin.* Camino," she repeated. "You walk to Rome?"

"*Oui! Oui!*" I was relieved they understood me and that one of them spoke some English.

"You want to sleep here?"

"*Oui. Oui!*"

"You walk alone?" the shorter lady asked in a serious tone.

"*Oui.* Just me." I nodded my head vigorously.

The two ladies and the nun spoke in French before they turned back to face me.

"She must speak with her superior. You go with her," the lady wearing glasses told me.

"*Merci! Merci beaucoup!*" I was so grateful for their help.

"*Buen camino,*" the short lady wished me. "You have much courage."

I followed the nun downstairs and through a doorway then sat on a wooden bench chair against the wall and waited for her to return. A minute later she came back with her superior. Sister Lucie smiled radiantly, her heart-shaped face framed by the white coif and black veil that covered her head. She spoke softly and sweetly in French. I understood that I could stay, and I followed her into her office where she inspected and stamped my pilgrim credential then led me out of the convent and across the bitumen car park to *l'hôtellerie,* the guest accommodation. I had expected at best a dormitory with bunk beds and was surprised when she showed me into a private room with a double bed, an old wooden writing desk and red-velvet padded chair near the decorative arched window that overlooked the tree-filled garden. Down the hall was a bathroom with a hot shower and downstairs was a kitchen where I could help myself to tea, bread and biscuits.

"*Dîner est à sept heures dans la salle à manger de couvent,*" Sister Lucie announced, after I dropped the Devil on the floor near the bed. I didn't understand. We muddled through some basic French, English, and charades until I understood that dinner would be served at seven o'clock in the convent. All I had hoped for was a simple bed for the night. I never expected dinner and a lovely private room.

Dinner was simple: vegetable soup and homemade brown bread to begin, followed by boiled white rice, a fried egg and baked endives for the main course, and apple compote for dessert. I shared the meal with Bernadette, a French woman I estimated to be aged in her thirties, and Marie and Jean-Claude, a married couple aged in their fifties from Belgium. Marie spoke some English and was able to translate for us. Bernadette was on a regular spiritual retreat, while Marie and Jean-Claude had been coming to the abbey annually for over fifteen years. After dinner, Bernadette rushed off for evening prayers. The couple followed Sister Lucie upstairs to talk about fabrics for upholstering, and I walked back to *l'hôtellerie* alone. In the dimly lit kitchen, I made a cup of hot, sweet black tea and sat on a wooden chair staring through the large arched window into the dark garden. As the bells chimed, I thought that we don't always end up where we think we are going, but we end up exactly where we should be.

In the morning, Sister Lucie cooked eggs while Bernadette, Jean-Claude, Marie and I set the table, made coffee and toasted white bread that we ate with jam made from the plums and apricots that grew in the convent grounds. The kitchen was jovial, thanks to Sister Lucie chatting and laughing as she cooked. I didn't understand what she said but her merriness was contagious. My body was sore but I felt happy in her company. After breakfast, I returned to my room to collect the Devil then found Sister Lucie standing in the garden talking with Marie and Jean-Claude. I didn't know what an appropriate donation would be, and as I had expected to stay at the hotel, I had little change with me. I handed her a large note, knowing it was too much but also that it would be returned to me in other ways.

"Oh no! *C'est trop!*" Sister Lucie exclaimed, indicating that it was too much.

"No, no. It's okay." I waved my hand at her. "*Tu tres généreux* to me … *et* …How do I say 'I liked my stay here very much'? … *Beaucoup!*"

I wished that I could communicate in French how I felt, but I spoke with my hand touching my heart and hoped she understood my sincere gratitude. She tucked the note inside her habit then retrieved her small compact digital camera from inside *l'hôtellerie* to take a photo first of me and then with me. Then she placed her hands on my arms and firmly kissed each of my cheeks. We couldn't speak each other's language but it didn't matter. Communication can transcend words.

Six—A pilgrim friend

Wisques to Auchel

I spent most of the day walking along narrow country roads with little traffic, past more golden fields with round bales of hay and herds of brown cows chewing cud as they stared at me curiously. Over the last few days, the landscape had been much the same as this, and I had read other pilgrims describe it as boring and monotonous, but I was never bored. The sky was ever-changing: clouds appeared then sailed overhead and disappeared past the horizon, and the sun cast magic spells, splitting clouds with silver majesty as it stroked the golden fields. Sometimes I had interesting interactions with locals, like just outside the small town of Wizernes, when an old man driving a rusty red 1970s Renault stopped in the middle of the road to find out who I was and where I was going. I attempted to tell him in French that I was a pilgrim walking the Via Francigena from Canterbury to Rome.

"*Que?*" he replied putting hand up to his ear.

"*Un pèlerin. Je suis un pèlerin,*" I repeated, speaking more loudly and slowly.

He shook his fedora-covered head from side to side muttering in French.

"*Je suis un pèlerin,*" I said again. "*Je marche* ... camino. Via Francigena. *Canterbury a Rome.*"

He shook his head and said something about Santiago de Compostela. I nodded vigorously and tried to tell him it was like that camino, except I was walking from Canterbury to Rome. He shook his head again. Behind him, two cars approached slowly, but whether oblivious or not caring about holding up the traffic, the old man kept talking and asked me where I came from.

"Australia."

"*Que?*" he asked, scrunching his face up and leaning his head closer to the open window to hear me.

"Aus-tral-ia," I shouted at him. The car behind him gave a single polite beep. The old man rambled some more then drove away. I waved and walked on with a bounce in my step, chuckling about our awkward conversation.

I arrived in Thérouanne in good time, walking 14 kilometres in three hours. My average walking speed so far had been four kilometres per hour, so I felt proud of my effort. As I walked towards the supermarket entrance, an older gentleman wearing a black suit and silver-blue tie approached me. It turned out that he was the mayor of Thérouanne, attending a wedding at the church just opposite the supermarket. He recognised me as a pilgrim and invited me to his office after the wedding so he could stamp my credential. I thanked him and told him I had to walk a long distance to Auchy-au-Bois so I must keep going. He shook my hand and wished me a *bonne journée*. Thirty minutes later, as I sat in a bus stop eating yet another ham and cheese sandwich for lunch, I heard a lot of tooting and many motorbikes revving. I stood up and looked down the street to see a convoy of fifty or more motorbikes turn the corner. Behind them was a white vintage wedding car.

After the clamorous wedding procession had passed, I continued walking, and an hour later the ever-present pain in my feet, knees and hips became unbearable. Every muscle in my body was tensed, anticipating the jarring pain that accompanied each step. I had walked 18 kilometres so far and still had another 10 kilometres to go. This would be my longest walking day yet. I passed a herd of brown cows sitting on the ground as they always did in the early afternoon. I looked at them longingly, wishing I could lie on the grass in the gentle sunshine enjoying rest and stillness like they did, but I had to reach Auchy-au-Bois so I pushed on. Ninety minutes later, I sat on dirty concrete steps built into the side of the old railway embankment and opened my emergency block of dark chocolate. My pain level was high and my energy was low. Desperate for a boost, I devoured two rows then rested into my tiredness and discomfort. Ignoring the pain didn't help, but there was no point giving into it either. I was in the middle of farmland with nobody around to help me but me. The only way I was going to make it to Auchy-au-Bois was to get back up and keep walking.

It was after five o'clock when I entered the outskirts of Auchy-au-Bois, reciting in my mind my French lines I needed to ask for a room. I arrived at the first of only two bed and breakfasts in the town, known as *chambres d'hôtes*, and wondered how I would cope if there was no room available. If I had to walk the extra five kilometres to the next town, I knew I would dig deep and just do it, but as it turned out, I didn't have to. I rang the doorbell and a buxom old woman with rosy cheeks and short hair dyed blonde opened the door.

"*Bonjour Madame. Je suis un pèlerin. Avez-vous une chambre ce soir?*" I asked.

"*Oui,*" she answered, her voice starting low and ending in a higher tone.

I could have fallen to my knees with my hands held together in prayerful gratitude before jumping up and hugging her. Instead I thanked her over and over as she ushered me inside.

She led me through a living room that was decorated with coral pink and cream polka dot wallpaper. Oil paintings, as well as silver trays and jugs, hung on the walls. We moved through to the dining room, where the apricot and dark pink polka dot wallpaper was adorned with painted porcelain plates. From the wooden beams hung dozens of copper jugs. A gentleman with short white hair that was thinning on top sat at the dining room table. He wore silver-topped spectacles and spoke French to my hostess. I assumed he was her husband until I noticed the walking poles and backpack resting up against the wall and saw a map of the Via Francigena spread out in front of him. He spoke not a word of English, but this did not stop him from talking to me in fast and fluent French. I was able to make out that his name was Jacques and he was walking north to Canterbury from his hometown of Besançon. He was near the end of his journey, while I had only just started mine. I was so happy to meet him, my first fellow pilgrim. He turned out to be an angel that night and also later in my journey.

Although I had purchased something resembling a pizza roll as my emergency dinner from a *boulangerie* I passed that morning, I wanted something more appetising and substantial. I told Jacques I was going to walk into town for a meal. He warned me I would find nothing, but our hostess mentioned there was a festival on and there would be food. Jacques abandoned his bananas and baguette and accompanied me. Night had already fallen as we walked along the dark and quiet street into the centre of Auchy-au-Bois. I knew from the guidebook that it was a very small village with no supermarket or *boulangerie*, and I saw no signs of any as we walked past residential houses. Jacques spoke non-stop in French and I listened attentively, trying to understand what he was saying and paying little attention to my surrounds.

We arrived at the festival area. It was early and the merry-go-round, laughing clowns with their heads turning side-to-side and a fairy floss stall were lit up and waiting for customers. We walked past them to a big white marquee that had been set up near the playing field. Inside were five long trestle tables covered with white tablecloths and individual place settings. At the back was a stage where a band was setting up their equipment. Rows of red and green triangle flags hung along the wall and beneath the ceiling of the marquee. At the front right side, a separate tent was a hive of activity, as people set up beer kegs and prepared food. It was the *Fête de la Biere*, a beer festival.

Jacques approached three women, all with short white hair, who were talking near the entrance to the food tent. I heard him say *pèlerin* and *Via Francigena* then he introduced me. We shook hands and I smiled warmly, trying to make up for my inability to communicate. I was desperate to sit down and get off my feet, but Jacques and the women kept talking for another fifteen minutes as he told them all about his journey from Besançon. I had only known the man for an hour, but already I understood that he liked to talk—a lot. Occasionally the women spoke to me and I did my best to understand and respond in French. Mostly I apologised for not being able to speak more fluently. The women left to continue their preparations and Jacques told me that food would be available when the festival started at nine o'clock. That was another hour and a half away. I didn't think I could wait that long and would have to eat my pizza roll back at the *chambre d'hôtes*. Jacques kept speaking, and finally I understood that the women were going to try and arrange something for us earlier.

As we stood waiting, a short, solid man wearing a navy suit arrived and was instantly surrounded by a small group of people. One of the ladies we had spoken to earlier ushered him over and introduced us. Jacques told me later that he was an important politician from the National Assembly, the lower house of the French parliament. He offered us an aperitif and we walked inside the marquee to the bar at the right of the entrance, where he bought us both a glass of beer. I accepted gratefully. If I couldn't eat, at least the beer would bloat me and make me feel full. Either that or I would feel tipsy on an empty stomach and not care that I was hungry. We stood around talking for a few minutes then the politician wandered off to speak to some other people. I left Jacques talking to a group of local men and sat down on one of the plastic chairs at the end of the nearest trestle table, happy to finally get off my feet.

"Jacques, food?" I asked him when he came over and sat down opposite me a little while later. It was interesting to be at the festival, but all I really wanted to do was eat and go to bed.

"*Dix minutes*," he answered. Ten minutes.

Moments later we were moved to another table and given two round white plastic plates laden with roast pork, potatoes and green salad. Jacques bought us each a glass of rosé, cold and sweet and dry. It dissolved the tightness in my body. One of the organisers came to ask if everything was okay then took our empty glasses and filled with more rosé before returning them. It was more than okay. It was wonderful. I could have been back at the *chambre d'hôtes* eating my cold pizza roll and drinking water. Instead, I had warm food, good wine and company. As we ate, people started arriving and were shown to their seats. The eight-person band came on stage. They wore traditional Bavarian dress and began to play traditional Bavarian music. Our empty plates were whisked away and we were presented with two slices of artisanal custard tart for dessert. When we finished eating, we found the ladies who had been so kind to us, to pay for our meal and say goodbye.

We walked back to the *chambre d'hôtes*, not as slowly as I would have liked. Jacques had a naturally fast walking pace and I assumed that, as he was a few weeks into his journey, his body was conditioned and free of pain, unlike mine. My body was groaning with pain, but my stomach was full and my heart bursting with happiness. I couldn't wait to see what the next day would bring.

After breakfast, Jacques and I walked together back to the main road. He was walking to the place from which I had come, and I was walking to where he had been. We said our farewells, but it was not a forever goodbye. As he lived close to Besançon, which was on my way to Rome, he gave me his phone number and told me that I should call him when I arrived and simply say, "Jacques. Kym. *Gare*," and he would come and fetch me from the train station.

It was quarter to nine when I left Jacques and started walking alone. This was a much earlier start than I'd had for the last couple of days. The light was softer and the world a little quieter and a bit more beautiful. I ambled along, enjoying the ease of being, the softness that surrounded me, and the sense that I had all the time in the world to arrive at my next destination, Bruay-la-Buissière. I promised myself I would get into the habit of starting out earlier on my walk. After an hour, I arrived in Amettes, the birthplace of St Benedict Joseph Labre, patron saint of the homeless. I visited the simple white stone church of St Sulpice, which holds the remains of St Benedict's kneecaps and the straw matting he died upon. I lit a candle at his shrine that was surrounded by fresh flowers. The morning light streamed through the stained glass windows, splashing the dark wooden pews and stone floor with soft pink and blue. I picked up a discarded order of service for the marriage the previous day of Claire and Ludovic. On the front was a photo of the couple. She rested her head on his shoulder and they both smiled contentedly.

I wondered if I would ever get married or feel that kind of contentment again. My relationship with my ex-partner in

Melbourne didn't work for many reasons. Some of our core values and the things we wanted out of life weren't aligned. I had also placed an incredible amount of pressure on him, making him the centre of my world and expecting him to make me happy instead of being responsible for my own happiness. The grief and pain I still carried from my mum's death also didn't help. It was a similar situation with David, in that we wanted different things in life. He didn't want children and I didn't want to give up on the possibility of one day having some of my own. I loved diving but didn't enjoy it as a job, and the only other work options in Phuket were teaching English or working in a resort, neither of which interested me. I was also tired of packing up my life in Melbourne to return to Phuket then having to start again and find somewhere to live when I returned to Melbourne. I needed to move on but David wanted to stay in Phuket. I also felt a calling to do more with my life. I knew that my happiness and the larger purpose of my life were not going to be found solely in an intimate relationship. I was seeking more than that.

For now, I was choosing to walk alone. This gave me the time and space to look inward and to sharpen and trust my intuition and inner guidance. Those inner tools I used to find my way along this pilgrimage path were the same ones that I must use to find my way in my life. In addition to this, I wanted to strengthen my connection with the Divine Spirit of this world, to discover a love that went beyond human relationships and would sustain me throughout my life, no matter where I was or who, if anyone, walked by my side in a relationship.

Seven—Rain, sun, pain, repeat

Auchel to Trefcon

In Auchel, I detoured to find a place to buy lunch. It was Sunday, so most of the shops were closed and the supermarket didn't open until one o'clock in the afternoon. I didn't know if I would pass another one that day and I didn't want to eat only my emergency supply of chocolate for lunch. That would, if necessary, get me through until I arrived in Bruay-la- Buissière for the evening, but I wanted to eat something filling and more satisfying. After walking 500 metres without finding the supermarket, I gave up and walked back to the route. I had no desire to add any further distance to my day. Thirty minutes later, I walked directly past a small convenience store, where I stopped to buy a sandwich. Another thirty minutes after that, I walked past another small supermarket and learned an important lesson. Everything I needed would appear along my path. I didn't need to go out of my way to find it.

In between towns, I walked through a variety of farmland: some flat, cropped fields scattered with the remains of loose, golden hay, and some green hilly areas on which cows grazed. I walked on quiet bitumen roads, grass, and even gravel. The hotel recommended by Jacques was some two and a half kilometres on the far side of town. I walked along the footpath beside Rue de la

Libération, lined with parked cars and three-storey brown brick houses that were spaced equally apart. Cars passed at regular intervals but the road wasn't busy. Just before reaching a large roundabout near the highway, I cut through a commercial area and arrived at the hotel just after three o'clock.

I showered, washed my clothes and hung them on the open window to dry in the last of the sunshine then lay down on the bed to rest before dinner. Over the past week, I had developed the appetite of a packhorse and was quickly developing the rump muscles of one too. Across the top of each buttock was a strip of bulging muscle where there had been none before. I wasn't sure how sustainable my current level of food consumption was for my bank account or my waistline, or if the distances I was walking really justified how much I was eating, but I was hungry again. There were few restaurants near the hotel so I ate at the Buffalo Grill across the busy highway. I was craving steak and chips, but when my meal was served, I sat looking at it, wondering if I had received the wrong one. It was a thick slice of pan-fried ham not beef steak. It was the wrong meal but I realised the mistake was mine. In my tiredness and confused by all the different types of steaks, I had ordered the *steak de jambon*. Ham steak. I ate it anyway.

The next day, I woke at half past six to pack and leave. I estimated that I had 38.5 kilometres to walk that day, taking the shorter alternative route. It would be my longest walking day yet. Only small villages lay between Bruay-la-Buissière and Arras with little accommodation on offer, and I couldn't find a way to split the next two days into three. The first 12 kilometres of the walk were easy. I stopped to talk to the curious cows that trusted me enough to approach. They lined up along the wire fence and stared at me as they chewed their cud. As the day wore on, my two remaining blisters burned, my arches and my heels ached, and my hip muscles went into spasm and screamed in pain. Tears burned behind my eyes but they did not fall. I kept telling myself that where there's a will, there's a way.

The last two kilometres into Arras were slow and painful, so very painful. I willed myself to keep taking step after step, to keep moving, no matter how slow I walked. I prayed to feel pillows beneath my feet and for the pain to soften just a little. I prayed for grace, for a way to accept the pain, to stop resisting it and making it worse. It took me an hour to hobble into town. I was so relieved when I saw the belltower and knew I had made it. The cheap hotel where I wanted to stay was just behind it in Place de la Vacquerie. I walked around the square but didn't find it. I checked the address then walked around the square once more. On my third round, I found the building, except it was now just a restaurant with a different name. Of all the days for this to happen, it had to be the day of my longest walk. I needed to get off my feet. I wanted to cry. Instead I studied my accommodation listing and map to find the next closest cheap hotel. After a five-minute walk to the train station and two minutes spent talking to the bar manager, I was upstairs in a non-smoking room that reeked of stale cigarettes. I flopped onto the spongy bed and my body began to relax. At last the pain began to fade.

Back in Melbourne, I had read *Italian Camino* by Maggie Ramsay and *An Italian Odyssey* by Julie Burk and Neville Tencer, about their experiences of walking the Italian section of the Via Francigena. I trawled blogs written by the Dutch adventurist, Henk Van Der Klok, and John Barrett's trail journal, *Slow Walker*, as well as joining the Via Francigena Yahoo forum, but I didn't remember one person describing how physically challenging and painful the pilgrimage would be. Perhaps they didn't want to put others off trying it for themselves, or maybe they didn't want to sound like they were complaining or whining.

Perhaps they just wanted to focus on the positive aspects of pilgrimage or they were superhero pilgrims who experienced no physical pain at all. Maybe there was an unwritten pilgrim law that stated, "Thou must not mention the pain of long-distance walking." I understood the nature of the path I had chosen and knew it wouldn't be a romantic stroll through Europe. The pilgrim path is a tough one that tests you physically, emotionally, mentally and spiritually. I had been tested in all ways that day.

After showering, I made my way back down the two flights of stairs to the restaurant, wincing with every step, but grateful that I didn't have to walk any farther to find food. After dinner, I went to the bar and asked the manager, who only spoke French, for some ice to take back to my room to put on my swollen feet. The best translation I found online was *pane au glacé*. The manager looked at me blankly when I first asked so I tried again.

"*Pane au glacé* … ice … ice blocks." I drew squares in the air with my forefinger. When that didn't work, I tried to scratch another sentence together from the limited French words that I knew. *My feet are not well. Today, I walk many kilometres.* Somehow, he understood what was wrong and what I needed, and he filled two plastic bags with ice cubes. Upstairs in my room, I alternated between resting my feet on top of the ice bags and sitting the bags on the top of my feet. After twenty minutes, the pain eased and I eventually fell asleep.

In the morning I took a coffee at the bar of the hotel then walked back to Place des Heroes without the Devil to look around and buy breakfast and lunch. Narrow four-storey townhouses of brick and stone, painted dark salmon and lemon cream, bordered the square. Dating back to the 15th century, they were built in the Flemish-Baroque style: the curved roofs had a high centre peak, the façades were decorated with sculpted ornaments, and sandstone columns supported the arches of the first floor. Cars drove around the perimeter of the square and some parked in its centre.

On my way back to the hotel, I stopped inside the cathedral. It was white and airy, the roof supported by two rows of white columns. I stood still and listened to a dozen people singing prayers in the chapel at the front. I didn't understand what they were singing but I didn't need to. Feeling the vibration of the words and the intention behind them was enough. I grew up in a Christian family. My mum's father, my papa, was a Church of Christ minister, with my nana by his side in combined ministry service before they retired. Although Mum stopped attending church because of her health, my dad played an active role in our local Church of Christ as an elder. I chose to stop going to church regularly when I was around thirteen. I didn't click with the other girls my age at Sunday school, and although I loved many of the Bible stories that were retold by the ministers, I remember one of them preaching about an angry God. It didn't feel right to me. Looking back now, I realise that it might have been a parable that I didn't understand properly. I still attended Easter and Christmas services and played the flute and organ when Dad led the Sunday service, but after Mum died I stopped going to church altogether.

When I closed my heart down around my grief and pain, I closed my heart to God. I didn't understand how He could allow life to feel so hard, unfair and painful. I never stopped believing in a higher source, but I stopped having a direct, heartfelt relationship with that source. I have continued to explore traditional and contemporary spirituality since my twenties, through courses and books. Although I understood the principles of what I read and learned, looking back, it never fully made sense without a direct relationship with the Divine. It was during my sabbatical year in Asia that I fully reconnected with that divinity through those tangerine sunsets that I watched almost religiously. The beauty I witnessed everyday was God speaking silently and directly to my heart. I learned to recognise the presence that underpins all of life and started to understand that I wasn't alone, that this presence was with me, that I was supported, and that the key to realising this was through my heart. When I looked back at my life, I could see how everything always turned out okay—often better than okay—in ways I could never imagine and how life supported me and brought me opportunities that led me to other opportunities, often ones I would never have thought of myself. This formed the basis of my spiritual faith in life.

While spending time in nature was my living church, I started visiting St Patrick's Cathedral regularly before I left Melbourne to walk the Via Francigena. The first time I went there, I was passing by it on my way home when my curiosity directed me inside. Golden light streamed through the arched windows, illuminating the wooden pews and stone floors. To me, churches are holy places where the Divine Spirit of this world has been invited to dwell and where I feel the same sacred energy I sense in nature when watching sunsets, or being on, near, in or under the ocean, or being in the stillness of a living forest. I felt the sacredness inside that cathedral and was transfixed. I sat on a pew near the altar for an hour, meditating and feeling the energy around me. I prayed for guidance and blessings and offered gratitude for my life and the journey that lay before me. In the ten weeks leading up to my departure, I visited the cathedral regularly, whenever I felt the urge to soak in that sacred light and space.

In Arras Cathedral, I strolled down the left side of the chapel beside the shrines and was again drawn to a statue of Mary, the epitome of the divine feminine and the mother of all mothers. It was the perfect place to light a candle for my mum. I did so and watched the flame flicker for a few moments before I left. I had 26 kilometres to walk to Bapaume that day. So much for my resolve to start walking earlier! It was half past nine when I left Arras in crisp air and brilliant sunshine. There was a bounce in my step, as my body had recovered surprisingly well after the previous day's painful marathon. Despite icing my feet, I'd still hobbled out of bed and around the room, packing and preparing to leave, but by the time I returned from town to put the Red Beasts on my feet and strap the Devil on my back, all pain had subsided and only muscle tightness remained.

It started to rain as I walked through the first of the First World War battlefields in Boisleux-Saint-Marc. This area was captured from the Germans by Commonwealth soldiers in March 1917. Part of it was lost to the Germans again a year later then finally reclaimed by Commonwealth soldiers in August 1918. Buried here are 416 Commonwealth soldiers and four Germans.[3] I put on Kermit and kept walking through the golden, fertile, peaceful land that was once filled with horror and bloodshed. As I left the Sunken Road Cemetery, where the names of so many young men were etched on simple crosses, I watched a fleet of sparrows skim the furrowed soil then suddenly dart skyward in perfect formation. I learned about the world wars in high school history classes and from watching movies, but it was almost impossible for me to visualise that here, where the sparrows flew freely, was where it happened, and to comprehend the scale of destruction and loss of life. There have been many wars since World War I, and there is still so much violence and conflict in the world. It seems that we still haven't learned history's lesson, or found a way to compromise, accept our differences and live together peacefully. As I walked upon that land, bearing its visible and invisible scars of war, I did the only thing I knew to do: feel the peace within my own heart and breathe it out into the world.

When the rain failed to eventuate into anything more than a shower, I took Kermit off again and didn't put it back on. The rain was light and not heavy enough to do more than dampen the surface of my clothes. For most of the day, the walking was relatively easy on my body. At one stage I mentally reviewed my packing process to make sure I hadn't left anything behind. Strangely, the Devil felt too light. Maybe I was getting stronger at last? However, thirty minutes outside of Bapaume, my heels started to throb and my hips cramped again. Tears stung my eyes but I observed the pain and kept walking. I was almost there and could rest soon.

Kermit cloak on. Kermit cloak off. Kermit cloak on. Kermit cloak off. That was the rhythm of the next day, as I walked to Péronne after staying overnight in Bapaume. I didn't mind that it showered periodically. I just wished that I could read the weather. I would walk for a long time with Kermit on, whipped by the almost constant wind that skimmed those lands, waiting to see if it was going to rain again. Then, within minutes of me deciding that it wasn't going to rain and taking Kermit off, it would do just that—rain—and I would battle against the wind to get Kermit back on and buttoned up over me and the Devil while it flapped wildly.

Despite the rain, it was a beautiful, peace-filled day of walking. I noticed all the small things: the worm wriggling its way along the rain damp bitumen; the small black cricket ambling beneath the grass; the white butterfly fluttering beside me; the crying gulls soaring over the ploughed fields; the pink, yellow, white and purple wildflowers dancing in the constant breeze while the bumblebees suckled their sweetness; and the white wispy dome of the dried dandelion, waiting for the perfect moment to shed what it no longer needed. These were all reasons I walked: to see, to wonder, and to be here in this world, experiencing it fully.

The pain in my feet was still present, but once again I accepted it was there, as resisting only made it worse. I took one step after the other, through open fields— some newly ploughed and others newly seeded—and past more fields of corn and more war cemeteries. I went on through more small villages that were daytime ghost towns, where there were parked cars but no people to be seen, only dogs that never failed to let me know it was their territory upon which I intruded. Once, I jumped in shock and fear when a giant Saint Bernard lunged repeatedly and forcefully against the metal fence that kept him in his yard.

After arriving in Péronne, I walked up and down a street several times, looking for my guesthouse, but eventually concluded that it had turned into a doner kebab shop. I walked back to the tourist office, hoping they could book a room for me, but the young man only offered a map listing all the hotels and guesthouses in town. I picked the cheapest option, one kilometre out of town, but when I arrived it was closed. I tried to phone the number on the door and was about to walk back into town when I noticed a movement in the kitchen at the back. I knocked on the glass door and a brunette lady walked over. I gave her my pilgrim spiel and was shown upstairs to a large L-shaped room with a double bunk bed against one wall and a single bed against the other. In the far corner was a bathroom with a shower and the toilet was just down the hall. The room was tired and in need of redecorating, but so was I. It gave me a roof over my head and a bed to sleep in for the night, and the restaurant downstairs offered *menu du jour*. I ate heartily for a mere 11 euro: a proper beef steak with *eschallots* sauce and French fries, a quarter carafe of red wine and a slice of plum tart for dessert.

The next day, it was only 19 kilometres to a little village called Trefcon that was no more than a cluster of houses around a church. There was no point in rushing to arrive, so I slept in until half past seven then wandered around Péronne. During medieval times, it was a fortified city, although all that is left of the fortification is Porte Bretagne, the archway to the road to Britain. It was burned and pillaged repeatedly during Norman times and virtually destroyed during World War I and again during World War II. [4] I roamed the grounds of the partly ruined castle, reading various informative plaques, and learned that in September 1918 during World War I, the 2nd Australian Division liberated the ruined town of Péronne from the Germans, and that out of a population of only 3.5 million, Australia sent 315,000 men to World War I. Péronne is still grateful for Australia's contribution to the war and their liberation, and it encourages its citizens to visit Australia. Even the young man in the tourist information office proudly told me that he was going to Australia next year to watch France play Australia in the rugby.

I took advantage of the late checkout at my accommodation and left Péronne at eleven o'clock. The gravel path out of town soon became a wide and long expanse of mud and puddles, too wet and muddy to walk along in my leaky boots. I walked back to the main road and picked up the trail again a kilometre out of town. Although it was a short walk day, it wasn't as easy as I expected. There was so much mud to dodge and trudge through. The weather was warm again. I was carrying extra supplies for dinner and lunch and couldn't get the Devil into a comfortable position. My left shoulder and upper back ached for most of the day, and my heels throbbed for the last two hours. After passing through the small village of Vraignes-en-Vermandois, I missed a turn and ended up walking 200 metres on the overgrown, grassy verge beside the road as cars and semitrailers passed at over 100 kilometres an hour. Simultaneously annoyed and humoured by my situation, I marched uphill, apologising to any slugs I may have stepped on and injured or killed. Relieved to be back on a quiet country road, I bounced along its rocky incline, and as I reached its plateau, I was greeted by an amazing sky of the kind where giant clouds cover the sun but the light streams through as if the silvery fingers of God are caressing the earth. In that moment, all mistakes were null and void. It was not a mistake to be there in that moment, witnessing that great sky.

My accommodation for the night was a dormitory at a *gîte*, a rural holiday house, where I was the only guest. The shower was barely lukewarm, too cold for my goosebump-covered body to stand under. I shivered as I splashed myself clean then put on most of my layers—thermal long-sleeved top, polar-fleece and windproof jacket—and wondered how my hosts could wear only t-shirts and long pants. It was going to be a freezing cold night in my light sleeping bag in my unheated room.

My hosts, an older couple with a teenage daughter, were friendly and helpful. They invited me into their kitchen to use the wi-fi so I could check my emails and Facebook messages from family and friends. We spoke in French and English of travel and walking and pretty homegrown pumpkins, of which they had several different varieties ripening in the kitchen. Daniela reserved a room in a small hotel in the next town for me, somewhere she knew to be decent and clean. She even gave me a massive slice of freshly baked plum cake, still warm from the oven, to take back to the dormitory. I ate it after my dinner, a shepherd's pie I heated in the microwave. In one of the kitchen sinks was a hairy spider the size of my hand with fingers spread. I washed my dishes quickly in the other sink without taking my eyes off it. Despite the simplicity of my accommodation, I was grateful it was available. It would have been an excruciatingly long walk to the next town. I climbed into my sleeping bag with two thick blankets over me to keep warm and drifted off to sleep, my mind filled with the vision of that amazing sky.

Eight—The power of brave

Trefcon to Reims

I left Trefcon early, shrouded in fog. As I walked to Étreillers, I was mesmerised by the hundreds of spider webs hanging between shrubs and blades of grass, adorned by dewdrops that glistened in the soft morning light. The bluebells looked frozen but the fine hairs of their closed buds held tiny dewdrops not ice. On my way out of the town, it started to rain and continued to do so constantly for the rest of the day. I hoped to pass a bus shelter so I could stop and eat lunch out of the rain. They usually appeared just when I needed one, but not that day. Not even singing '(Are You Ready) Do The Bus Stop' by Fatback Band and dancing as I walked could manifest one. Instead, I sat on a metal cabinet between two shrubs with the Devil loosened but still on my back while rain dripped from my hood onto my nose and then onto my ham and cheese sandwich. I reminded myself again that it is the weather of one's heart that matters. I had no control over the weather, but I was still happy and content. I was here by my own choice, doing exactly what I wanted to do, living my dream, and I felt free. Although a very different experience, this was the same happiness and contentment I had felt when I was living in Thailand, riding my scooter through the jungle-covered hills, watching a sunset, floating in the sea, going out on the boat to go scuba diving, even when we were rocking and rolling over big waves. I was living my life in a way that felt true to who I was, living one day at a time, one moment at a time, and away from the merry-go-round of Monday to Friday corporate city living.

I spent the last hour of the day's journey walking beside the dark green waters of the Canal de St Quentin. Excited that I had almost made it to another town and was pain-free except for the ache in my heels, I put on some music and sang and dance-walked as I stepped over and around the orange slugs out on rain patrol. The hotel that Daniela had booked for me in Tergnier was easy to find on the main road, beside the railway line and above an Indian restaurant that was closed. I dreaded making the phone call and having to converse in French to let the hotel owners know I had arrived. I found it even harder to understand someone over the phone than in person, but I didn't want to wait three hours for the restaurant to open, so I rang the mobile number for the hotel that was on the door. I didn't comprehend much of the man's response, except that maybe he was coming to let me in, I hoped. I sat down on the step to wait. Five minutes later a short, stocky Indian man opened the door from inside the restaurant. It took only a few minutes for me to register and pay then I was upstairs in a modern renovated room that was relatively quiet, given it faced the main street and busy railway. I inspected my poor feet. My Red Beasts were turning out not to be as waterproof as they were meant to be. My socks were soggy, my feet white and prune-like, and I had one new blister. I enjoyed a long, hot shower, making up for last night's meagre splash with lukewarm water, and then went out into the cold and rain to buy supplies from the supermarket to have a picnic dinner in my room.

Despite the hot shower, wearing all of my layers and eating, it felt like ice was running through my veins so I crawled beneath the bedcovers for extra warmth. I suspected that my body was in shock from walking 34 kilometres that day. When I felt warmer, I sat up in bed and typed an email to the makers of the Red Beasts to tell them, politely, that their boots weren't waterproof as advertised and asked what could be done about it. I didn't expect a reply or that they would have a solution for me, but I was sick of walking with wet feet. With my frustration out, I curled up to hug my own warmth then fell asleep.

I woke to grey light filtering in through the gap in the curtains. The weather forecast on my phone said there was a 90% chance of rain from eight o'clock and a 70% chance that it would rain all afternoon. I got out of bed and pulled back the curtains to look out the window and confirm what I suspected: it was already raining, although only lightly. I glanced at the Red Beasts. They were still dark red, which meant only one thing. They were still wet. I would be walking in the rain all day, wearing wet boots that were going to get even wetter. Tired tears pooled behind my eyes at the thought, but in the moment just before they fell I started laughing, because I was doing this voluntarily. It was my choice each day to get out of bed and walk for kilometres through rain and mud. Today's additional challenge and choice was to walk in wet boots. While the idea was unappealing, it was a small price to pay for the freedom and joy of walking on this pilgrimage path.

With the Devil harnessed onto my back, I walked outside into the dull light and drizzle and headed straight into the bar next door for a *café-au-lait chaude* (coffee with warm milk). I added sugar and savoured its hot sweetness in quick sips. I wasn't eager to walk in the rain but I had 31 kilometres to go today and I needed to get started. As I paid for my coffee, the bar lady spoke to me in English about my pilgrimage.

"Aren't you scared of walking alone?" she asked.

"No. No, I'm not. Most of the time I'm in the countryside, and there is no one around. I make sure I am alert and aware of my surroundings. I'm more scared of walking on the roads. They can be dangerous."

"You are very brave."

That is not a word that I would use to describe myself. It's not that I'm not brave; it's just that I don't always feel brave. I'm far from fearless. When I started seriously contemplating this pilgrimage after I was made redundant, all my fears surfaced as 'what if' statements. What if I didn't make it? What if it was a huge waste of money? What if I were injured? Over the years, I have discovered my own unique dance with fear. I feel it, I back away from it, and then I dance up to it again, allowing myself to feel the fear a little more before retreating. I repeat this dance until I am ready to take that final step into what is unknown, uncomfortable, scary or painful. There are people who take a flying leap right into or over their fear, but that's not me. I dance with it until I am ready to act. Brave is the power I summon to take that final step. I have learned that my authentic desires are more powerful than my fears. Therefore, instead of focusing on my fear, I focus on my dream and how it would feel to live that dream. This way, my desire grows stronger than my fear, and it makes the decision to take that final step much easier. This was how I decided to embark on this journey in the first place. I summoned the power of my bravery to make the decision. Everything else was just walking, faith and resilience. Still, I appreciated the bar lady's kindness. I thanked her, said goodbye and walked back out into the rain.

At the end of the road next to the supermarket, I walked into the *pâtisserie* and bought a croissant and *pain-au-chocolat* for breakfast, a double indulgence to compensate for the rain. The lady who served me gestured at my bag and said something in

French that, as usual, I didn't understand. She seemed to know I was on a long journey, maybe she even knew I was a pilgrim and wished me *bonne journée*. These good wishes buoyed me above my early morning despair over walking in the rain in wet boots. It would be another week before I realised that *bonne journée* didn't translate literally as 'good journey' and wasn't used as a specific and special pilgrim wish just for me, but that it just meant 'have a good day'. I preferred my own translation.

Walking along the footpath as I ate my croissant, I realised something completely awesome: the rain had stopped. Ten minutes later it started again, and an hour later it was pouring, but that didn't wash away my good mood. My spirits remained high. As I approached a paddock, the herd of white and fawn cows in it galloped away from me, scared of the bright green blob moving towards them. I laughed out loud. When their curiosity eventually overpowered their fear, they walked towards me slowly until they stood in a long line against the wire fence. With the rain falling on me and around me and dripping from my nose, I stood for a while, speaking to the cows. When I continued walking, the cows followed me for 30 metres then stopped, huddled together and watched me leave. I realised that walking in the rain in wet boots and socks wasn't as bad as I thought it would be. The rain was just doing its thing, watering the earth. I had the Kermit to keep me mostly dry and although my feet were a little damp and getting wetter, I was fine. I was better than fine. I was walking through the French countryside, fuelled by coffee, croissant, the *pain-au-chocolat* I had just eaten and the kind words of strangers. I was living my dream and befriending French cows.

Late in the morning, I walked through the forest of St Gobain. Surrounded by tall, slim trees wearing ivy dresses, I sat on a fence made of round pine poles next to the road, watching and listening to the soothing patter of rain on leaves and the sound of the breeze rustling the high branches. Once I had passed the village of Cessières, I had a clear view of Laon, a medieval town on a tabletop hill, surrounded by dense trees. Over the next two hours I watched the town get larger and nearer. Having a visible target made the walking easier. Bursts of traffic rushed by me and the grassy verge was too overgrown and wet to walk through, but at least the road was flat and I had only one busy roundabout to navigate before arriving.

My hotel was in the new part of town at the bottom of the hill. I showered and washed my clothes quickly so I could explore. It was a 100 metre climb on steep paths and steps to the top of the hill. Without the Devil, I felt free and light, if a little lopsided. I wandered the narrow paved streets past the towering Notre Dame Cathedral, the Church of St Martin and the crumbling abbey. The Picardy plains surrounded the hill and the earth stretched on forever, punctuated by towns and green squares of farmland. I felt blessed to be exactly where I stood.

The next morning after breakfast, I walked back up to the old town to walk its cobbled streets and visit the cathedral one last time. After I returned to my hotel room to collect the Devil and checkout, I discovered that I had to walk back up and through the old hilltop town anyway. I had assumed the way to Corbeny would be around the hill, not up and over it. This was the equivalent of climbing forty-eight floors before I even left town, and it was much harder walk with the Devil on my back. I breathed heavily and paused twice on the way to let the lactic acid burn in my thighs subside.

Although there was a shorter route out of town following one of the main roads, I decided to follow the guidebook so I could give my feet a break from the punishing bitumen. I was soon pleased with my decision as I passed through quiet woodlands with ivy clad trees, listening to the crackling of twigs and branches and the drilling tap-tap-tap-tap-tap of what I assumed was a woodpecker somewhere nearby. The muddy forest floor held day-old tyre prints of four wheel drives and dirt bikes. Alone in the woods, I felt vulnerable. There was no one around for miles. My imagination told me fearful stories, but I really was alone in the woods. There was just the woodpeckers and me, and maybe if I were lucky, some wild deer.

As I walked down a wide dirt and grass track, I heard the sound of tyres on earth and the hum of an engine. A small white car approached from behind me. My heart beat a little harder against my chest as I stepped off the path to let it pass. Driving the car was a male in his forties, wearing a white t-shirt. He drove past slowly and kept going until he was out of sight. Five minutes later, I once more heard rubber on dirt and the hum of an engine as the car returned. My heart pounded again. I wondered why he was coming back. This time the car stopped and the man wound down the window. My breath momentarily caught in my lungs as a 'stranger danger' alarm sounded in my head.

"*Avez-vous un peteetkien?*"

I tried to decipher what he said, but he spoke quickly and the words blended into one another.

"*Non comprende,*" I replied.

"*Un peteetkien?*" he asked again, holding his hands 30 centimetres apart.

"*Non,*" I said and shook my head. It was pointless to tell him again that I didn't understand.

He wound up his window and continued driving slowly back towards the road. I continued walking in the opposite direction and tried to make sense of what he had said. *Peteetkien. Peteetkien. Peteetkien.* Oh! *Petit chien!* Small dog. He was looking for a small dog. I released the breath I had held shallowly in my lungs. There was no danger here.

By the end of the day I was back on bitumen, feeling it pounding my feet and knees. I was tired. My feet were throbbing. I felt like I was never going to arrive at my destination for the night. There was little traffic on the road so I read poetry on my iPad and even wrote my own poetry, typing with my index finger on the in-built keyboard as I walked, to remind myself that the goal is never about arriving, that there will always be a long road, a coming and going. The quiet of the woodlands was broken by the occasional passing car and the crack of gunshots nearby. I prayed for the safety of the animals, wishing them speed and agility to avoid the hunters' bullets.

If I followed the guidebook's directions out of Corbeny the next morning, I would have started my day walking through farms and woodlands and the vineyards of the Champagne region. I would also have walked a total of 40 kilometres, comprising 24 kilometres to Hermonville then a further 16 kilometres to Reims. I had neither the desire nor determination to walk that far, so I studied my map and found a shortcut that would save me 2.7 kilometres. The D1044 road ran straight from Corbeny to Berry-au-Bac, where I could return to the trail. Theoretically, it made perfect sense until I saw the soggy, overgrown verge and all the semitrailers and cars speeding along the road in both directions. I turned back to follow the guidebook's trail, but after only ten steps, I turned around again. I really didn't want to walk 40 kilometres. This shortcut beside the road was only for eight kilometres, and I would be in Berry-au-Bac in about two hours. I could handle it.

At times, the verge was very narrow and the traffic too close for comfort. Chased by black clouds laden with rain, I wore Kermit, expecting a downpour at any second. Unfortunately, Kermit was no match for the hurricane winds that were generated by the trucks speeding past and that ripped the green poncho open. I marched as if my feet were on fire so I could get off that horrible road. My poor feet were once again wet from the long grass that had been saturated with last night's rain and they worked hard while soggy. Despite these difficulties, I made it to Berry-au-Bac by ten o'clock and didn't have to walk 40 kilometres that day.

I rewarded myself with a large hot coffee with milk at the local bar while I studied my map. Although I planned to continue on the official route, there was a dashed line beside the Canal de l'Aisne à la Marne, indicating a path running all the way from Berry-au-Bac to Reims. It was shorter than the route to Hermonville, which was not one of the towns documented by Sigeric, so I decided to take a chance on it. During the day I cursed the weather frequently. Melbourne is renowned for having four seasons in one day, but on this road it was four seasons every hour. Kermit cloak on then off, warm layer off then on again. Repeat, repeat, repeat! As frustrating as the weather was, it had its blessings too. A sudden shower forced me to put Kermit back on and then five minutes later the sun came out scorching, leaving me cursing as I ripped the Kermit off again. I rounded a corner and saw a host of yellow and purple wildflowers glistening in the sun. My cursing turned into cries of amazement.

Trusting my instincts paid off. I walked only 30 kilometres to Reims, although it was still a long day and took me almost eight hours. In the afternoon I was more tired than usual and walked much slower than my average pace of four kilometres per hour. I spent the last hour of the day mud-skating beside the canal, and then when I thought I had almost arrived in Reims, the Avenue de Laon stretched on and on forever with no end. I arrived, eventually, as I always did, but not without stepping in my first pile of dog poo. I guess it had to happen sooner or later, but I was annoyed and grossed out by the smelly brown mess clinging to the sole of my boot. I had been so careful to watch where I was stepping, especially when walking through towns. It was only a momentary glitch in attention, and I landed my foot in the wrong place at the wrong time.

After drying and resting my soggy feet and tending to my blisters, I walked straight to the Reims Cathedral. The sheer size and intricacy of this cathedral was breathtaking. I sat in a wicker chair for thirty minutes, staring at the ceiling and absorbing the enormity of the space, until my eyes were drawn to the Marc Chagall windows in shades of violet-tinged sky blue. They were the prettiest stained glass windows I have ever seen. At the St Thérèse chapel, three dozen candles burned before a statue of the saint, breaking through the darkness. The unexpected beauty of it led to unexpected tears. I lit a candle for my mum in this chapel. She would have loved it too. As I left the cathedral, I knew that Reims was the place for me to take a rest day. I had walked for sixteen consecutive days. I was tired and my sore body needed a break from carrying the Devil. There were a few days of long, hard walking ahead and I needed to arrange accommodation. Aside from all of that, there was something beautiful and special about this small city, and it wasn't just the champagne.

Nine—Goodbye tent! Hello new boots!

Reims to Châlons-en-Champagne

On my rest day in Reims, I decided it was time to say goodbye to Tent. The weather had become too cold for camping, as it was dropping down to around 6°C at night. I had not used Tent since Guînes. The August holidays were well and truly over, and I had no problems with securing accommodation, even when I turned up without a booking. The guidebook warned me about places where I might need to phone ahead, and Canon Clare had told me that if I were ever really stuck I could ask the town's mayor for help. So there really was no need to keep Tent anymore.

After breakfast, I took Tent to La Poste, the French post office, to send home. However, Tent wouldn't fit in their largest box, not even after unwrapping it and trying to cram it in. The poles were too long.

Madame Postmistress said that if it didn't fit in that box then it was *non possible*.

"Où?" I asked her, wondering where I could go to send it home. She shook her head. There was nowhere. Not ready to give up, I walked to the tourist information office. Someone there would speak English and might know what I could do. Madame Tourist Officer kindly spent the next fifteen minutes searching for a solution for me. Eventually, she found a courier and phoned them. It sounded promising until I heard her say, *"Non."* Madame hung up and told me that couriering Tent home would be very expensive with taxes and that I needed to have a company in order to sign documents. It could not be done.

There was only one other option and that was to leave Tent behind. Madame directed me to the parish office across the road and I handed Tent over to the secretary, hoping it would find its way to someone who needed it. I didn't expect anything in return, but she asked if I needed help with accommodation. As it happened, I did. The hotel I had stayed in the night before was fully booked. I'd left the Devil in storage with them while I disposed of Tent and found somewhere to sleep. The secretary made a phone call, and a few minutes later I left the office without Tent but with somewhere to sleep for the night. As I walked away, emotion filled my belly and tears welled. Letting go of Tent meant I was instantly lighter by almost two kilograms, but it also meant that I was more vulnerable. My security blanket was gone. I had no choice except to trust that all my needs would be met and that I would always find the most important and basic of our human needs: shelter.

It was supposed to be a rest day for me, but I still managed to walk 18 kilometres around Reims. Without carrying weight on my back, my ankles and heels didn't ache, but I missed the Devil hugging my back and the freedom of walking out into open space and solitude. I felt conflicted, with an urge to rest and an urge to keep moving forward, but I also feared that by moving forward, my journey would end too soon, before I had my answers. After checking into the hostel, I logged onto the internet to check my email and received some unexpected good news. The makers of the Red Beasts had sent a message and were apologetic that there had been "a failure in the production process" of the boots. They wanted to send me a new pair... for free! I just had to tell them what size and where to send them. But where? I moved towns daily and couldn't commit to being anywhere by a certain date, and they couldn't promise delivery by a precise date either. Then I remembered Jacques. Jacques lives near Besançon, and I would be there in two weeks. I sent him a text message to ask if I could have the boots delivered to him. In the morning, I woke to great news. Jacques had texted me back, agreeing that I could have the new boots sent to him. He gave me his address and told me to call him as soon as I arrived in Besançon. Immediately I replied to the Red Beasts' makers with his address and my size. I was excited. In a couple of weeks, I would be walking the rest of the way to Rome with dry feet.

I left Reims the next morning, and after following the Canal de l'Aisne à le Marne for ten kilometres, I found myself walking through hilly Champagne country. Grapevines stretched as far as I could see up and down the hills of Montagnes de Reims. Each village I passed through—Verzenay, Verzey, Villers-Marmery and Ambonnay—were filled with champagne-makers and cellar doors. As I walked amongst the vines, I plucked a small but bulging plum-coloured grape from a small bunch. It tasted sweet and had a tiny pip inside.

I was almost two kilograms lighter now that Tent was no longer with me, and I thought the day's walk would be easier despite the long distance and hills, but it wasn't. I felt off-balance without Tent on my right hand side. It took a few kilometres and much jiggling and adjusting of straps until I started to get used to walking without it. Then a new and pointed pain developed in the ball of my left foot, below my third and fourth toes. No matter how I stretched or massaged, the pain kept returning. I knew it would be a long walking day, and it took me just over nine hours, with a coffee break, *pâtisserie* stop, stretching and massage stops, and a fifteen minute lunchbreak. As I tracked my progress in the morning, I felt stressed that I was 'behind schedule.' I tried to breathe through it and let it go. I reminded myself that I had no schedule, but I was worried that I would still be walking in the dark at seven o'clock. Only when I reached the vineyards and was captivated by the beauty and sheer area they covered did my anxiety drop away for a while. Then I was distracted by the physical activity of Kermit on, Kermit off, Kermit on, Kermit off. It didn't bother me the first time. I was overawed by the rain I could see sweeping towards me over miles of grapevines. I put Kermit on in preparation for its arrival and marched up the steep rocky hill between rows of vines. The rain soon passed and I took Kermit off.

I was also accepting the second and third times I put Kermit on then took it off again after the rain passed over. But an hour after lunch, my patience with the continually changing weather ceased. I had just taken Kermit off after another shower when the sun revved it up a notch and I needed to take layers off. I developed timesaving techniques that meant I could do this while standing up or even when walking, without taking the Devil off my back. I used the first method when standing still. By undoing the chest strap then slipping my arms out of the shoulder straps while leaning forward at 45 degrees and balancing the bag upright on my hips, I could slip out of my jacket and pull my long-sleeved top off over my head. I used the second method when I wanted to keep walking. In this version, I undid the chest strap and slipped my right arm out of the shoulder strap then out of the jacket sleeve, letting the jacket drop down between the bag and my waist strap, before pulling my right arm out of the long-sleeved top and dragging it over my head. I would then put my arm back into the shoulder strap and repeat the manoeuvre on the left side until I was free of the jacket that I tied around my waist and the long-sleeved top that I tucked into the Devil's waist strap.

I had just completed the standing still method and walked a couple of hundred metres when the cold wind returned, followed by more rain. I wrestled with the backpack straps and a billowing Kermit to get everything back on again. The wind whipped Kermit into a frenzy as the rain battered the vines, the ground and me, falling at the perfect angle to penetrate the gaps between Kermit's right-hand side buttons. My right leg was saturated and cold and I had hours of walking left. I growled and cursed at Kermit as I attempted to wrestle it into a position so the rain couldn't get through the gaps. I didn't succeed. The rain passed again and I took Kermit off because at last the sky looked reasonably clear. I should have known it wouldn't last, and it didn't. This time, big rain came and it bucketed down.

I was grateful that I approached a picnic shelter, the first one I had seen, just as the torrent started. I sat on the picnic table, hunched over and hugging my body for warmth, trying to limit the area the sideways spray could wet. I was seriously over everything: the rain, the wind, the pain, the cold and the fatigue. As the rain poured down, so did my tears. I sobbed, letting go of my frustration and pain. I didn't always cry so freely. I used to be ashamed of how hurt and broken I felt and tried to keep it all inside, unseen. Through my counselling with Myree, I learned how necessary it is to feel and release my emotions, as holding onto and suppressing them only causes me greater pain. Once my tears subsided, I reached into my bag for the emergency supply of chocolate to get some extra energy and channel it into the only thing that would really help me, which was to keep walking. I waited fifteen minutes for the rain to stop. It didn't. I had to keep going to make it to Condé-sur-Marne by nightfall, so I put Kermit back on and walked out into the rain that had eased a little. Ten minutes later it stopped.

As I walked the last three kilometres to Condé-sur-Marne, I

stopped to admire the awesome black clouds skimming the earth and the towns of Ambonnay and Isse behind me. I love an amazing sky. However, I prefer if this kind of amazing sky keeps its distance. It was chasing me, so I picked up my walking speed to a fast march, looking over my shoulder every few minutes.

"Please let me win just once today," I prayed repeatedly.

A few minutes after I arrived at my *chambre d'hôtes*, so did the black clouds and the rain. I didn't care. I made it there first, so I won, and now it could rain all it liked. After a long, hot shower, I paused for a moment in front of the mirror then raised my arms above my head in a V. I had made it to another town, through another challenging day. It was a small victory.

When I left Condé-sur-Marne the next morning, it was sufficiently chilly that I wore my polar fleece mittens for the first hour of walking. It was 19 September. Summer was almost over and autumn was about to begin. I made my way out of the small village on the path beside the Canal latéral à la Marne. The sun was trapped behind a thick silver veil and the still water of the canal reflected everything that lined it: trees, bridges, a factory building. I promised myself that I wouldn't rush, that I would let my body find its natural walking rhythm. I only had to walk 18 kilometres to Châlons-en-Champagne and I couldn't check into the youth hostel until after three o'clock. It was easy to walk slowly, surrounded by the gorgeous light and reflections.

After the rain comes sun. It managed to break through the clouds for large parts of the day. I welcomed its warmth on my skin, pausing to bask in the simple pleasure of it. Yet after the rain also comes wet grass and mud. Although my map showed that the canal path continued all the way into Châlons-en-Champagne, I followed the guidebook's detour via Juvigny and trudged through 500 metres of thick, gunky mud that clung to the soles of my boots, gluing my feet to the ground. I hated the mud to the point of repulsion. I hated how it felt under my feet and I hated getting dirty. After stomping along for a time, I was relieved to turn onto a gravel path, but after 900 metres the gravel led to more wet grass and thick mud. The last 100 metres I walked through were a tangled mess of knee-high grass and blackberry bushes. The Red Beasts were wet again and so were my feet. My soles were clumped with mud and my pants smeared grey-brown. I missed the turn onto Rue St Martin that led to another field, but I didn't mind walking along the hard bitumen for a while longer. At least my feet weren't getting wetter or coated in more mud. Two kilometres down the road, I turned onto a gravel track back towards the main trail that became four more kilometres of clay and wet grass.

If I had to choose between walking all day in the rain on bitumen roads or walking in the sunshine on muddy wet tracks, I'm not sure which I would choose. They were both short straws: the bitumen punishingly hard, the rain a pain and the mud just plain repulsive. I tried to find something positive about mud and wet grass but couldn't. It was annoying and gross and that was all. I was so happy when I finally turned back onto the concrete towpath and scraped the mud off my boots with a small stick. I had never spent this much time outdoors with limited shelter, exposed to whatever weather swept through, and with the need to keep moving. Unlike the week I walked through Tuscany in summer, when it was hot and hot only, I was experiencing four seasons almost every day, often numerous times each day, and it was testing my ability to accept what is.

Ten—After the rain

Châlons-en-Champagne
to Le Meix-Tiercelin

The sun was just beginning to rise when I left Châlons-en-Champagne to walk to Le Meix-Tiercelin. It was yet another small town with no shops or even a bar. There were no hotels or guesthouses in the town or within a 16-kilometre radius, so I had pre-arranged by email to stay the night at ESAT Les Antes, a home for people with disabilities. The guidebook instructed me to carry all food and water for the day, so I carried two lunches, dinner, breakfast, snacks and over two litres of water. The Devil was fully laden and a heavy burden, even without Tent. As I walked towards the river, the almost full moon was still visible, a luminous milky white against the lavender dawn sky. Seeing it unexpectedly at that time of morning shocked me and I realised it had been more than a month since I had seen it last. When I was scuba diving, it was second nature to pay attention to its cycle so I could anticipate the strength of the ocean currents. Since starting this journey, my eyes searched at night only for somewhere to eat and for the way back to my room again.

I walked into the wet and muddy fields towards Sogny-aux-Moulins. As I trudged along, with the mud clinging and compacting to the soles of my boots, I unexpectedly discovered something positive about mud. As I walked and watched the ground, choosing the least muddiest place to step, I noticed the footprints and tyre marks from bikes and tractors and wondered who it was who had gone before me, where they were going and how long ago they had trod in this same mud. Sometimes when I saw a footprint, I liked to imagine there was another pilgrim just ahead of me, and I wondered what it would be like to meet them. I passed through Sogny and reached the Voie Romaine, the Roman road. It stretched for miles before me, a straight road of pale clay that passed through the wind turbine farm and disappeared over the horizon. It was an exposed area. On both sides of the road were gentle undulating fields, occasionally broken by a line of small shrubs. I set off, one step after the other, along the long straight road whipped by the wind that ruled it, feeling a sense of awe in knowing that for centuries before me pilgrims had walked this road and that I would spend most of the day and half of the next walking along it.

The wind farm comprised a dozen white turbines, each around 80 metres high, with three giant blades steadily churning. I expected that the turbines would be loud, but here the wind was louder than the soft hum of the engines. I walked past a dozen workmen, digging up the road with a backhoe to lay cables, and greeted them with bonjour. They turned and stared at me as I passed. I crossed a road into another wind farm and passed a warning sign written in French. I glanced at it, wondering if I was allowed to enter but kept walking. This was the way the guidebook directed me to walk so I assumed it must be okay. As I exited the farm, I saw another sign and this time I stopped and tried to interpret the words and pictures. It seemed that only authorised personnel could enter the area where the turbines stood, as there was a risk of being electrocuted. According to the translator application on my iPad, there was also a hazard of downfall of ice cream. I chuckled. Then I read the last warning, which featured a big exclamation mark inside a red triangle. Pedestrians and vehicles should not stop beneath the wind turbines.

"Oops," I said aloud to myself. It was too late for that. I had already stopped numerous times to take photos.

Despite these unknown dangers, I survived my visit to the wind farm and continued walking happily. Yellow butterflies fluttered beside me and flitted from flower to flower. Grasshoppers played chicken in front of my feet, jumping out of the way a split second before my foot hit the ground. The Roman road climbed skyward towards the giant marshmallow clouds hanging low as if ready for picking, and then it would drop away, leaving the clouds out of reach. At one point, a mountain-sized mound of harvested potatoes sat beside the road. Pots of bright pink and purple pansies and golden marigolds greeted me as I arrived into Coole. On my lunchbreak, I sat on the side of the road on a metal bench with flowerpots at either end filled with yellow carnations and marigolds, buzzing with bumblebees. I took off my boots and socks and laid them on the seat next to me then made my ham and cheese ciabatta roll. I warmed my bare toes in the sun as I ate.

As I walked that afternoon, I stopped often, pausing to listen to the wind rushing through the fir trees, sounding sometimes like a bubbling brook and at other times like a speeding car. I wanted to soak in the calm and solitude and the awe of having all this space to myself. It was my twentieth day of walking, and besides meeting Jacques almost two weeks ago, I hadn't crossed paths with any other pilgrims. I wasn't surprised. From my research, I knew the route wasn't as popular at this time of year, for I was walking in autumn rather than in spring or summer. I watched as a hundred crows scattered into the sky like black confetti and as an eagle circled and landed in a far field. At the top of a low hill, I took off the Devil and lay down on the rocky ground from which sprouted sparse grass. I soaked in the sun and I read one of my favourite Rumi poems, 'Love Dogs', out loud, lingering over and repeating my favourite lines. On a farmyard track next to a field of golden grass hedged by bushes, I took a quiet moment to celebrate having walked my 500th kilometre. I thanked my feet and my body for enduring it and bringing the Devil and I all that way, through all sorts of conditions and terrain. I was one quarter of the way to Rome. I felt the pain and knew I was really doing this pilgrimage, yet it still seemed surreal. Everyday I got up and packed and walked and made it to the next town, and all of those steps and kilometres and days now added up to 500 kilometres.

ESAT les Antes was easy to find. A dark-skinned orderly with a huge white grin welcomed me warmly. He spoke in a flurry of French, which as usual, I did not understand. I told him I only spoke a little French, and he actually spoke more slowly but still used words I didn't understand. He told me I should follow him to meet the director. Monsieur Dido shook my hand and welcomed me. Our communication was awkward. A heavy fog of tiredness made it difficult for me to recall the few French words I could actually speak. He stamped my pilgrim passport and gave me a metallic purple pen with ESAT les Antes written on it. I wished I could tell him how much this meant to me. Purple was my writing colour. Over the last few years I had been drawn to writing in purple journals with purple pens. Purple is the colour associated with those seeking spiritual fulfilment and with the crown chakra that connects us to the universe and the Divine. Monsieur Dido had given me the perfect gift and all I could say was merci beaucoup and très généreux.

The orderly led me out of the office, downstairs along corridors, and then into a room with a single bed and its own bathroom. I was surprised but happy. In his email Monsieur Dido had said that they could offer me a couchage, which I assumed was just a bed or literally a couch that I could sleep on. I didn't expect to have my own room and a bathroom. As an added bonus, the shower was even hot. I was clean and warm for five minutes until the coldness set in. The room was unheated. I put on all my layers: merino t-shirt and long-sleeved wrap top, polar fleece, synthetic-fill jacket and even my beanie and gloves, but I was still chilled to my core. My body was in shock once again after the long walk. I had been walking for almost three weeks and was still waiting for my body to adapt. I was starting to think it never would. A throbbing in my lower body woke me in the middle of the night, and my crippled feet could barely take my own body weight in the morning. I was constantly tired and chilled at night, but at least it wasn't getting any worse. It probably couldn't get any worse unless I sustained an injury. Still, I was on track to make it to Rome by 1 December, and at this rate I could allow myself to take two more rest days or put in some more long days to make up more time and ground. All I could do was take one day at a time, one step after the other, and see where each day would take me.

Eleven—The house of horror

Le Meix-Tiercelin to Brienne-le-Château

Breakfast at ESAT les Antes was simple: coffee that I drank French-style out of a bowl, and a baguette with apricot jam. I ate in the dining room with the residents, who cheerfully wished me *bonne journée* as I left. I emerged into the misty morn and walked along the sleepy street to the main road, past residential houses and a small group of men wearing bright orange safety vests, preparing to repair the road. I crossed over the road towards open fields to take a closer look at a small field of sunflowers. Their giant heads had no petals and were bowed towards the ground. They were dead, awaiting harvest of their seeds. I had never seen a field of dead sunflowers before, and while there was something sad about seeing them like this, they were still majestic, even beautiful.

The remnants of fog hovered above the horizon as I continued along the Voie Romaine, surrounded by open fields with neat rows of new seedlings. I had the ancient road all to myself. Even the lonely factory buildings I passed between were deserted. The five wind turbines to my left stood still, while spiders had been busy decorating the shrubs that lined the road with more fine lace webs dotted with dewdrops. As the morning deepened, the haze lifted and the sky rippled as if the ocean tide had run over it in an effort to sweep the cloud away. I loved the sun and warm weather, so it was much easier to find blessings when walking on sunny days than in the moments I was being pelted by rain and whipped by wind. On those two days walking the Voie Romaine, I experienced such beauty in the world and in my own solitude.

As I approached Brienne-le-Château late in the afternoon, the main road was lined with parked cars and more were arriving, looking for somewhere to park. I walked on the embankment until it became too steep, and then I had no choice but to walk on the busy road. The oncoming traffic slowed and veered away from me, sometimes heading into approaching traffic. In town, the main street was lined with stalls selling clothing, regional and artisanal delicacies, and lollies and fast food like sandwiches, soft drinks, hot dogs, waffles and crepes. There was an area with carnival rides, dodgem cars, merry-go-rounds and games. A number of outdoor beer barns had been set up, and there were champagne stalls as well. The street was thick with slow moving people, Sunday-shuffling along, browsing the stalls and stopping to speak with friends they met along the way. It was the Fête de la Choucroute, a festival celebrating sauerkraut.

The crowd was my worst nightmare, especially at the end of the day, when all I wanted to do was find the tourist office and secure a bed at the communal pilgrim house. My walk became a shuffle and weave through the sea of people. Of course the tourist office was located right up the other end of the street, in the section where there were no stalls. If I had known this, I could have turned off the main road and bypassed the crowd. In normal circumstances, I would have rejoiced at the opportunity to experience a local celebration, but my feet were sore, I was tired, and I just wanted to get the Devil off my back, have a hot shower and get off my feet.

In the tourist office, a young blonde-haired woman with a cool demeanour registered me. After I paid the fee, she stamped my pilgrim credential, gave me the key and a map of the town, and explained how to find the house. It was a ten-minute walk away, but it was easy to find on the road behind the château. The three-storey house was rendered a pale salmon-fawn colour and sat squarely in the middle of a large block of land, hemmed by a hedge at the back and sides and by a picket fence at the front. The two lower windows had white roller shutters drawn all the way down, while the window above the door was uncovered. Perfectly placed above each lower window was a stag head. In the fading light, the house looked eerie.

I walked through the unexpectedly unlocked front gate and down the white gravel path and let myself in, after fumbling with the key in the old lock. To my right was a small kitchen equipped with a stove, small table and chairs, kettle and a fridge. In a room to the left were three hospital beds and a mattress on the floor. I dumped the Devil on the floor then climbed the stairs to the second storey. There were two more bedrooms on this level, one with two hospital beds in it and the other with only one hospital bed. To my surprise, there was a sleeping bag laid out on this last bed and beside it a backpack on the floor. The lady at the tourist office hadn't said anyone else would be staying here, but this explained why the front gate was unlocked. Surprise gave way to a little kick of elation. This meant I would meet another pilgrim, only my second one in 21 days. I closed the door and walked up the last flight of stairs to check out the bathroom. It obviously had hot water, as the mirror was still steamy. I must have just missed the pilgrim. I decided to sleep in the downstairs bedroom to leave some space between us and laid out my sleeping bag on the bed on the left-hand side of the room.

After showering, washing my clothes and resting briefly, I strolled back into town to find dinner and experience the festival. I sampled the local champagne and ate French fries, as well as crepes with Nutella. I browsed the stalls, but by half past eight I was tired and returned to the communal house. It was dark and there was no sign of the other pilgrim. I stayed up for a while, writing and reviewing the map and guidebook for the next day's walk. At half past ten I prepared myself for bed, but strangely there was still no sign of the pilgrim. I couldn't believe a pilgrim would arrive then stay out so late when they had so many more kilometres to walk the next day, but perhaps this guy was young and had more stamina than me. To ensure that he would know there was someone else staying in the house when he finally returned, I hung my towel and red t-shirt on the hooks in the hall. Unable to lock the front door from the inside, I left it unlocked. I felt uneasy, but I didn't know what else to do. I couldn't bolt the front door or the other pilgrim wouldn't be able to get in. I returned to my room and bolted it closed instead.

I had just fallen asleep when I was woken by two male voices speaking French loudly. They stood in the hallway outside my door talking then started turning the handle, trying to get into my room. I lay still, barely breathing. The handle kept turning from side to side and someone leaned forcefully against the door. There was only meant to be one pilgrim staying upstairs, but there were definitely two males trying to get into my room. My heart pounded faster and harder. I had done the wrong thing in leaving the front door unlocked. I had allowed strangers to enter the house. Now there was some bumping against the door, as if they were trying to ram it open with hip and shoulder. They spoke French to each other, or was it to me? I couldn't be sure.

"Hello!" I called out, wanting to let them know someone was inside. "Hello!" I called again, hoping it was loud enough for them to hear me.

They kept twisting the door handle from side to side and bumping the door. I didn't think they were ever going to stop, so I got out of bed and while leaning up against the door, I unbolted the lock and let the door open against my shoulder. Fifty centimetres from my face was a guy in his twenties. His clothes reeked of strong, pungent cigarettes and the mild sweetness of alcohol wafted off his breath. I looked into his eyes that I remember only as being pools of blackness. He was drunk. My vision expanded and I saw another young guy standing a metre behind him. He wobbled on his feet, drunk. They spoke French to each other then to me. I stared at them dumbly and kept leaning my weight up against the door.

"...lits," one of them said, pointing into the room.

I was tired and alarmed and not thinking clearly. I looked at him blankly for a few seconds until my brain understood. They wanted to come into the room, to sleep in the beds.

"Non," I shouted and shoved the door shut in his face, bolting it to keep them out and me safely inside.

My heart raced and adrenaline started to course through my veins. My body automatically tensed itself like it was a giant fist ready to punch someone and my heart pounded my chest like it was trying to escape a cage. I was ready to run or ready to fight. This was meant to be a house for pilgrims, but they weren't pilgrims. I forced myself back into bed, breathing shallowly and straining to hear what was happening outside, above the boom of my pounding heart. A mobile phone rang. One of the guys answered and spoke for a minute then ended the call. From what I could hear and roughly translate, someone else was coming. Finally, the two of them went upstairs. I heard them talking then there was the sound of metal scraping on the floor as they dragged the beds around. It lasted for several minutes. I imagined they were trashing the room and that I would end up in trouble for all of this. I was the registered pilgrim. I had left the front door open. This was my fault.

I heard a car pull up and one more person entered the house. The stairs creaked as they walked upstairs. Maybe this was their friend from the phone call, or perhaps it was the 'pilgrim' with his stuff upstairs, except he had arrived by car and not on foot. I was still terrified and ready to run, but I had nowhere to go and I didn't want to leave in the dark. I realised that I didn't know the number for the police and no one back home knew exactly where I was. I could disappear and my family would only have a vague idea of where to start looking for me. I sent a text message to my eldest sister, Julie, in Melbourne, telling her where I was, that I was scared, that there were three drunk guys in the house, and that I needed a reassuring word and the phone numbers for the police, just in case. I clutched my phone to my chest like a security blanket, waiting for a response. Upstairs, the scraping stopped but the men were still talking. I started planning my escape at first light. I would get up at quarter past six, quietly pack everything back into the Devil, tiptoe out of the house, and then run down the road so I would never have to see these guys or the house again. Julie texted me back with a message praying for me to be safe and reminding me that I was brave. She also gave me the phone numbers for local police.

Thirty minutes later the house fell quiet. The men upstairs were asleep, and I was safe but still scared and thinking about my escape at first light. I wouldn't brush my teeth or use the toilet upstairs or even fill my water bladder. I just wanted to get out of there as quickly, quietly and invisibly as I could. As I thought about my escape, sleep finally came and stole me away in his grey prickly arms, three hours after the first two guys entered the house. In the morning, I woke before my alarm, blinked my eyes and remembered where I was, what had happened and that I needed to get out of there before the guys got up. I unzipped my sleeping bag halfway and climbed out of it slowly and quietly. The room was dark but my eyes adjusted so I could see in the grey fuzziness. The temperature continued to drop down to around 6°C overnight, so the air was cool but I didn't care. I just wanted out.

I dressed in the previous day's hiking clothes then gathered up the clothing I had hung over chairs and bed ends to dry and air, piling it onto the bed, ready to pack. I started with my sleeping bag, slowly stuffing it into its cover. Then, as I shoved it inside the Devil, I heard the two guys talking and the stairs creaked as they descended and stood outside my door. I froze, not wanting to breathe, not wanting to give any clue that I was in there and awake. They spoke for a few minutes then the front door opened. Footsteps crunched along the gravel path. Car doors opened. There was more talking then car doors closed and the engine started. Tyres crunched over fine gravel and the hum of the engine faded as the car drove away. I stood frozen for a minute longer, wanting to make sure they were both gone. When I was sure they had and were not returning, I continued my packing. I only had the towel and t-shirt that were hanging on the hooks in the hallway left to pack when I heard the stairs creak again as the third guy walked downstairs. I froze once more, listening and waiting. He walked straight out the front door, closed it and locked it with the key. The metal flap of the letterbox lifted, followed by a tinny ring as the key was dropped in. I heard footsteps on the path and the click of the gate. A car door opened then closed and the engine fired. Its hum faded as it drove away. They had all gone. It was 6.45 a.m.

With the Devil packed and harnessed, I walked towards the front door. As I did, a key rattled in the lock and the handle turned. I froze again. They had returned, except I hadn't heard a car. My heart pounded and my breath caught in my throat. I stood there like a deer in headlights. When the door finally opened, my shoulders dropped and I released my breath. It was just a family: two middle-aged men, a couple of teenage boys and a young girl.

"*Bonjour,*" they chirped brightly as they walked through the door.

"*Bonjour,*" I replied on autopilot and stood blinking. I asked if they would sleep here tonight because of the festival.

"*Oui,*" the older man responded then added a flurry of words in French. The others started bringing in bags and pillows and sleeping bags from the car outside the gate.

I told them I was a pilgrim and that I was leaving. I walked my right index and middle fingers through the air. They moved out of the way and I stepped through the door, dropped my key into the letterbox and continued on the gravel path and out the gate.

Everything looks different in the morning light, except that house didn't as I turned to look at it one last time. It still looked eerie, especially with the two giant stag heads that were like beady black eyes with their antlers like thorny eyelashes. The window in between them, above the front door, was positioned like a square nose, glowing amber. It reminded me of the house on the cover of *The Amityville Horror*. One of my sisters read parts of that book to me when I was five years old, and I remember having nightmares just from looking at the front cover.

As I started to walk back towards the town, I realised that the whole situation might have been one big misunderstanding. They were just guys, probably locals from somewhere outside of town, who knew they were going to drink at the festival or stay late and had arranged to stay at the house in advance so they wouldn't have to drive home. I was alone, in a foreign country where I barely spoke the language, in a strange big house by myself, with two drunk guys wanting to come into my room in the middle of the night when I only expected one lone pilgrim to walk straight upstairs. I wished the woman at the tourist office had thought to tell me that other people would be staying at the house too, but it was too late for that now. The night had passed and I was safe. I texted Julie to let her know I was okay and that in my vulnerability I had misread the situation. I said I hoped I hadn't scared her.

The morning was crisp. I passed a dew-dropped grassy field that had a pair of auburn horses standing in the hovering mist. The orange glow of the rising sun kissed the thick tree trunks and gently lit the town surrounded by fog. Its beauty softened my heart and I started to let go of the memory of the night. I meandered my way into town, viewing it in the light of a new day and through new eyes. I followed a sign to a viewpoint over an old brick bridge patched with moss and stood above the village. The bridge led to the gate of the château that was once a strict school attended by Napoleon Bonaparte but was now a museum housing important paintings from the 17th and 18th centuries. On the main street, I discovered the town was waking up, preparing for another day of the festival. I walked into the closest bar, sat down at an empty table with the Devil on my back and was studied by the dozens of locals already drinking their coffee. I ordered my normal coffee but the waitress didn't understand.

"*Un café au lait chaude,*" I said again.

She shook her head and handed me a menu. It appeared my coffee had changed its name in this region.

"*Un café crème grande,*" I ordered instead.

As I walked between fields to the next village of Brienne-la-Vieille, mesmerised by the beauty of sun on fresh dew, I started to cry. My tears were soft and gentle at first but soon became wrenching sobs as I released the fear and nervous tension built up in my body. I sobbed until my body was free of convulsion and my breathing returned to normal. The night had passed and I was walking in this beautiful countryside, just a little more discerning now about where I would stay.

Twelve—The beauty in confusion

Brienne-la-Vieille to Langres

That day was filled with blue skies, soft sunshine and mostly hard bitumen on quiet country roads. I could hear gunshots as I approached woodlands, and I walked into the thick of the woods on narrow tracks that I dared not stray from. I ate my lunch in the gardens of the Saint-Léger church in Dolancourt, a very small village with a population of only 140. I took off the Red Beasts and laid my socks on the ground so the sweat could dry from them, and then lay down on the bench to soak in the gentle sun as I listened to the cheers and screams of kids playing in a pool.

On the outskirts of Bar-sur-Aube, I lost the trail in a field but managed to find my own way into town beside the railway line. There were only three options for accommodation, two of which were affordable and one was over my budget. I chose the cheapest hotel and walked to the other side of town only to find the reception unmanned. I rang both phone numbers on the sign but nobody answered. The attached restaurant was also closed and not due to open until six o'clock. I couldn't wait that long so I walked back into town to the other affordable option. I walked up and down the street several times, searching for it with no success. There was only one other option, and it was the expensive hotel just around the corner.

"Stuff it, Kym. After the night you had, you deserve a little comfort," I told myself.

The male receptionist spoke fluent English and escorted me to my room in a separate building out the back, past a small swimming pool that was green with algae. The room had cornflower yellow walls and an indigo blue carpet with gold spots. The bedspread on the queen bed was a matching cornflower yellow with dark green stripes. There was thermostat controlled heating, wi-fi and a big bathroom with a bathtub. After the receptionist left, I dumped the Devil on the ground and fell backwards onto the bed, still in my hiking clothes. The bed was comfortable and the building so secure that I couldn't even leave until reception opened at seven o'clock in the morning. I knew I would sleep safely that night and I did.

There were two options the next day to walk out of Bar-sur-Aube: the hard way, with a very steep climb into les Côtes d'Aube, the forest on the outskirts of town; or the easy way via the road that reduced the distance by 1.2 kilometres. The guidebook stated the main route would be challenging for riders and walkers with heavy packs but the reward would be a beautiful view over the Aube valley. The shortcut was tempting. The Devil was heavy and the day would be long with 38 kilometres to walk, but there was that possibility of the beautiful view over the Aube valley to consider. I only hesitated for a minute before I chose the harder route.

In the early morning light, Bar-sur-Aube was a different town to the one I had walked into the day before. The spires of the Saint-Maclou church were only just visible through the fog that hugged the town, and the round peach sun had just peeked above the bushy trees lining the riverbank. I continued across the bridge, following a group of students uphill. Out the front of the school, cigarette smoke drifted towards me from the clusters of teens standing around and talking before class. I continued past them and into the woods. The dirt track was moist not muddy and covered with leaves and twigs. I walked for 100 metres then paused, panting heavily. The guidebook was right. It was steep and hard going for walkers with heavy packs, but I wasn't going to give in. I walked another 100 metres, taking one slow step at a time until I arrived at an almost vertical drop into a deep gully. This couldn't be the right way. I retraced my steps back to the last sign I had seen and started again. Between some trees to my left was what I guessed could be a path. I followed it and a minute later found another sign. It was the right way. A few minutes later I stood exactly where I wanted to be. I had found the view.

Just beyond the border of trees, the hill dropped away to a valley I couldn't see because it was covered in a thick blanket of fog. Above, the sun spliced like a diamond against the pale blue sky streaked with jet streams. I stood staring, my breath stolen by the wonder of the scene before me. I felt like I had hiked above the clouds. The hard path was worth it. As I stood there, spell-bound by the incredible beauty, I remembered what my life used to be like before I started scuba diving and walking and paying attention to the world. Before that, I was merely surviving in the city, my vision restricted to four walls, computer screens, televisions or the car ahead of me as I drove to and from work. Now my life was reduced to few belongings, finding food and shelter, and making my way from town to town, but I was no longer just surviving. I was alive. As I stood and wondered what the Aube Valley looked like without the fog, I heard that wise voice from within and beyond speak to me once again.

"Don't be so desperate to see so clearly. The beauty is in the confusion."

For four years, I had struggled to find a clear vision for my life, not knowing what I was going to do. Now that I stopped wrestling with the questions, I understood that the confusion was not bad or a problem to solve but a gift that had led me into the magical unknown and to where I stood in that moment.

Eventually, I walked away from the amazing view, past a young man sleeping in his car then down a grassy track between fields towards the woods. The path was thick with sludgy mud that was impassable in places, but somehow I managed to skirt around the edges, and for once I was not repulsed by the mire. It was worth it for that view. The woods were quiet except for the rhythmic tapping of the woodpeckers. The silver-fingered sun infiltrated the tall trees, their leaves luminous and singing with life. The grass was again covered with lacy webs dotted with diamond dew. I emerged from the woods into sweeping vineyards and the valley that was still covered in fog. As I walked downhill between grapevines, I whispered the word *wow* again and again.

The locals in the area were keen to help me find my way. As I stood confused at a gravel intersection between the vineyards, a four-wheel drive passed and the male passenger pointed downhill on the right fork. On the other side of Fontaine, an old couple fixing the trellis of some vines stopped working to give me directions to Châteauvillain. The man spoke in a flurry of French as he gestured over the grapevines. I nodded my head, smiled and said *oui* frequently. I understood little of what he said but appreciated his kindness.

I arrived at Clairvaux Abbey just before midday and walked beside its crumbling brick walls to the gabled gateway that was only wide enough to allow a single car to pass through into the outer court that was now a car park. The abbey was once a Cistercian monastery founded by St Bernard but is now a tourist attraction, except for the high security prison that occupies the rear of the complex. A number of the original buildings remain standing, including the chapel for children, *l'hostellerie*, the cloisters, dormitory, refectory and the barn. I was keen to explore the abbey buildings but I had just missed the eleven o'clock tour and the next one wasn't until half past two, so I left. As I walked out of the abbey gates, I turned around and took a photo on my phone. A few minutes later, a plump dark-skinned woman caught up with me and accused me of taking a photo of her. I showed her the photo on my phone. Satisfied she wasn't in it, she turned around and walked back towards the abbey. I wondered why she was so upset then realised she probably didn't want to be photographed leaving the high security prison.

The rest of the day I walked on gravel tracks and roads, through meadows, past woodlands, through small villages, past shallow but fast running rocky rivers, and past locals working on small plots of land thick with growing vegetables and colourful flowers. Just outside the small town of Aizanville, I sat on a bridge over the River Aujon, admiring the cascading branches of the weeping willow dangling into its jade green waters. In Pont-la-Ville, I lay on the concrete retaining wall of the river in the shade of a tree. My final approach into Châteauvillain was past fields of corn and dead sunflowers all facing the same direction with their heads bowed towards the ground. I walked along the quiet bitumen road lined by old brick houses towards the cathedral. Its dark grey tiled spire topped by a cross was visible above the two- and three-storey buildings. According to my guidebook, there was only one *chambre d'hôtes* in town. My hosts, Maggie and Steve, were a friendly English couple who also ran the bar and restaurant next door. I followed Maggie upstairs and chose the first room she showed me. Sunlight streamed through the window past a chair. A floral bedspread covered the bed, and the cushions propped near the bedhead invited comfort. I showered then lay down to rest before dinner.

I had just one task left to do. The following night I would stay in the tiniest village of the whole trip and I needed to phone ahead to ensure I could stay in the only accommodation available. I still hated making telephone calls in French because I rarely understood anything more than *oui* or *non*. While I could have asked Maggie or Steve to make the call on my behalf, I wanted to be able do this for myself. I braced for five minutes of confusion except the lady answered my question quickly and simply.

"*Oui,*" the reply came back when I asked if she had a room tomorrow night. *Oui!* Finally, someone answered a question with a simple yes. She said many other things I didn't understand, but I asked again to confirm I had a room the next night and again she responded with *oui*. I thanked her and told her I would arrive after four o'clock then hung up feeling pleased that I had managed to arrange accommodation in French by myself.

In the morning, I walked away from Châteauvillain along a gravel road, excited to be on the road again, walking into another day of adventure with something new to be witnessed and experienced. As I approached the woods, I heard one gunshot then nothing more, but I was wary. The guidebook specifically warned that hunting of wild boar and deer could take place on any day and recommended that I wear bright colours and not stray off the paths. I entered the woods and passed a sign that read *Chasse tous les jours sauf mercredi prudence*. I was confused about whether I needed to be careful on Wednesdays or if it was safe on Wednesdays. I exercised prudence anyway, staying strictly on the paths. I took off my black jacket so I could be more visible in my bright red t-shirt, but I didn't hear another gunshot for the two hours I spent walking through those woods. If I were to worry about anything that day, I should have been more concerned about the possibility of getting lost in the woods. I zigzagged along wide and narrow tracks following the guide-book instructions and the signs painted on trees. Unusually, my map showed the forest as a pale green blob without any paths. If I got lost, I would be wandering around blindly trying to find my way. As it turned out, I lost my way only once, and as soon as I realised, I turned around and retraced my steps back to the last sign.

That afternoon, I walked through another woodland, happily shaded from the sun. The last five days had involved mostly road walking, where I was exposed to the constant but beautiful sunshine. Although I wore my cap and put on the SPF50 sunscreen every morning, my arms and face were becoming deeply tanned while the soft skin around my eyes remained noticeably paler, with a look I called the reverse panda. The woods were a beautiful place to walk. The earthy floor was damp, often muddy, and carpeted with rotting leaves in hues of yellow, tan, and paper-bag brown. There were toadstools big and small, in clusters and alone, some tan and others pale grey, thriving in the decomposing muck. The leaves that grew thickly on the upper branches of the trees caught the sun and glowed radiant green, filtering softer light to the forest floor. The woods were quiet with only the soft sound of subtle movements. Beetles climbed under and over leaves that rustled under their weight. The wind occasionally whooshed through the treetops. Twigs crackled as they fell. Occasionally, invisible birds chirped.

By mid-afternoon, I emerged from the woodland into the little hamlet of Mormant. After walking past some crumbling brick ruins, I was approached by an old lady with white hair. She was broad and short, no taller than the middle of my chest, and was slightly hunched over. She spoke in French and gestured for me to follow, leading me towards a two-storey house. I tried to ask her if she were the woman I had spoken to on the phone the night before. She said something like *ma belle fille*. I thought she meant her 'beautiful daughter', but a friend later suggested it means daughter-in-law. Whatever it meant, I was relieved the *oui* from my telephone conversation really meant I had a room. She led me upstairs to a large bedroom with a double bed. Downstairs was a large kitchen and living area with a television that I had all to myself. She left and I understood that *ma belle fille* would come later, which she did. Her name was Annicka and she was an angel. She made sure that I had dinner with me and telephoned the presbytery in Langres to arrange a bed for me for the next night.

Mormant was just a cluster of old houses, a farm and the ruins of an abbey. It was small in size, but big on crumbling charm and beauty. Some of the abbey's brick structure was still standing although much of it was reduced to large piles of brick and rubble. In a field, two kids played with two brown horses. A black cat with glowing yellow-green eyes sat primly on a brick wall like she were queen of the village. As I returned to the house, the golden sun dipped behind a naked tree. I ate my shepherd's pie in front of the television, watching the news. I felt so rested and peaceful and blessed to be there in that village, to have spent so much time deep in the woods alone, and by the kindness of the people I was meeting on my journey.

Despite the peace and tranquillity of my surrounds, I slept badly, tossing and turning, and waking up too hot beneath the blankets. After finally falling asleep, the throbbing and aching in my feet, knees and legs woke me again. I walked to the bathroom for some water and on my way back to bed I stopped to look out the bedroom window. The sky was cloudless, a dark silver blue revealing galaxies of stars shining brightly. The Three Sisters were the brightest, perfectly aligned in front of my window. The half moon was luminous and milky. Below it, the village was dark except for the incandescent light shining from the second floor window of the house diagonally opposite. I wondered briefly who else was awake at three o'clock in the morning and why.

Thirteen—Desperate distances

Mormant to Dampierre-sur-Salon

Without intending to, I set my alarm an hour too late. Perhaps my subconscious knew my body was tired and needed some extra rest, but I had agreed with Annicka to have breakfast at half past eight and I didn't want to be late. I woke from my deep slumber with only fifteen minutes to dress and pack. I didn't rush but moved swiftly and with intent. In twenty-five minutes I was ready and went downstairs to enjoy breakfast only a little late. I poured a large mug of coffee, dropped in two perfectly white sugar cubes then sawed off a chunk of baguette that I split down the middle and slathered with creamy butter and sweet raspberry jam. Annicka hovered around the kitchen washing dishes and tidying. When I finished eating, I wrote a message of sincere gratitude in her guestbook, paid her and went back upstairs to fetch the Devil.

I walked slowly out into the day, feeling no need to rush. Those first two hours, when the light was still soft, were the best part of the day. The pink-tinged dawn had brightened and the low-lying sun filtered through the crisp air, softening everything. Once on the main road, I stopped and looked back at the ruins of the abbey. I hoped I would always remember the peace I felt at being in this little pocket of the Earth that I never would have visited if not for the pilgrim way I was walking. I continued along the main road but soon veered off onto a narrow bitumen road that led back towards the Voie Romaine then back into the woods. I passed through an electric fence, opening the gate with great care, unsure if it was unearthed or if I might get zapped. The morning was filled with glistening dewdrops, purple wildflowers and more fields of dead sunflowers with their heads bowed towards the ground but still radiant in their death.

The guidebook instructions didn't match the signs in the woods and I wasn't sure which path to take. I walked along, trusting that I was going the right way, until I lost my way in the middle of the woods. Unexpectedly, a dozen or so guys and girls in their late twenties and early thirties stood chatting in a clearing next to three stationary four wheel drive vehicles. I asked for help and eventually got them to understand that I was looking for the GR145 by showing them the guidebook. Two of the guys read it, nodded then looked over at the woods and pointed directly in front of me. It didn't look like a path to me, but they insisted it was. I thanked them and walked through the wild grass and underbrush and within a minute I saw a sign. They were right and I felt embarrassed that I had lost the path directly in front of me.

I continued on, stepping over toadstools pushing their way up through the damp earth, avoiding a worm wriggling its way through the mud, and of course walking around more muddy paths. When I finally emerged from the coolness of the woods, giant fairy floss clouds hung in the sky, providing sporadic shade from the sun's stinging rays. I walked along the quiet bitumen road, noticing all the purple wildflowers, thinking there really is something ethereal about all the different shades of purple. After lunch, I reached the dark jade waters of Lac de la Mouche, a 400-metre-long dam. I sat beside it for a while, watching the sun's diamond-studded rays bounce off ripples as two men fished from a small boat. Then I continued up the steep path into the surrounding hills. My thighs burned and I had to pause to catch my breath. Before long, I was back in the countryside, walking over cracked, parched earth that was scattered with white feathers. Descending the woody hills, I emerged onto a road to see the walled city of Langres perched high up on a hill before me. I paused at the base of the hill before I commenced my ascent. It seemed like the steepest climbs were always at the end of the day. Fortunately, this one was short. I put my head down and marched on without stopping until I was standing on the flat path that lead me victoriously into the town through Porte Neuve.

Three-storey beige terraces with white window shutters lined the street. Shops occupied their ground levels while the upper ones appeared to be apartments. Langres Cathedral was partly obscured by scaffolding. Bright red doors brightened its dirty stone façade. I walked along the pavement towards the presbytery, feeling nervous about staying in pilgrim accommodation after my experience at Brienne-le-Château, but I didn't need to worry here. The presbytery offered only two beds for bona fide pilgrims with credentials, and the priest locked the gate at half past eight at night, not opening it again until seven o'clock the next morning. Reading through the guestbook, I saw there had only been a few pilgrims who stayed there over the last couple of weeks. I was the only pilgrim to stay that night. The last few days had been pain-free. It was only at night when my feet and body ached. The regular resting, massaging of my feet and airing of my socks and innersoles so they could dry all helped. I had read that long-distance walking causes foot-spread, but I didn't really know what that meant or that you could see it. My feet looked fat and wide as the muscles and flesh bulged. They were becoming strong feet.

I left Langres the next morning through an avenue of birch trees. The leaves were turning from lime to lemon, except for the rusted tan leaves that lay already abandoned beneath my feet. In a clearing beyond a house on the Voie Verte, I watched the sun rise in a swirl of gold and apricot above thick white cloud on the horizon. As I turned onto the road after Saints-Geosmes, I walked towards more thick silvery clouds that shrouded the sun, resulting in summertime cool air with a promise of heat to come. After lunch, by which time I had clocked 25 kilometres, I walked on minor roads where there was no shade from the scorching sun. There wasn't any breeze either. I wore all black as usual and was hot. The pain that had returned again crippled my body, but I still had another 16 kilometres to walk. I cried then let it go and accepted that all I could do was take one step after another and keep going. Soon, my rhythm came back and I felt more at ease.

The last kilometre was a constant incline that was really tough on my aching feet and legs that were tired after walking for 40 kilometres. I knew from my pedometer that I averaged 1417 steps per kilometre, so I counted each step. This distracted me from the pain and made it easier to keep going, knowing that with each step I counted I was closer to arriving. I continued past the grand château—now an arts museum with manicured lawns divided by a wide, white gravel path that was lined with bench seats and blue wooden tubs planted with lollypop shrubs—then straight to the first hotel on my list. The receptionist gave me their basic room. It looked like it hadn't been painted or redecorated since the 1990s, which appeared to be a common theme in the area. I had a small window overlooking the inner courtyard and a television that could only be switched on by a remote control that didn't work. I didn't have the energy to walk back downstairs to reception and ask for new batteries. Instead, I stripped off my dirty, sweaty clothes and lay naked under the bedcovers.

I was already cold, going into shock after the long walk. I needed to have a shower and wash my dirty clothes, but I didn't have the energy or desire to stand up just yet. My body rejected the 41-kilometre day. My spirit rejected it too. To my surprise, I found that walking at a rate of four kilometres per hour was too fast. I wanted to walk slower, to meander and rest a little more, to drink in my surroundings and fully absorb these moments that I would experience only once. I did not want to march on and on relentlessly to reach my next destination, but I was walking through a non-tourist section of France where the distance I covered each day was dictated by where I could find accommodation.

I slept until half past seven the next morning then lay in bed for another hour, enjoying the stillness and the knowledge that I didn't need to leave until after eleven o'clock at the earliest. I rolled out of bed tentatively, expecting the electric pain to shoot through my feet, but there were only a couple of twinges in each arch that ceased after the first few steps. I lingered over my simple French breakfast then went to the supermarket to pick up dinner and lunch for two days in case there was no supermarket, restaurant or bar in Dampierre-sur-Salon. The supermarket was small and not well stocked. There were only a few unappetising, pre-packaged sandwiches, so I bought a baguette, some mortadella and cheese and what I hoped was butter. It was a plastic tray with ten small rectangles covered in gold foil with *levure de boulangerie* written on them. I knew it had something to do with bread because of *boulangerie.*

By the time I returned to my room, I had only twenty-five minutes until I had to checkout and I hadn't even packed. I moved quickly and had just piled the last of my things into the Devil when the female receptionist rang to hurry me. She said she needed the room fifteen minutes ago. As I closed the bag, I realised that I forgot to fill my water bladder. I pulled a few items out of the Devil then dragged it to the bathroom and used the complimentary plastic cup to fill the bladder with nine small glasses of water, hoping that would be enough to get me through the day. I rushed to put my socks and boots on then and made it down to reception at 11.02 a.m., two minutes after my checkout time.

I promised myself that it would be a slow day. I relaxed and didn't rush, knowing that I would arrive when I arrived. The day before, I walked with a subtle essence of desperation and a subconscious voice reminding me that it was a long walk and I still had far to go. I felt like I was never going to make it but I had to make it, so I kept pressing on even when I wanted to rest. I knew that I needed to be aware of that voice and to change its message when necessary.

In the absence of any bus stops or any other seats or walls in the shade, I sat for lunch on the front porch of a vacant two-storey house near a factory. I untied the baguette from the side of the Devil, cut it in half then took out the plastic tray of little butter packets. I opened one of them, but instead of finding pale lemon butter inside, I was presented with a hideous, pale grey substance. I didn't have to taste it to know it wasn't butter. I put the tray in my rubbish bag and made my baguette with just the mortadella and cheese. As I ate, I typed *levure de boulangerie* into my translator app and pressed translate. The answer came back: bakery yeast. Nothing like butter.

That day I saw at least six eagles circling majestically above the woodlands or swooping into trees. I usually heard them first then followed the sound of their unique cry to its source. Gone now was the vivid green of lush grass, to be replaced by the dusky green of seedlings and ploughed earth like pale pumpkin-coloured sand. I watched a tiny ladybug walk silent across the dry earth at my feet, and I helped a crazy cricket to the safety of the grass after it kept falling onto its back and flailing its legs about, unable to navigate the bumpy bitumen. Butterflies with a violet cat's eye on each brown and auburn wing fluttered over wildflowers. Being outdoors helped to heightened my senses. Somehow, I always looked down at my feet just in time to avoid stepping on critters, slugs, crickets, beetles, snails, worms and even toadstools. Goliath is not God, and everything has a right to life. As a child and even a teenager, I would pick up worms and snails that crossed my path and put them safely on grass so they wouldn't be squished accidentally by a careless foot. But it was travelling and scuba diving that really awoke my environmental awareness, as I saw how destructive human beings can be, how we use and abuse our earthly home, and how we harm our domestic and wild animals.

Although I felt like I was walking more slowly than the previous day, I still arrived at Dampierre-sur-Salon just after four o'clock, averaging four kilometres an hour, as usual. However, this was a more enjoyable experience and not as emotionally strenuous as the previous day, not because it was shorter but because of how I walked. I crossed the bridge adorned with trays of red, pink and white geraniums then turned onto a quiet residential street to my *chambre d'hôtes*. My white-haired host greeted me as soon as I walked into the courtyard and showed me into the kitchen where he gave me a glass of cold orange juice. My bedroom upstairs was a large room containing two single beds, each with a bedside table and lamp. I dumped the Devil and put my waist bag on the table near the ensuite bathroom. The dark floorboards creaked as I walked over to the bench seat under the window that had a view of grassy paddocks beyond the back garden.

"*Bien*?" My host asked, checking to see if I thought it was okay.

"*Tres bien, merci.*" It was quiet and quaint; the perfect place to stay.

Following breakfast the next day, I set off along the quiet main road. Being early on Saturday morning, there was little traffic. I walked past an apartment building several stories high. From an open window, I heard raised voices that were verging on angry. A bare-chested man leaning out a window next to three large pumpkins sucked on a cigarette. I pretended to ignore him and kept walking, looking ahead for the left fork I was meant to take. When I didn't see it coming anytime soon, my gut started protesting. Something wasn't quite right. I checked the map and decided to geolocate myself. My gut instinct was right. I had walked for twenty minutes the wrong way out of town. I shook my head and laughed. It could have been worse. I could have walked for another forty minutes or an hour. The mistake cost me three kilometres, but that was better than any more.

As I marched back towards town, I stepped off the road to look at a concrete statue of Mary. She wore a draping gown and had a halo of stars above her head. A weeping willow dotted with lemon leaves bowed behind her. Mary's eyes were closed and she smiled as if she were experiencing a serene and beautiful moment of pure love. In that moment, I had that experience too. Tears burned the back of my eyes. I understood then that there was no wrong way to walk on this pilgrim trail, just as there is no wrong way to walk in life, except to be asleep with eyes closed to the beauty around us and within us, thinking that we're meant to be somewhere other than exactly where we are.

Fourteen—Keep calm

Dampierre-sur-Salon to Besançon

It was a charming day of walking through petite farming villages along quiet country roads and between woodlands. At lunchtime, I stretched out in the sun next to a *lavoir,* the old public space that was once used for washing clothes, and read a book, relaxed by the sound of the running water and the warmth of the sun on my skin. I arrived into Gy just after half past three, and passed a family playing bocce on the grass as I walked towards the quiet main street. The first *gîte* on my list was closed. I rang the phone number on the door and asked for a room but was told they weren't open that night. I was surprised but not concerned and walked farther along the road to the hotel that other pilgrims had given good reviews. One described it as a three-star hotel for the price of a two-star hotel. I looked forward to a night of inexpensive comfort, and as I passed the pizzeria, I could already taste the pizza with anchovies and capers and the icy cold beer I would have for dinner.

I arrived at the front door of the hotel to find it was locked and unattended. On a metal A-frame sign was a phone number to call for information. I sat down on the step and rang the number. It rang once and disconnected. I tried again. It disconnected again. I sat and waited for a few moments then tried again, and again it disconnected. I turned my phone off then on and tried again. The sixth time I dialled the number, it rang for a long time until eventually a woman answered. I gave her my usual spiel about being a pilgrim, but when I asked if they had a room, instead of answering a simple *oui* or *non,* she responded with a string of sentences that were beyond my comprehension. In French, I told her that I didn't understand and spoke only a little French, but this didn't help. She kept rambling and I still didn't understand.

"*Non comprende,*" I told her again, starting to feel exasperated. "*Une chambre ce soir, oui?*"

She still didn't answer yes or no but rambled on.

"*Une chambre ce soir, non?*" I tried again. I just wanted her to answer with a simple yes or no to having a room, and then she could ramble as much as she liked. I listened intently, trying to understand. I thought she said something about 'late' but wasn't sure. Finally I heard *non* and took this as my answer. I thanked her, said goodbye and hung up.

I still had one more option: the Office de Tourisme. They could help me find somewhere to stay. I walked back along the street and found the small shop, except it had a closed sign hanging on its glass front door. On Saturdays, they closed at two o'clock in the afternoon. It was now four o'clock. A little pot of panic started to simmer in my belly, but that voice from within and beyond told me firmly to keep calm. And so I did. I walked to the bus stop, sat down with the Devil still on my back and studied the guidebook. There was one last option in Gy, a rural *gîte* just outside of town on the other side of the highway. I rang the number but there was no answer. I tried the mobile number. It diverted to message bank so I left a message in French, hung up and hoped they would call back immediately. Just like a watched pot never boils, a watched phone never rings. Starting to feel desperate, I proceeded to stalk both numbers, ringing the landline, and when that wasn't answered, hanging up and trying the mobile again and again. Finally I stopped trying. It was a sensible decision, as I never received a return call from either number.

It had to happen sooner or later, that I would arrive into a town and not be able to find accommodation. It seemed that today was the day.

"Keep calm," the wise voice within reminded me, against my rising panic.

Okay, but now what?

There was nowhere else to stay in Gy. The accommodation listing indicated that the Association of St Joseph provided emergency accommodation in Frasne-le-Château, except I couldn't find Frasne-le-Château on my map. There were a couple of accommodation options that I passed hours earlier, but I didn't want to backtrack and make the next day's walk to Besançon 40 kilometres long. I could keep walking, but the next accommodation on the route was at the end of the next section, which was 15 kilometres away and uphill. That was unattractively too far. I would arrive in the dark, after half past eight, but if I didn't want to backtrack or sleep in the bus stop then maybe I had no choice.

Can I do it? I asked myself as I blinked away tears. Of course I could, but I didn't want to.

I checked the list one more time and saw a *chambre d'hôtes* in a town called Choye. I expected that it would be over the hill or too far away, but I looked for it on my map anyway. When I found it, hope flickered. The town was south-west of Gy, only four kilometres away. It was off the official Via Francigena route and in the wrong direction, but I had only two feasible choices: to walk 15 kilometres uphill in the dark, making the total distance I travelled 44 kilometres for the day, or walk four kilometres off the trail and retrace the same four kilometres back in the morning.

I dialled the number in Choye and a lady answered after only three rings. I told her I was a pilgrim who had arrived in Gy to find there was no room for me here and asked if she had one available. I sounded desperate, a mere step away from begging.

"*Oui*," she answered.

Oui! I was saved.

"*Merci! Merci beaucoup!*" I gushed. I was ecstatic and told her I would arrive in one hour.

I jumped up with the Devil on my back and walked straight to the *boulangerie* to buy supplies for dinner and lunch. There would be no pizza and beer for me that night. Instead, I would eat something that looked like a cheese roll, with a chocolate éclair for dessert. I marched to Choye with a smile on my face, grateful for having found a room and amused that I almost didn't have one. The smile faded as I marched on the damp, grassy verge of the busy road, but it returned when a car stopped and a couple offered to give me a lift. I declined with genuine thanks.

I walked into the warmest welcome by my hosts, Jean-Noël and Samia. They were generous-hearted country folk and horse people. Jean-Noël often went riding in the nearby woods and the two of them occasionally had people stay who brought their own horses. They welcomed me with big smiles and I put my hands together at my heart and thanked them, telling them I thought I wouldn't have anywhere to sleep that night. They laughed, perhaps at my bad French. Samia showed me straight to my room. I had a big double bed, a lounge area, television and a bathroom all to myself.

After washing my face and taking the Red Beasts off my feet, I joined Samia and Jean-Noël at the table in the courtyard and drank a glass of cold and sweet homemade cordial. Neither of them spoke any English and my French was far from fluent or correctly pronounced—I had called Choye *choy* when it is actually pronounced *shwah*—but I was mastering the art of stringing individual words together with a lot of charades to communicate. We sat around the table in their courtyard for an hour and a half, chatting about my pilgrimage and about horses, walking, their children, and the route I could walk tomorrow back to the trail. The sun was close to setting and the air a little chilly when they got up to go inside to prepare their dinner and we said *bonne nuit*. I showered and ate my cheese rolls, musing over what had almost been the night I had no accommodation but wasn't. These lovely people were the first proper company I'd had since meeting Jacques three weeks ago. In only one more day, I would see him again.

Jean-Noël and Samia waved me farewell from their front gate the next morning and I set off in high spirits. Eight hours of walking and I would see Jacques again and receive my new boots. No more leaky Red Beasts. No more white soggy feet. The morning sky was clumped with silver cottonwool clouds. Low on the horizon the sun glowed gold, but the layer of cloud was too thick for it to break through. Fifteen minutes after I left, the sky started to spit and then to stream. I expected rain so I had attached Kermit to my waist belt for easy access. I covered the Devil and myself in its bright greenness and continued walking.

I mapped a network of country roads, tracks and forest trails that would enable me to cut back onto the official trail and save a couple of kilometres instead of walking all the way back to Gy. Jean-Noël told me the way could be steep and muddy, and I knew there was a chance that the trails on the map might not really exist, but I decided it was worth the risk. I walked up a steep hill with the rain still tumbling down, past the blue and yellow scallop shell signs of the St James Way, the more popular pilgrimage trail to Santiago de Compostela. As I approached the woodlands that were the final obstacle between the official trail and me, it stopped raining and the sun burst through weak clouds on the horizon in a glow of golden apricot. I was surprised to hear cars approaching behind me. The first car contained a middle-aged man and two teenage boys. The next car had two more young men. I wondered where they were going but assumed that, as they were driving towards the forest, the road must lead somewhere. Then I walked past an old white Fiat parked on the side of the road. The passenger door was open and a white-haired man wearing khaki pants and a shirt and a bright yellow vest sat with his legs outside the car, drinking hot coffee. In the back of the car in a cage was a hound, and a rifle leaned up against the boot of the car. It was Sunday. Hunting day.

I passed eight parked cars then two hunters carrying guns as I entered the forest. It was disconcerting to be alone in a foreign forest, knowing there were men with guns wandering around. I had no service on my mobile phone but I continued on anyway. I draped Kermit around my shoulders and over the Devil to make myself more visible, and I stayed on the path. The forest was beautiful, full of young birch trees, tall and thin. On the path of damp dirt that was soaked to mud in places were scattered leaves of tan and rust. Some of them were still tinged green and yellow. The forest was silent. Not a single bird chirped, but I heard no gunshots or human voices either. I assumed the hunters were stalking *la chasse* in stealth or were in a section of forest far from me.

As I bent down to take a photo of the forest's autumn carpet, I felt a sudden urge to look up. I don't know what made me want to do that, but I think that the more time we spend in nature, the more attuned we become as it silently speaks to us. Just 50 metres ahead of me, two deer appeared at the edge of the path, ready to cross into the next section of forest. The stag was dark brown with jagged antlers sticking out each side of his head. The fawn doe was smaller and had no antlers. They looked directly at me then crossed the path and walked off into the trees. Slowly and quietly, I walked to where they had stood. I looked among the thin trees, hoping to see them once more but they were already gone. A minute later, a lone hunter walked towards me with his rifle slung over his shoulder. I was glad that the deer were out of sight and I prayed that they stayed safe. I walked on, buzzing with awe and gratitude.

The path through the woods was flat until it suddenly descended into a steep gully with a gradual but longer climb out the other side. The drop was impossible for me to walk down with the Devil without slipping or falling, so I zigzagged my way into the gully through the surrounding trees and undergrowth where it was less steep and then cut back onto the trail to climb back up the other side. I reached the top and stood there for a minute, catching my breath and waiting for the burn in my legs to subside before continuing on, only to find the path disappeared completely. In front of me where there should have been a path was nothing but trees, both standing and fallen. I tried the path to my right then the path to my left, but they each wound away from the road. With no other option, I climbed through the undergrowth and beneath the fallen trees near the road, where I waited for a car to pass before breaking out of the forest by squeezing myself through the thick hedge.

Later in the afternoon, I arrived in Besançon and found my way to the train station. I leaned up against the concrete base of a light pole and rang Jacques.

"Jacques, c'est Kym. Je suis ici, à Besançon, à la gare."

"...cinq minutes," was all I understood of the numerous French words he spoke in reply.

I took the Devil off my back and sat on the concrete base of the light pole, waiting the five minutes for Jacques to arrive. It was a moment to celebrate. Today was 29 September and I had walked 783 kilometres in 29 days and finished the first of the three guidebooks for the Via Francigena. I had made it this far alone, through mud and rain and with searing pain. As I sat there reflecting on my journey so far, I realised that I no longer doubted I could make it all the way to Rome.

Fifteen—Pilgrim solidarity

Besançon to Mamirolle

Jacques appeared suddenly in front of me. I greeted him with a joyous *bonjour*. He kissed me on each cheek then hoisted the Devil off the ground and deposited it in the boot of his car. I climbed into the passenger seat and we set off. I assumed we would go directly to his place. I wanted to shower and get out of my mud-splattered hiking pants, but Jacques wanted to give me a guided tour of Besançon... in French. Not slowed down or simplified French for my beginner's level of understanding but normal, everyday, fast French. He parked the car and we got out, just as it started raining lightly. I sheltered beneath my tiny travel umbrella as I trotted behind him.

We started at the old pilgrim entrance to the town then walked past an old pilgrim refuge and across a bridge over the river Doubs into the old medieval town centre. We visited Besançon Cathedral, where we admired the gilded altar and the stained glass windows, before emerging back into the grey pre-dusk to visit Victor Hugo's house and the Palais de Justice. Along the way, we stopped to chat with the numerous people that he knew. I was grateful for the tour, but more grateful to be sitting back in his car and driving to his house, which was ten minutes away. It was a two-storey townhouse behind a high-rise apartment complex facing a huge grassy park with a view to the Jura Mountains. It was tidy and was furnished with modern but elegant furniture. Jacques presented me with a box then went outside to brush the dirt off our boots. Inside the box was my new pair of bright red boots: my Red Beasts version 2. I pulled them out of the box and clutched them to my chest. Finally, my poor feet could walk in dry comfort. I tried them on and walked around. They felt firmer but more cushioned than Red Beasts version 1. Many kilometres of walking had worn them down significantly. Jacques came back in and put our boots down near the door.

"Jacques! Look!" I gushed pointing down at my feet. "*Nouveau* boots!" I smiled and hopped from foot to foot. "Feel *beaucoup differente. Merci beaucoup!*"

While I danced around in my boots, Jacques brought out some snacks from the kitchen: olives, breadsticks and four bottles of wine for me to choose from. We drank champagne and chatted about our journeys, him in French and me in Frenglish. While I showered, Jacques cooked us steak and potatoes for dinner. After we ate, he printed off a list of all the *donativo* (donation-based) accommodation between Besançon and Vercelli. Then he showed me the photos from his walk. *All* the photos. We would get to the end of one batch and then there was another batch then another. I was so tired I could barely keep my eyes open, but he was so excited to show them to me that I didn't have the heart to stop him. I was relieved when the show finally finished and he guided me to my bed for the night.

When I went downstairs for breakfast the following morning, I found Jacques packing his daypack. He wanted to accompany me for part of the walk. I didn't expect this and to my surprise I had mixed emotions. I wanted to preserve my solitude while walking. I wasn't sure that I could maintain my strong connection to the world around me unless I was alone, as the company and chatter of another human would be too distracting. But Jacques' company wasn't optional—he was coming with me. As we left, Jacques gifted me a pair of navy blue canvas and rattan slippers to wear at night. They were at least another 300 grams that I didn't need to carry, but I didn't have the heart or language to decline the gift. Instead I thanked him and crammed them inside the Devil, along with the pear and banana he gave me. I was weighed down with kindness.

As we walked to the car, Jacques carried the original Red Beasts in a plastic bag to throw in the rubbish. I knew they were just boots, inanimate objects, but I felt sad to part with them. They had been with me every step of the way for thirty days, even if they did let me down and leak, at first a little and then a lot. It was time for them to pass the baton and permanently retire. Jacques decided that we would drive up to Chapelle des Buis and walk from there. I didn't know how to tell him that my intention was to walk all the way, which meant I wanted to continue walking from Besançon up to Chapelle des Buis, even if that meant walking four kilometres up the steep hill. Sometimes we have to let go of our ideas about how things should be, and this was one of those times. Still, my subconscious voice chastised me for a good part of the morning, telling me I was cheating and that I wasn't walking all the way. I couldn't change what happened, so I noticed the thoughts and let them go.

Jacques parked the car near a bus stop then marched me a small way down the hill to show me the steep steps I would have walked up from town and to point out a Via Francigena sign he had personally nailed to a tree, as he ran the region's Via Francigena Association. We walked back to the car, put on our backpacks and started walking, although marching might be a better word to describe it. Jacques walked fast, taking each step with conviction, strength and a joyful bounce. I liked taking photos, but Jacques wouldn't stop to wait for me. He just kept marching on and I would jog-march to catch up to him. I took few photos that morning.

The path was undulating and slippery, not ideal conditions to break in my new boots. They wouldn't grip on the rocks, and I slipped several times. Jacques instructed me to put my weight down on the balls of my feet when walking downhill. Doing so stopped me slipping, but it hurt the ball of my left foot where I had developed a Morton's neuroma, a thickening of the tissues around the nerve between my third and fourth toes. During the four hours we walked together, he pointed out almost every Via Francigena sign and noted whether it was pointing towards Rome or back to Canterbury. He really loved the trail and the work he had put into it to help others find their way.

Although Jacques led the way, I still liked to check my guidebook and map, interested to see exactly where we were and if the guidebook's route matched the way we were walking. Every time I checked, Jacques rolled his eyes and said something in French that I translated as "Bah, guidebook, map! You don't need them". Then he would chuckle sarcastically. After a while, I only checked when I lagged behind him and he wasn't watching. We stopped for coffee at his friend's workplace. I was grateful for the fifteen-minute reprieve from the rain and the chance to sit in the warmth. Jacques also called his friend in Nods to arrange accommodation for me for the night. They chatted for ten minutes before he hung up.

"*Jacques, une chambre ce soir?*" I asked when he didn't offer any information. There wasn't a lot of accommodation on the trail along this section and I wanted to know I had somewhere to stay that night. He confirmed that I did have a room for the night and that my hostess spoke English. I made him write down the address for me and I tucked it safely into my waist bag.

After we stopped at the general store in Mamirolle to buy baguettes for lunch, I thought Jacques would turn back, but he continued walking with me uphill and out of town. I was ready for a proper rest break to sit down and eat my lunch, but Jacques marched on, so I followed behind him as he continued to point out signs he had placed along the way. When we reached the top of the hill, he showed me that the path split in two directions and indicated that I should follow the old traditional route straight ahead. Then he told me that he wouldn't walk any farther with me and was turning back. Suddenly our time together seemed so short. I was ready to walk alone again, but not ready to say goodbye. I felt like I was leaving an old friend I would never see again. Jacques had been so generous with giving me accommodation and food and receiving my new boots for me. I felt it was only right to offer him something, but he waved away the money I offered him.

"*Non, non.*" He shook his head. "Pilgrim solidarity," he then said in English.

Yes. Pilgrim solidarity. Tears burned my eyes and I blinked them away as I hugged him and he kissed me on each cheek.

"*Au revoir,*" I said.

"*Au revoir,*" he replied then turned and walked back in the direction from which we had come. I turned around at the same time and kept walking towards Rome, alone, without looking back.

Sixteen—To the border

Mamirolle to Jougne

Alone again, I could walk my own pace and pause to take photographs as often as I wanted. I started doing so straight away, taking pictures of the heart-shaped leaves of the flowerless common morning glory, the first wild holly I had ever seen, and yellow and brown leaves lying beneath a canopy of green. I ignored the rain, not worried about getting a little bit wet from the few splatters that managed to penetrate the thick canopy overhead. When I reached a clearing, I put up my travel umbrella. It kept the rain off my head and mostly off the Devil until five minutes later it started pouring. Rain streamed like a waterfall off the back of my umbrella and down onto the Devil. There was nowhere to shelter. My backpack and pant legs were getting soaked. I needed to put on my Kermit poncho. I tried to wrangle it off the right side of the Devil where it was stowed without taking the pack off my back and while still holding on to my umbrella, but I couldn't. I took off the Devil and rested it on my boots to keep it out of the puddle that was growing around my feet. I unbuckled Kermit, threw the Devil back on then put down the umbrella and pulled Kermit on as quickly as I could. With Kermit on and the umbrella back in place over the Devil and my head, I continued on my way, damp but no longer getting wet.

I was ravenous by the time I arrived in L'Hôpital-du-Grosbois in the rain. I had been looking for somewhere I could sit and eat lunch and I had my hopes pinned on a bus stop, but there were none to be seen in this town. Instead, in the square next to the town hall, I sat on top of Kermit under a plastic shelter with notices pinned to its back wall and ate a baguette. The wind chilled my clothing that was damp from rain and sweat. I put on my windproof jacket, zipped it up to enclose my neck then leaned back against the shelter until the rain started to drip from the roof down my back. Directly opposite, a man walked out onto his verandah and gestured with a summoning wave and a friendly nod of his head for me to come over. I smiled and waved back dismissively, shaking my head side to side and he walked back inside his house. A few minutes later he walked out onto the verandah and gestured again.

"*Non, c'est bon ici, merci,*" I declined.

It wasn't really good, there where I was sitting. I was on the verge of an I-hate-walking-in-the-rain breakdown. Tears burned my eyes, ready and waiting for the okay to spill down onto my cheeks. The man's offer was kind, but I knew if I went over I would feel obligated to sit and chat when I just wanted to eat then start walking again and arrive in Nods. I had just stuffed the last of my escargot pastry in my mouth when I looked up and saw the man walking over towards me.

"*Venez pour un café,*" he said with a kind smile, inviting me to come back to his place for a coffee.

I couldn't argue. He had already picked up the Devil and had started walking back to his house. I stood up, brushed the crusty breadcrumbs off my chest and pants, picked up my rubbish, Kermit, my umbrella and waist bag, and followed him. He put the Devil down at the door and walked in. I took off the Red Beasts and went after him into the kitchen.

He was tall and solid with an obvious enjoyment of food, as indicated by his rounded belly that was pushing out the front of his white t-shirt. I felt awkward and wary. Like so many, as a child I learned stranger meant danger. The programming was still there, but I knew there was no danger here. The man just wanted to give me a coffee and a dry place to sit. We sat on his cream leather lounges and drank espresso. There were moments of awkward silence, but I reached back into the archives of my high school French to break it. He invited me to use his toilet, have a shower, connect to wi-fi and even sleep, but I declined all of these offers. Rain or no rain, I needed to get to Nods. I stood up to leave and he offered to drive me. I thanked him but declined and proceeded to put on the Red Beasts, the Devil and Kermit. He stood at his front door as he watched me walk away in the rain.

My energy was renewed and I started to see the blessings of walking in the rain, like the dozens of spider webs holding giant globules of glistening raindrops that hung like horizontal nets in the ivy growing around the base of the birch trees. Without the rain, this beauty would not exist. I wanted to remember this moment the next time I found myself walking in the rain with dampened spirits. There was a lot of mud around, but I found my peace walking in the rain and I started to find peace with the mud too. I couldn't avoid it on this trail. It kept showing up time and time again. Mud is a part of life, which isn't always clean and smooth travelling. You just have to keep walking through it until you get to the other side. Sure, it might stick for a while and it might be messy, but it doesn't last forever and it does wash off.

When I could no longer match the guidebook directions to the landmarks around me, I decided to follow the GPS track on Pocket Earth. For 600 metres, I trudged along the busy highway with cars and trucks speeding past me as the occupants turned to stare at me in my bright green cloak. From my research, I knew that a number of pilgrims had walked to Rome predominantly along the major roads instead of the trails and tracks in order to shorten the distance. There is no right or wrong way to walk, but I never enjoyed walking along the busy roads. I was always anxious, sometimes afraid and often prayed to be kept safe. I was relieved to turn onto a quiet country road then onto farm tracks again, passing curious cows. If I had studied my map a little closer, I would have seen that the farm tracks didn't connect. Instead, I was surprised when the path ended at a fenced-off paddock. My only option was to climb under the rope and take my chances with the cows and bulls and hope that I didn't get caught trespassing. I picked up the rope and was zapped. Shocked, I dropped it. It wasn't ordinary rope but an electric fence without any warning signs. It didn't deter me. I removed the Devil, pushed it under the fence then clambered beneath the rope, using my hands to stay off my knees. As I walked across the paddock, I alternated between scanning my surroundings for bulls and looking at the ground to dodge the fresh khaki cow pats. When I reached the other side, I pushed the Devil beneath another electric fence then clambered out behind it and continued on a gravel path.

I arrived in Nods just after four o'clock and walked up and down the Grand Rue for ten minutes, trying to find my hostess' house. The numbers weren't consecutive and Jacques had written down the wrong house number. Fortunately, I saw a pilgrim sign out the front of a house and walked into the large garden where a lady was pruning fruit trees. Her curly brunette hair with silver streaks was pulled into a low bun. She wore a loose cotton dress and moved with assuredness and ease. There was something beautiful and earthy about her. She greeted me and we introduced ourselves then she took me to the front entrance on the other side of the house. I took off the Devil then my new boots. They were wet on the outside from all the rain and had also leaked a little inside so that the toes of my right foot were damp.

That night I shared dinner with my hostess and her family. We ate homemade pumpkin soup with fresh bread followed by a type of French-style cannelloni stuffed with pumpkin in a cheese sauce. We talked about Australia, about refugees, and even about Tasmania. And we spoke about Nods and France. I started to realise how much I have taken my 'lucky' country for granted: our liberty, opportunity and the rugged beauty of it. I had already met many French people whose children had left to live in Australia. Many more told me they would like to visit or live there one day. As I walked through the villages in France, I felt envious of the sense of community in them that I felt Melbourne lacked, yet I was learning there was poverty and unemployment here too. One cannot judge a place merely by looking at it or passing through. It may not be all that it seems.

After dinner, the kids helped clear the table and my host and I discussed the way I would take out of town. There were a couple of tricky places coming up where the signs wouldn't be clear, so he gave me specific instructions to follow. I listened and made mental notes. There was nothing wrong with getting lost. Getting lost is how we find our way. Still, with so far to walk, I preferred to avoid it if I could. I left my hosts the next morning after a simple breakfast of coffee and bread. The town was quiet, with few cars and people on the streets. As I headed towards a pine forest, a lone crossbred dog walked straight towards me, barking. It stopped in the middle of the path, snarling and blocking my way. I pointed Right Rodney directly at it.

"Go on. Get!" I growled as I walked slowly towards it. "Go on." He kept barking but walked in an arc onto the grass to the right of the road, out of my way.

The pine forest was magical. The conifers were like tall pencils covered in fine green moss. I stood for a moment, looking up to their tips reaching towards the silvery sky. Now that the dog had stopped barking, the forest was quiet. No wind. No birds chirping. I was enveloped in deep stillness. A middle-aged woman wearing a red tracksuit power-walked towards me using hiking poles and her small brown terrier trotted behind. Ten minutes later, I was startled as a man with bare muscular legs ran past me. I was so absorbed in my wonder of the forest that I hadn't heard his steps crunching along the gravel road.

I emerged from the forest into fields of grass and followed the winding road uphill towards some farm buildings. A farmer emerged from behind one of the buildings and my face flushed guiltily. Although I was on a public road, I felt like I was trespassing.

"Via Francigena?" I asked him and shrugged. He nodded and pointed at the path to the left.

I stepped over mini streams and tiptoed through the mud, following the path down to a barbed wire gate held in place against the sturdy fence by a wire loop. Undoing it was challenging, however, closing it again seemed almost impossible without injury. I wrestled with it, trying to stretch it close enough to the fence to slip the loop back over the pole without spearing my hands on the barbed wire. Ten minutes later I succeeded, just.

I walked along the gravel track into another pine plantation and followed the signs deeper into the woods until the trail stopped. I looked around, trying to discern a trail heading somewhere but couldn't see any. This was probably one of the sections my host in Nods had warned me about, but I couldn't remember his instructions and it was too hard to zigzag back. On the map, the forest was another patch of green with no marked trails. I turned right, hoping I could find my way back to the road, and walked through knee-high thistles patched with spider webs, feeling the thorns grabbing at my pants. I was starting to worry that I might be lost for a long time in the forest, when I heard the mixed jingle of cowbells and followed their sound to a clearing where some brown cows grazed. From the clearing, I walked down to the road then turned onto a gravel track and passed a Via Francigena sign stuck on a tree. I clapped my hands together. I had found my way back.

I arrived in Pontarlier too early to check into the youth hostel. As usual, all I wanted to do was shower and rest immediately, not in another two hours. I looked for another place to stay. One hotel was nice but far too expensive. The other was above a dodgy-looking bar and was asking too much for that privilege. Instead, I walked to the church and sat on a pew, resting until I remembered that I needed to replace the waist belt clip on the Devil that was bending out of shape. To my dismay, I walked two kilometres to the sports store only to discover the clip was sewn into the belt and could only be replaced by cutting it out and sewing the new one in. I walked back into town, chastising myself for not checking that in the first place and consequently walking four extra, unnecessary kilometres. The only positive was that I arrived back at the youth hostel just as it opened for check-in.

I hoped I would have a place to myself, but as soon as I entered the room I realised I would be sharing. A blue night jacket and a towel hung on hooks on the wall opposite the door and the bottom bunk bed closest to the door was already made up with a blanket neatly tucked over the mattress. I met my roommate after dinner. I was lying on the opposite bed, writing in my journal when the door opened and in shuffled an old lady with a thickly wrinkled face and white hair tied back in a bun. She was slightly hunched over and carried shopping bags in both hands.

"*Bon soir,*" I greeted her.

She spoke in the standard flurry of French that I didn't understand. I explained I spoke only a little French, but it didn't matter. She continued to speak the same anyway.

She shuffled around the room, humming as she unpacked then changed into her pastel blue nightie and night jacket. She shuffled outside to use the external toilet and when she returned, she apologised that she would have to get up in the night to go to the toilet. I apologised that I had to leave by seven o'clock the next morning and said I would try to be quiet. She nodded then offered me food, using her hand to demonstrate putting food into her mouth. I had just eaten dinner so I declined. Then she walked over to the cupboard and pulled out a package and offered me cake. I thanked her but declined again. She put it away and shuffled over to her bed, humming again, then climbed under the covers and started to read. Within minutes she fell asleep and snored softly. I continued writing in my journal for another twenty minutes then closed it, set my alarm and snuggled down under the sheet and blanket. Just as I started to fall asleep, my roommate stirred, sat up, put her light on, put her slippers on, stood up, shuffled to the door, opened the door, shuffled to the toilet, flushed the toilet, opened the door, closed it again, shuffled back to bed, sat on the edge, took off her slippers, turned off the light, lay down then started softly snoring once more. So started the two-hourly pattern for the night, but I could not feel annoyed by it or her. One day I would be old too.

I woke at half past six, got out of bed as quietly as I could and walked to the bathroom. When I came back, my roommate was awake and told me it was okay to turn on the light. As I didn't use my sleeping bag, it was quicker and easier than usual to pack. With the Devil on my back, I said goodbye. The lady offered me food again but I was ready to leave and declined. As I stepped towards the door, I noticed that my bum felt oddly cold. I touched my pants. They were soaking wet. Then I touched the bottom of the Devil. It was wet too. My water bladder was leaking. I dumped the Devil on the ground, pulled out the hydration bladder and examined it for the source of the leak. The tube was fully inserted, the lid was in place, and I pushed on the bladder but no water came out. Unsure as to why it leaked in the first place and not trusting that it wouldn't start leaking again, I put it inside a plastic bag, hoping that would contain any future leaks. Then shoved it back into position inside the Devil. The base of the bag was still wet and dripping water but there wasn't much I could do about it. It would dry out during the day.

The morning's walk was serenely beautiful, but at times challenging. I passed beneath the Château de Joux, craning my neck to look up at the castle on top of the rocky hill. I was grateful that I was walking at its base, until I realised that I had to walk over it. Walking up was easier than I expected, but I winced at the pain in my knees with each step down the steep, rocky path. I walked on through lemon-tinged forests on leafy carpets the colour of a burnt sunset. I followed muddy tracks no wider than my two feet and clung to sturdy vines to keep steady as I descended. When the path was fully flooded, I walked between the trees, their branches grabbing at my clothes as I stepped over roots and toadstools. I walked on the old railway covered in dirt and then beside the scenic railway line and even on the tracks themselves, but I followed the line too far into Les Hôpitaux-Neufs and had to break out of the holding yard by squeezing my way between a wire fence and a locomotive. I climbed to an altitude of 1000 metres and walked straight towards the long, sausage clouds that were always just out of reach.

In Jougne I bought lunch and tried to arrange accommodation in Orbe, where there were few places to stay. I called the

Catholic parish but was told that they didn't accommodate pilgrims. I tried to call a chambre d'hôtes but there was no answer. I trusted that it would all work out when I arrived. Forty-five minutes later, I stood with one foot in France and one foot in Switzerland. I had walked 870 kilometres in 32 days across France and was about to walk into the third country of my pilgrimage.

Seventeen—Unstable ground

Jougne to Vevey

I made my way past the unmanned frontier guard box. It had been disused since 2008 when Switzerland joined other European countries in the Schengen Area, thereby abolishing the need for internal controls at their mutual borders. Soon I was walking back on the remains of the Voie Romaine. It was unlike any section of a Roman road I had walked so far. At first there were just clumps of moss-covered rocks on the ground, but soon there were unbroken sections where the deep grooves worn into the rocky path by chariot wheels were visible. The afternoon was spent walking at the top of a gorge, listening to the Orbe River rushing along its bed many metres below the trees and out of sight. With only four kilometres left to walk, I found a metal barrier suddenly blocked my way forward. A sign said the path was dangerous and closed, while an arrow pointed a detour uphill to the left. I checked my map. It looked like the only way out was to walk all the way back uphill to the road and follow it into town, adding at least two kilometres to my day. I started crying as I followed the detour. I had already walked 35 kilometres. I didn't want to walk the long way. I didn't want to walk any farther at all. I just wanted to be in Orbe to rest my tired and aching body. At the top of the steep path another arrow appeared, directing me not up to the road but parallel to the gorge in the same direction as the river. My tears ceased as I followed all the arrows along the winding trail that merged with the original path. The detour only added 700 metres to my day.

Once in Orbe, I walked into the first of only two hotels in town. Behind the bar, an old lady with bleached-blonde hair was busy putting drinking glasses away. She looked up at me but didn't greet me or offer me a smile, only a tired stare. I asked if they had a room. She responded in French. When I told her I didn't understand she grabbed a brochure from the counter, put it in front of me and pointed at the tariff. It was 145 Swiss francs for a tired room for which I would have only paid 45 euros (45 Swiss francs) two days earlier in France. I walked out and went straight to the tourist office a few doors down the road to see if they could find me anything cheaper. The young lady inside told me the other hotel was even more expensive. I would have no choice but to pay the inflated price. I turned to leave but stopped when she called out to me.

"Wait!" she commanded then flicked through a book and made a phone call. She conversed in French for a minute then put her hand over the phone's receiver to tell me that I could stay at a private house for only 25 Swiss francs. "Do you want to take it?" she asked.

"Yes!" I replied so enthusiastically I almost shouted.

She wrote down the address on a large map of the town and showed me where the house was. I was so grateful for her help that I thanked her then thanked her twice more. I bought a pre-packaged chilli con carne with rice for dinner from the small convenience store then walked a weary and painful kilometre uphill to my accommodation. A pretty girl wearing jeans and sneakers, who I estimated was no more than eleven years old, was leaning up against a wire fence, waiting for me. I followed her into the apartment on the third floor where she showed me my room and the bathroom, whispering all of her explanations. I didn't understand why she was whispering or much of what she said, except that Madame would come later and that I should put the key back in the dresser on the landing when I left. She closed the door behind her and left.

It felt strange staying in a private home without ever having met the owner. I showered and ate my dinner alone at the kitchen table, before washing my dishes and retiring to my room. I laid my sleeping bag on the single bed next to the window then lay myself down to rest and write. Later, I heard someone enter through the front door and walk down the hall. A door opened and closed then a phone rang and I heard a male voice. After a while, I heard him come back out into the kitchen and return to his room again. At half past eight, there was a knock on my door. A young woman with shoulder-length dark blonde hair, wearing dark-framed rectangular spectacles, told me that Madame said I should leave the money and key on the table in the kitchen when I left in the morning. Then she went back to her room. She was the only resident I met.

I was done with walking 35-plus-kilometre days and now the need for them was over... hopefully. Accommodation from Lausanne to Rome was said to be plentiful and I was on track to make it to Rome within my visa. I had learned the hard way that day that there is a big difference between walking 39 kilometres through flat countryside and slogging 39 kilometres on hilly terrain. My whole body was in pain except my head and my arms. With shorter days, I expected the walking to be easier on my body, but I probably should have thought more about where the path was about to take me.

In the morning, I scribbled merci beaucoup on a piece of paper that I tore from my journal and put it on the kitchen table, along with the money and key. I left Orbe on a bicycle path that ran beside the busy road and watched the tramcars ferry people to Chavornay some four kilometres away. I daydreamed about being on one too so I could be in a café drinking coffee in five minutes instead of in an hour. The day's walking was relatively easy, through woodlands beside a quiet river with some steep climbs up into the forest. I stopped frequently, not to catch my breath but to admire the different fungi growing beneath the trees and in the middle of the paths, and to marvel at the vivid red and green mottled foliage of the autumn trees. I walked along bitumen paths from village to village in between fields of canola and purple flowers. Just outside Le-Mont-sur-Lausanne, I passed a roadside hut selling pumpkins, some larger than basketballs and others as tiny as cricket balls, and an orchard laden with rosy apples ready for picking. A little while later, I found myself walking downhill to Lausanne.

In my room at the youth hostel, I sat by the window, looking out over the tops of the surrounding buildings as the sun set into a thick blanket of grey cloud that was hovering above the horizon. I gasped when the clouds dissipated momentarily to reveal the Alps. That's when reality set in. The Alps were big—really big—and in only a few days I would start climbing them. It wasn't the first time I had seen them. This was my third time in Switzerland, but I had forgotten exactly how big and foreboding they were. I am gutsy and determined, but I was becoming nervous about crossing them. In her blog, *wheresnetia*, Australian pilgrim Venetia Bowen, who walked the Via Francigena a year earlier than me, wrote about a section between Martigny and Orsières that was really challenging. Her guidebook had described it as "treacherous". Mine described it less ominously as "not liked by some walkers". Venetia's photos showed steep and narrow trails. I felt alarmed, especially as photos often make things look less steep than they really are. Netia and her walking companion even sent their backpacks ahead by taxi so they didn't have to carry anything. The Devil was double the weight of the bag Netia had carried, and my knees had already been grumbling and whining with every steep downhill step. I wasn't sure if I could do this, but I didn't have to worry yet. I was still five days away from its treachery.

I spent the next day following the shoreline of Lake Geneva. It was stunningly beautiful; so much so that any pain and tiredness in my body was overawed as I walked beside the calm silvery waters. I climbed up high into the UNESCO World Heritage listed vineyards of Lavaux and watched in wonder as the haze hovering above the lake cleared to reveal the jagged purple shadows of the Alps. I ate my ham and cheese sandwich high in the vineyard terraces, sitting on a brick wall with my feet dangling towards the vines below. I couldn't stop staring at the Alps or looking back towards Lausanne.

I walked back down to the lake through the village of Cully then continued on beside the rippled waters before climbing back up into the vineyards around Espesses. As I paused to take a photo and catch my breath, a gentleman walked up the steps behind me, his hair as silver as the hazy lake. His name was Maurice and he was a retired doctor taking his regular walk from Lausanne to Rivaz, where he told me the air was fresher. It was a pleasure to have company and have an English conversation. We walked together all the way into Rivaz then he turned back to Lausanne. I continued on alone into Saint-Saphorin, down yet another hill only to climb back up into the terraces once more. I was hot and tired but my spirits were high from the company and the beauty that surrounded me.

That night, I ate a picnic dinner in my hotel room as I studied the guidebook and the weather forecast for the coming week. It was 4 October and I was approaching the Great St Bernard Pass, the place where I would cross over into Italy. It felt like the climax of the journey, being halfway and the highest point. At an altitude of 2469 metres, I would be on top of the world, surrounded by beauty and completing a rite of passage like so many pilgrims before me, but I needed good weather. If it snowed, I wouldn't be able to walk up to the Pass. I had no experience of walking in snow and no idea how to use snowshoes. Alone in the Alps was not the time to teach myself these things. The alternative route was to walk along the main road through an enclosed avalanche gallery that was four kilometres long and offered no sidewalk or safety for pedestrians. The guidebook warned that this could be dangerous too. Only the day before, I had felt daunted by the prospect of climbing in the mountains on steep and narrow paths with the heavy Devil on my back, especially given that I am scared of heights, but I had received a message from a fellow pilgrim who had walked this section, reassuring me it was not as bad as it seemed. The walk from Lausanne with the Alps in view made me excited at the prospect of being in them, foot to earth. The Pass was still a week away and weather is fickle; anything could happen.

In the meantime I needed to rest, and Vevey was the right place for that. It was a smaller town than Lausanne with not as much to see. After so much walking and constant movement from place to place, I craved stillness. My initial plan was to sit somewhere quiet and absorb the beauty of Lake Geneva and the Alps, except the lake was whipped by a wild and cold wind. Instead, I spent the afternoon stretched out on my bed, catching up on emails with friends and family, uploading photos so I could delete them from my iPhone to free up space, and writing my blog and private journal. Every day I walked, I was becoming clearer on my purpose, especially when I wasn't thinking about it. I heard the whispers when I was tired and in pain or in awe of the beauty around me. These whispers were encouraging me to write and to teach. I started to write these ideas down, to get them out of my head and capture them to build a relationship with them so they weren't just passing fancies. It felt right, except for the fear and doubts that jeered softly from the shadows. Who was I to think I could inspire others? I wasn't an expert in anything. What could I possibly teach? I had a long history of doubting myself, a response I learned in my childhood.

My mum became bedridden from the time I was aged eleven, after she slipped a disc in her back. This was the beginning of a downward spiral. The muscular dystrophy deteriorated her physical condition so she couldn't lift her arms above her head, and she couldn't walk very far, as she was prone to falling. She lived in constant pain, especially in her legs. I helped by cooking dinner and ironing, even if I didn't like doing it at times. I made sure Mum had tea and coffee and anything else she needed when Dad wasn't home. I ran errands for her down at the local shops, buying her chocolate and craft supplies, and picking up her medicine from the pharmacy. I took her shopping in her wheelchair and accompanied her to the hairdresser for moral support. Mum had always been particular about her appearance, as the muscular dystrophy caused her face to droop. A trip to the hairdresser usually battered her self-esteem. I felt her distress as she spent hours afterwards trying to fix her imperfect hair. For days she would be upset and complain about the cut, even though there was rarely anything wrong with it. Her distress and annoyance reflected how she felt about herself and her diseased body. Sometimes I was called home from school after she had fallen on the floor and was unable to get back up. I would look after her until Dad got home from work or we called an ambulance as well as clean the blood and skin from her knees off the carpet. At night, my brother and I would take turns pummelling her legs with our fists to try and ease her pain. Meanwhile, I enjoyed school, studied hard and received good grades. My parents never had to nag me about doing my homework. I tried to make sure that I was more helpful than in need of help myself.

Mum's physical condition deteriorated in stages. She would go downhill then eventually stabilise for a while before going downhill again. She was angry and grieving as she lost control of her body and suffered constant pain. Struggling to accept her emotions and what was happening to her, she often took it out on me and tried to control me to compensate for her loss of power. Sometimes there were signs of trouble brewing, like when the way she spoke to me started to become short and snappy, but a lot of the time I was caught by surprise and only knew trouble was coming just before it hit. I would be summoned down to Mum's bedside, where I was subjected to a tirade of angry, hurtful words from her that burst in my heart like invisible grenades. I no longer remember the words themselves, only how I felt: bewildered, frightened, hurt and ashamed. Any attempt to explain or defend myself only made it worse. I should have been able to handle 'being told off', as Mum described it. As the daughter of a church minister, Mum, along with her brothers, was expected to behave impeccably and set an example for others. Nana was known to be very strict. I suspect Mum treated me in a way that was similar to how she had been treated growing up.

Frozen by shock and fear, I would stand there and listen to everything Mum had to say about what I had done wrong that upset her. Too young to recognise that she was overwhelmed and unable to deal with all her emotional and physical pain and loss and was taking it out on me, I took her words to heart. I believed that I wasn't good enough, that I could never get things right, that there was something inherently wrong with me, and that I had to earn her love. I believed that it was my fault when others were upset and that despite my best intentions and efforts, whatever I did would probably end up being wrong, criticised and attacked.

Her words hurt, but the days that followed when Mum wouldn't talk to me were even worse. I just wanted everything to be okay again, but it took Mum time to normalise. I couldn't avoid her or her silence, as I needed to look after her while Dad was at work. I would walk down the hallway to her bedroom with overwhelming trepidation, unsure of the welcome I would receive. Somehow I held it together on the outside, but inside I trembled with fear. Sometimes she would grunt at me. Other times I received a blunt yes or no, or a nod or shake of her head to my offers. During those silent periods, she would barely look at me. I was petrified that from her silence she would launch into another attack, yet I walked down that hallway time and time again, hoping that everything would go back to normal and she would start loving me again, only to be reminded once more of how unworthy I was when she couldn't even look at me or speak to me.

For a few days after these episodes, I would tiptoe around the house, trying to be quiet and invisible, worried that I might do something to set her off again. Eventually, when Mum was ready, she would start talking to me. We never spoke about what happened. I was so relieved that it was over and didn't dare mention it in case it triggered her and she became upset again. Our relationship would slowly go back to our version of normal. We'd watch movies together, decorate woven baskets with lace and flowers, and talk and laugh. Sometimes Mum would be generous with gifts, maybe to try and make up for what had happened. She loved dolls and so did I. She bought me several Cabbage Patch Kids and even an expensive handcrafted porcelain life-like baby doll. Life started to feel okay once more, until the next time I did something wrong, but I could never completely relax and let my guard down. I was always on the lookout for signs of trouble coming, and I was always second-guessing what I did in an effort to try and stay out of trouble.

I never really understood why Mum was so upset with me. It always felt so confusing. I know now, through counselling and conversations with my dad, that I didn't really do anything wrong and it was related to Mum's deteriorating physical condition. At the time, though, all I understood was that I had upset Mum again. It was my fault. I wore the blame and I felt ashamed. Over time I found ways to cope with my experience. As crying in front of Mum only made things worse, I learned to brace myself for the impending attack and hold back my tears as best I could, although I didn't always succeed. Afterwards, I retreated to my room or sometimes sat outside on the back step with our dog, Penny, an Australian silky terrier crossed with an Australian terrier. She always knew when I was hurting, and she sat silently by my side while I cried quietly and told her about my troubles. It wasn't just a matter of hiding my feelings. The attacks were too overwhelming for my child self to be able to process, so my most sensitive and precious spirit went into hiding in an untouchable, safe world that nobody knew existed, and I developed a tough armour of silent, fierce stubbornness and resistance. These were my only powers against my mother.

I didn't know how to process my emotions as a result of being attacked, and I couldn't talk about them. There was so much going on in my family that I felt like I needed to be strong and not a burden. I hid my distress. I also believed, just like Nana told Mum her whole life, that I shouldn't feel the way I was feeling. I was simply supposed to get over it, and that's what I attempted to do. I squashed my grief and hurt down into a tight black ball in my stomach that I hid for years, and I wore a mask that told the world I was okay, but whatever you suppress you carry with you until it is tended to with love. For most of my life, I felt like there was something wrong with me. I thought it was related to lingering grief from Mum's death. Even as an adult, when I had everything to be happy about—a successful career, a loving partner, money in the bank, holidays, a great lifestyle—grief and sorrow constantly lurked in the background. I felt broken in some way and was ashamed of my feelings. I thought I was being ungrateful for the wonderful life I had. I didn't know that the way I felt was because of trauma.

When I was sixteen, I started becoming my own person. If I wasn't at school or doing homework, I was spending time with my friends. Learning to become independent and making your own decisions is a natural and necessary part of growing up in your teenage years, but Mum couldn't bear me pulling away from her. She was housebound due to her disability and had few external relationships, so I was central to her world and fulfilled multiple roles as daughter, carer, friend and confidant. Although Mum tried to individuate from Nana, she never succeeded. Nana couldn't let her go, probably due to her own unresolved grief and trauma from the death of her mother when she was a child. Nana continued to play a dominant role in Mum's life even when Mum was a middle-aged woman with three children of her own and four stepchildren. As a result, my relationship with Mum became more tumultuous during my last two years of high school.

In a last-ditch effort at being independent and denying the reality of her condition, Mum moved out of the family home and attempted to live by herself in her own house. The distance from her was a relief, and I started to feel more relaxed at home. However, during this time, Nana died, and so Mum was grieving the loss of her mother and the complicated nature of their relationship at the same time as I was grieving the loss of my grandmother and pulling away from Mum to become my own person. This probably made the process harder than it otherwise would have been. I was occasionally summoned to see Mum at her home, but she mostly chose to express her frustration and hurt through letters. It was a little easier to digest this in writing. I focused on my high school studies, determined to achieve high marks and get into my university of choice. I succeeded in this and was offered my first preference, a place in a Bachelor of Commerce degree at the University of Melbourne.

Unable to live independently any longer, Mum needed to move back in with Dad so he could care for her. However, the layout of our family home was no longer suitable. Mum needed a more compact house that enabled her to access the kitchen and living areas without having to walk too far because she was prone to falling. They spent several months looking for a suitable new home and finally found one, except there was one catch. It didn't have enough bedrooms for the four of us: Mum, Dad, my brother and me. Within days of finding out about my university acceptance, I was summoned to Mum's place and told that I had to move out of home. I was shocked and devastated. I hadn't been given any warning that this was even a possibility, and I hadn't seen it coming, despite the fact that my four older half-sisters from Dad's first marriage had all moved out by the age of eighteen. Naïvely, I had assumed that I would be able to live at home until I finished university.

At eighteen, I was suddenly catapulted into an independent adult life. I had no idea of where I was going to live or how I was going to support myself while I spent the next three years studying to complete my undergraduate degree. I felt panicked. It was a lot of change all at once, but after the initial shock subsided, I found my way out into the world and discovered that the universe was actually on my side. My friend's parents had moved to the agricultural country town of Shepparton in northeast Victoria, where her father got a job as a food technologist. My friend, her older brother, her sister and her sister's boyfriend were still living in the two-storey family home with attached granny flat just around the corner from my childhood home. There was a spare room, and I was able to move in with them. I received student payments from the government, at times, and financial assistance from my dad when my payments were cut off due to his financial situation. I also obtained a job filing land titles at the Victorian Land Titles Office at night, thanks to a referral from a university friend. I started to enjoy university life and the freedom of being an independent adult.

After settling into my university schedule, I began visiting Mum on Fridays, which were my day off. The conflict of our mother–daughter relationship ended, and slowly we found a new way to relate to each other that was loving, peaceful and accepting, although we never spoke in detail about what had transpired between us in the past. After years of battling her muscular dystrophy and failing body, she finally accepted herself as she was and stopped directing her pain and frustration outwards. Intuitively she knew that her days were numbered, and she started to talk often about dying and about our lives going on without her. Despite death hovering in the background, this was the most calm and loving period of our relationship. I looked forward to visiting Mum. At first, I caught the bus or walked the forty minutes from my home to hers, until she helped me buy my first car and I could drive there. We spent the afternoons talking about my university life, work, craftwork, family and friends. Mum had always cared for and been interested in my friends, and they always enjoyed and appreciated conversations with her. She was a kind and compassionate listener who treated my friends as grown-ups, and she always offered empathy and sage advice. Mum was also my source of greatest compassion and support when my little Maltese Shih Tzu dog, who was my best friend for four years, was hit by a car before my eyes, and had to be put to sleep. It was Mum's idea to lay her out in the lounge room and mourn her. She wrote a heartfelt poem expressing her grief for my grief and loss.

Although Mum tried to prepare us for her death, it was still a shock and immensely painful when she died six days before Christmas in the following year. I felt like I had just gained my mum back, only to have her taken away from me. It was so painful that I experienced what I could of the grief and then shut down and ran from the rest. I was only twenty years old. I carried the grief of her passing, along with the invisible wounds inflicted by her words and silence for all those years, until I started unravelling it in counselling sessions. With Myree's support, I finally felt safe enough to be able to face those painful events, to feel the hurt that had been trapped in my body and psyche, and to heal and open my heart. That hadn't been the reason I sought counselling in the first place, but I discovered it was a necessary step on my path. I was able to recognise the gifts of this painful relationship. Among them were strength, resilience, determination, compassion, empathy, understanding, spiritual power, maturity, wisdom and courage. I began to see how much my life had called me to live with great courage, to live through and heal deep wounds, to live with uncertainty, to leave the safety of my career and the life I knew, and even to walk this pilgrimage path alone, but this was something I still downplayed. Playing small was my way of still tiptoeing through life, hiding and protecting myself. People I met along the way kept telling me I was courageous. Perhaps it was time for me to acknowledge and own this quality within myself.

Eighteen—Into the Alps

Vevey to Martigny

After my brief rest in Vevey, I was happy to have the Devil on my back and get back on the trail again. I felt off-balance, like a part of me was missing, when I walked without it. Unlike the grief and emotional pain I had carried since Mum's death, this was a burden that I consciously packed and carried, and one that I mostly enjoyed bearing. I left my hotel prepared for rain and was instead blessed with sunshine for most of the day and a mild temperature of 18°C. It was perfect weather for my final hours of walking beside Lake Geneva before I veered south, away from the lake and into the valley between the mountain ranges. I felt emotional as I walked towards the lake. There I was in Switzerland, having walked almost 1000 kilometres since my journey began. I was almost halfway and about to walk through the Alps then across the Great St Bernard Pass into Italy. I was finding my own way, supported by the kindness of strangers, comfortable and content in my own company, and in love with this world.

The lake had calmed after the previous day's windy fury. It was flat but rippled, and the sun splashed dancing diamonds on its surface. I walked past the Giant Fork sculpture stuck into the lake near the Alimentarium museum and through Montreux where the famous jazz festival is held, marvelling at the luxurious

Le Montreux Palace hotel as I passed. I deferred my lunch break until I arrived in Villeneuve, but I had forgotten it was Sunday. The best I could find to eat in the small town was reheated kebab. The next few hours were spent walking on the east side of the Rhône valley at the base of the rising Alps, with flimsy cloud drifting over their rocky peaks, until I arrived in Aigle to spend the night in a *chambre d'hôte* surrounded by vineyards.

My walk to Saint-Maurice the next day was on a bitumen bike track beside the dark jade waters of the Rhône river. The banks of the river were thickly vegetated with trees and bushes, and the dark grey clouds clumped around the mountains threatened rain. The path was popular with cyclists, some in full biking gear riding for fitness, others in casual dress using their bikes as a means of transportation. I watched a platoon of army cadets marching on the other side of the river, carrying their packs. I walked slower than my normal pace, yet I still walked faster and with more purpose than they did. My accommodation for the night was at l'Hôtellerie Franciscaine, the guesthouse of the Franciscan Order. I checked in and paid for the half-board option. It was good value and meant that I didn't have to leave the building to find somewhere to eat dinner. Before I went to bed, I checked the weather forecast again. It had changed and wasn't looking favourable. Snow was forecast for the day I would climb up to the Great St Bernard Pass. I would have to push hard to beat the snow, but I didn't know if my body could handle condensing the long steep climbs into fewer days. The path ahead was shrouded by both uncertainty and adventure.

The low rocky hills of the Alps were veiled by misty cloud as I meandered my way out of Saint-Maurice. The clouds hugged the hills all day, but it was warm enough for me to wear a t-shirt and it didn't rain. I lost and found my way through the woodlands, following my instincts to make my way back onto the path and across the narrow river rushing over its rocky bed. I walked past a cage of five alpacas, all staring at me curiously with their giant brown doe eyes, and past a roofless carport covered in kiwifruit vines that were laden with the bronze fruit. Ninety minutes into the day, while walking beside a quiet road six kilometres outside of Saint-Maurice, I hit a new milestone: 1000 kilometres. There was no one to witness or acknowledge the moment, just me saying to myself, "Holy wow." Then I kept walking.

Later, I stood beneath the base of the giant cascading waterfall, Pissevache, watching and listening to the water tumble to the ground then through another section of lemon-coloured woodlands. Despite the traffic noise from the nearby expressway, the woods were still steeped in stillness and calm. I ate my sandwich in the courtyard of a modern church as I watched the eagles circle and cry in front of the Alps' rocky peaks. After lunch I entered another woodland. Maybe I was mesmerised by the tranquillity, or maybe I was looking at my iPad to check the way ahead, or maybe it was inevitable and would have happened regardless of where my attention was, but I caught my foot on a raised tree root hidden by the leaves littering the forest floor and fell. Instinctively, I put my hands out. I knew that whatever happened, I needed to protect my iPad that I wore around my neck in a clear waterproof case or it would smash and there would go my map and blogs. It might have been the lopsided weighting of the Devil or perhaps I pushed myself over, but somehow I rolled and landed on my butt so that I was leaning back on the Devil, dazed. One second I was up, the next I was down. The iPad was unscathed but my hands were lightly grazed and bruised and my right knee throbbed too. I took a minute to recover from the shock then pushed myself off the ground and back onto my feet. My right calf twinged, as did my hip flexor. I started walking again, slowly, hoping they were just strained and nothing worse. Fortunately, the pain soon eased.

I entered the centre of Martigny after crossing the narrow river via the covered bridge. My room for the night was a studio apartment. There was a table and chairs and even electric hot plates stored in the cupboard, but without pots or pans they were useless. From a food hall in town, I bought takeaway barbeque chicken and roast potatoes. As I emerged, I saw the rocky peaks of the Alps above the three-storey buildings, showered gold by the waning sun. They were magnetic. I marched down the street towards the railway station, hoping for a clear view, but the platforms blocked my way forward and the shelters obscured my view. I walked back to my room, regularly glancing over my shoulder at the golden peaks rising majestically above the buildings.

Nineteen—Pass the Pass

Martigny to Bourg-Saint-Pierre

The next morning, I checked the weather forecast again as soon as I woke up. Snow showers were still forecast for Friday. I checked another forecast and another and another, hoping for positive news. They all had slight variations on temperatures and the amount of sunshine and clouds, but they all agreed that snow was on the way. I really wanted to walk up to the Great St Bernard Pass and complete that rite of passage. All I could do was hope. I took breakfast in a bar then left Martigny with the low-lying clouds hugging the mountains again. I had no idea what the day would bring. I could study the guidebook and read other people's experiences, but I didn't really know what it would be like until I walked it and experienced it for myself. I passed through the town of Le Bourg then entered the lime and lemon woodlands and started climbing. My heart beat solidly in my chest, partly from the climbing but mostly in excitement to see the 'treachery' that lay ahead. The trail, littered with rusted leaves, was narrow, barely a line on the edge of the mountain that quickly and steeply dropped away to my right. I could stand on it with both feet slightly parted but not much more. I used both Rodneys to help me climb, to take some of the weight of the Devil and to keep me stable.

Twenty minutes into the climb, a fallen branch blocked the trail. It had snapped from the tree but had not broken off properly. It was impossible to move and there was no way around. To my left, the hill ascended almost vertically and to the right it was a vertical drop. Walking back to the road was not an option. It was a busy highway with a constant stream of traffic. The only way forward was through. I snapped off some of the smaller branches to create a gap then took the Devil off my back and pushed it through, followed by the Rodneys. I climbed through behind them, shoving the remaining branches out of the way so they wouldn't scratch my face. Once on the other side, I hoped there wouldn't be any other impassable obstacles that would force me to turn back. I resumed walking along the narrow mule track, surrounded by the trees in their colours of lemon and lime, alone on the side of the mountain. I laughed. It was exhilarating. I felt so alive.

The path became steep. Using my arm as a protractor, I estimated the gradient was around 60 degrees. There were sections of earthy steps held in place by planks of wood hammered into the ground. I climbed slowly and steadily, huffing and puffing, my thighs burning, hoping the way would level out for a while, but there were more steps to climb, up and up the mountainside. Finally it levelled out at a clearing in the trees. Far below was the railway line with a bright yellow repair locomotive and the tiny figurines of men wearing bright orange and hammering the track. Opposite me, a village of blue, pink and green chalets nestled into the mountainside. At length, I reached the section of the track described as treacherous. The narrow dirt path slanted towards the edge of the hillside that dropped away sharply. A chunky metal chain fence ran low beside the path, perhaps as a means to break one's fall or provide something to hold onto if you were short or crawling. I looked down the steep slope and my heart pounded. I felt a rush of buoyant energy. I was thrilled by the adventure of facing this treachery on my own. I shuffled along the path, stepping carefully. Occasionally I looked down at the village in the valley far below and my heart pounded a little harder as fear threatened to take hold. I could see why some people wouldn't like this, especially if it had been raining and the track was slippery.

Winding its way down, the path was just as steep as it had been on the climb up. I almost had to resort to sliding down it on my bum, but the Rodneys helped to keep me stable and I was able to descend on my feet. When I looked back at where I had just walked, it looked like there was no trail, just a steep wall of dirt. I climbed up and down sheets of flat rock that looked like they had been deposited by an avalanche, although not recently at least. One hour and forty minutes after I entered the woods and started climbing the mountain, I emerged into Bovernier, feeling triumphant amid the grapevines growing in orderly rows on the steep mountainside. I survived the treachery and decided it wasn't as bad as I'd thought it would be. You can listen to the opinions of others, but it is your own opinion and experience that matters. After passing a flock of mountain sheep with thick greasy fleeces that were eating the lush grass on the steep slope, I sat down at a picnic table beneath a wooden shelter to eat a muesli bar and an apple and rest my feet. I thought the hardest part of the day was over. I didn't know then there was more to come.

The trail led back into the pine forests. At first it was narrow but flat, and there was the occasional fallen tree to climb over. Then it was made up of moss-covered rocks and the steep drop-offs returned. Yellow diamonds painted on some of the rocks marked the way. I stepped carefully, wary of the tree roots that jutted out of the earth, the loose gravel beneath my boots, and the steep inclines on which I could easily lose my footing or injure my knees. I emerged into a clearing, only to climb a narrow rocky ridge with the mountain to my right and the enclosed motorway to my left. Then I walked back into the mountains on yet another steep and narrow trail among hundreds of fallen pines.

It took me twenty minutes to find the correct trail after passing through the village of Sembrancher. I wound my way into the farmland hills along gravel roads, past Tibetan prayer flags stretched across a backyard garden, and past sheep with thick curling horns wearing bells. I arrived at my hotel in Orsières, tired and starving. According to the guidebook I had climbed 1.6 kilometres and descended 1.2 kilometres. No wonder I was physically tired, but I was mentally tired as well from concentrating on each step to keep myself upright and safe. I ate a pizza in the hotel's restaurant and studied the weather forecasts. They still differed, except on one thing: there would be rain and possibly snow tomorrow. The weather and my timing were bad. I went to bed knowing I might not be able to walk to the Great St Bernard Pass.

As soon as I woke, I jumped out of bed and hobbled over to the window. It offered a postcard-perfect view of the village nestled between the rising slopes. The skies were silver and puffs of cloud floated over the arching back of the Alps, but it wasn't snowing or even raining. I reached for my phone to check the weather forecasts, hoping for good news. As usual, they all varied, but the general consensus was that I should expect rain and maybe snow later in the day. By the time I started walking to Bourg-Saint-Pierre, the sun had broken through the clouds. It was a beautiful morning and I forgot about the forecast. I walked out of town past the local fire brigade where a practice fire was burning on a giant mound of dirt and mulch. After crossing the river, I climbed uphill and stopped frequently to look down at the village and the valley patched with green grassy paddocks and trees. I continued climbing into the pine forest mountain, and exactly thirty minutes into the day's walk and three and a half hours from Bourg-Saint-Pierre, according to the sign I stood in front of, it started to rain. At first it was just spitting and I ignored it, hoping it would pass, but it soon fell steadily. I put on Kermit and continued on, happy despite the rain. There was no wind to batter me and I was surrounded by beauty. I passed small chalets, surrounded by stacks of logs for winter fires, and clumps of sunflowers, still alive and blooming despite the coolness of the air. Above the little town of Fornex, I sat on a seat to take in the spectacular scenery. I was almost as high as the thick sheet of cloud that was hovering above the valley below.

The trail soon veered away from the highway and deep into the forest, back on the narrow mule tracks etched into the mountainside that dropped away steeply. This was not a day to fall. I walked through the glorious forest with its varied colours of dark green, lemon, rust, honeyed apricots, dry gold and red. All was silent and still, except for the river bubbling along its rocky bed. There were more obstacles on the path. The first was a pine tree that hung low over the track, its fine, prickly branches blocking the way ahead. I took off the Devil and pushed it beneath the tree to the other side then I crawled through behind it. Ten minutes later, I walked beneath two trees that had fallen over the track, a little nervous that if I knocked them or my timing was bad, I could end up pinned beneath one. While I was in the thick of the forest, the trees blocked the tumbling rain, but I was splattered by it when I emerged into clearings. It didn't bother me. The beauty surrounding me negated its impact.

On the way out of Dranse, I sheltered from the rain in a rotunda with half-brick walls that appeared to be used as a chapel or memorial. I apologised to the Virgin Mary statue on the altar, but I needed somewhere dry to rest and eat. I ate quickly and rested for only fifteen minutes. The cold bit my fingers and nose and infiltrated my bones. I was shivering, so I put on my polar-fleece gloves and neck-gaiter under my windproof jacket and the Kermit and started marching up the gentle rise, hoping the exercise would warm me quickly. It was another half an hour before I stopped shivering. In the meantime, my fingertips ached and my nose went so numb it was hard to draw in breath through my nostrils.

I passed a reservoir of jade-coloured water then entered the forest once more, walking alongside a brown river surrounded by pencil pines 30 metres high. Red berry bushes and ferns that had rusted brown from the cold covered the ground. I had taken few photos so far that day because of the rain and trying to outrun the cold, so I sheltered now beneath a tree to take some, to remember forever the beauty of the forest's contrasting colours. I noticed the rain began to soften then fall more slowly to the ground, as if it were in slow motion. I stood mesmerised, watching it fall, then realised it wasn't rain. It was snow. It had actually started to snow! This was the first time I had ever seen snow fall. I can count on one hand the number of times I have been to the snow and it never fell while I was there. Watching the snowflakes float to the ground was hypnotic. I was in my own real-life snow dome in the autumn forest I had all to myself.

The cold started to tug at my bones so I started to walk again but stopped beneath another tree to watch the snow tumble and blanket the ground and trees. The snow shower became heavier and visibility decreased. As I entered Bourg-Saint-Pierre, I could barely see anything more than a few metres away with all the snow flying into my face. I took shelter under the eave of a nearby house and tried to locate the hotel on my map. A silver Audi wagon pulled up and the male driver offered me a lift. I looked at him. He was in his fifties and probably married with kids, given the car he drove. I was not going to find my hotel without help, so I accepted his invitation.

The hotel, up on the main road to the Pass, was Swiss chalet style and was so warm when I stepped inside that I immediately needed to start shedding layers. I checked in and the manager booked a table for me in the restaurant for dinner. I told him I was a pilgrim and planned to walk up to the Great St Bernard Pass and asked him if he knew the weather forecast. He told me that thirty centimetres of snow was predicted, that walking was *non possible,* and that I should take the bus. My heart sank. I was a day too late. If I had pushed harder, I could have been here earlier and walked up to the Pass before the snow, but I wasn't ready to give up hope yet. Up in my room, I showered to get warm and then hung all of my clothing on every available hook, chair and door to dry. I put the Red Beasts up against the warm radiator then I lay down on the bed to study and make plans.

I checked all the weather forecasts, hoping that at least one of them would predict sunshine. I also searched for an alternative route. If the paths were covered in snow, it would be unsafe or even impossible for me to walk. I posted in online forums, seeking the advice of others who had walked before me, hoping desperately to find a way to walk up to the Pass. I was only 11.6 kilometres away from it. That was just four or five hours of walking uphill. I was so close yet so far. I glanced often out my window. The snow fell consistently for two and a half hours, and when it eventually stopped and the clouds cleared, I was completely surprised by the view. Opposite my hotel, I could see a steep mountain ridge with pine trees covered in snow, but not for long. It didn't snow again, but the clouds repeatedly swept over the mountain, completely obscuring them from view then eventually clearing to reveal them once more. I am no mountaineer, able to understand the weather or how to read the snow on the ground, but as mesmerised as I was by the snowstorm that welcomed me into Bourg-Saint-Pierre, I realised its danger as well. The snow and the fog I had passed through that day completely obscured my view until I was walking almost blind.

Past pilgrims slowly started to respond to my post in the forum. "Use snowshoes," one advised. "Walk the road," another said. There was also the same message given to me by the owner of the hotel: "Don't take the risk, take the bus." I considered my options. The closest place I could hire snowshoes was back in Orsières. The road to the Pass was still open to traffic, but the guidebook warned it was dangerous to walk through the four-kilometre-long enclosed avalanche gallery. I went to bed, preparing myself for the reality that I would have to take the bus to Étroubles in Italy and continue walking from there. That meant I would miss the pinnacle of my journey and the rite of passage. There was part of me that was sad and disappointed. If I couldn't walk the Great St Bernard Pass, it felt like there would be a gap in my pilgrimage and that I would have failed in my mission to walk all the way from Canterbury to Rome. But there was that voice inside me, reminding me that it is the journey that is important and not the places I passed through; that how I managed uncertainties and challenges and how I responded to the unexpected situations that arose on my path is what mattered; that from time to time, pilgrims of old would have taken other means of transportation too. The voice also reminded me of the sacredness I had experienced that day, standing mesmerised in a dark green forest splashed with red, gold and rust, as the snow began to fall and blanket everything around me, including myself, in soft white.

I woke at 6.40 a.m. and hobbled as fast as I could to the window to pull back the heavy drapes. It was still dark. The pine-covered mountain opposite was a fuzzy outline, but it wasn't snowing. Hope flared in me like a match just lit. Maybe I could walk up to the Pass. I dressed and packed then went downstairs for breakfast, eager to talk to the manager, to ask his opinion again on the weather. Twenty French people had recently arrived by bus and they sat at a long table, chatting noisily. The manager was busy behind the bar making their coffees. I sat down at my reserved table beside the window. A young waitress brought over my breakfast: a croissant, rye bread with butter and apricot jam, and a pot of freshly brewed coffee with hot milk. I tried to eat slowly, but I was anxious to find out if I could walk up to the Pass.

As soon as I saw him standing idle, I walked over and asked the manager for his verdict.

"Thirty centimetres of snow. Better to take bus."

"I don't mind walking through snow, but I am worried that the weather might change, that a snowstorm might come over so I won't be able see."

He shrugged, shook his head then walked outside, leaving me standing at the bar with the young waitress. She brushed back her shoulder length blonde hair.

"I am not from here so I don't know. Maybe you can walk the road," she offered.

The manager strolled back in. "It might be okay on the road. The path, no. You might miss a sign. But the road, lots of traffic."

"Maybe I could try and if it is too hard, I could come back and catch the bus tomorrow?"

The manager shrugged again. That was his only answer as he walked off.

I walked up to my room and called the hospice that provided food and shelter to pilgrims on the Pass. My balcony was still blanketed with snow, although it had thinned a little since it had fallen so there was still hope.

The caretaker priest answered the phone. He told me he spoke only a little English, so I spoke French to ask him if he thought it was possible for me to walk up there from Bourg-Saint-Pierre that day. He paused before he answered in English.

"Lots of snow... very difficult. Better on bus."

Sadness clamped down on my lungs. Two locals had now told me not to walk. I had to heed their advice. I thanked him, hung up, then lay down on the bed and started to cry. Some describe disappointment as bitter. For me, it was just a weeping release as I let go of a dream. I had been looking forward to walking up to the Pass, to complete the rite of passage, following in the ancient steps of pilgrims and armies from as far back as 390BC, and to arrive at the halfway point of my pilgrimage on foot. Now it would forever be the missing middle piece of this long and winding walk. I felt like I was so close, but in truth it was another world away.

If we feel, cry, release and let it go, acceptance eventually comes, and then peace. My tears stopped after a few minutes and I prepared to catch the bus through the tunnel to Étroubles. In anticipation of the cold, I put on all my layers of clothing except my gloves and beanie that I carried in my hand to put on when I finally stepped outside into the snow. Downstairs, I settled my bill then walked outside into a winter wonderland just as it started to snow again.

It was hard to feel glum when surrounded by so much wonder. I held out my hands and watched as the snowflakes landed on my black gloves. The Christmas trees were powdered white, and both the ground and long sloping roofs of the chalets were thickly blanketed. I walked carefully along the road. It was clear of snow but icy, and occasionally my foot slipped before my boot gripped. The road was quiet. Only one car passed towards me before I found the path that cut from the main road down into the village. The ground beside the path was covered with snow so thick I had no idea what lay beneath it. I knew that walking the path up to the Pass would be too dangerous, and there was the risk of a snowstorm or the fog rolling in and blinding my way. Given the circumstances and choices, I knew I'd made the right decision even if it wasn't what I really wanted to do.

I was the only person waiting for the bus. It arrived on time and reversed into the parking bay. When the door opened, I stepped up into its warmth.

"Étroubles," I said, handing the driver a ten franc note. I took a seat near the back of the bus. It had only twelve passengers: four couples, three individuals, and now me. I took off the Devil, my beanie, gloves and jacket and waited for the bus to drive me into Italy.

Twenty—Out of the Alps
Étroubles to Châtillon

The bus passed through the six kilometres of the Great St Bernard Tunnel. When it emerged in Italy, I felt like I had time-warped. Gone were the overcast skies carrying snow and the blankets of white that covered the roads, the trees, the cars and the houses. In its place were blue skies and sunshine. The only snow was on the surrounding mountain peaks. Much as I tried to deny them, the 'maybes' tormented me for a while. *Maybe* I could have walked up to the Pass. *Maybe* it would have been safe to walk on the road. *Maybe* I should have just tried. *Maybe* I should have waited until tomorrow. I got off the bus at Étroubles, bypassing 23.8 kilometres of walking in just forty minutes. The maybes stopped. The Pass was already past. I was going forward not back.

With only 16 kilometres to walk that day, I strolled from Étroubles to Aosta, pausing often to absorb the beauty around me. As I left Echevennoz Superiore, I walked in the company of an older gentleman and was suddenly thrown into communicating in Italian. I studied basic and elementary level Italian during my relationship with David, but over the last six weeks I had become conditioned to responding in French, so my mind felt linguistically scrambled. I listened attentively but understood little of what he said until he asked me where I was from and what I was doing. We parted ways at Chez-Les-Blanc, where he stopped to supervise some construction work being undertaken on the track.

"Ciao," I said as I left him behind. Belatedly, I remembered that was too informal a farewell for someone I had just met and who was older than me, but perhaps using the wrong Italian word was better than no Italian at all.

I continued on, alone once more, on the narrow mule track beside the ancient aqueduct that ran through the hills. The trees were mainly pines with intricate natural markings on their trunks. I felt excited to be back in Italy, my fourth and final country on my journey, and one that I adored. I was now more than halfway through my pilgrimage. I stopped for lunch in the square opposite the terracotta church of Gignod and lay in the sun, facing the sweeping mountain range, listening to the fountain bubble behind me and the birds chirping and the humming of a car engine as it wound its way down the hill. When I resumed walking, I hit dead-ends finding my way out of town.

First, I climbed the hill of the castle to avoid the narrow road with blind corners at its base, only to discover there was no way down the other side. Then I followed the GPS trail onto private property and found myself blocked at the bottom of the stairwell of the public walkway by a locked metal gate. My next attempt took me to a hill that was too steep and thick with trees to descend to the road below. I backtracked and walked along the road, despite its blind corners and narrowness. I climbed up into vineyard-covered hills, from where I could see Aosta sprawling in the valley below, then wound my way down the hillside and into the town and straight to a cheap hotel. The day had not turned out the way I had hoped, yet I was still content. My path was still leading me to Rome. Acceptance had crept quietly into me while I was looking with wonder at where I was now.

With 29 kilometres to walk through hills, I planned to leave Aosta early the next day, except my room was cold when I woke and I wasn't inspired to leave the warmth of my bed. If I knew the beauty that I was about to walk into the Valle d'Aosta, I would have leaped out of bed. The scenery stunned me. Clouds hovered over giant snow-covered peaks on both sides of the lush green valley. On the left were vineyards, on the right were pastures, and through the centre ran the motorway. As I walked into the valley away from Aosta, the clouds grew thick over the peaks crowding behind me. I wondered if the weather was going to turn, bringing rain or even snow, but the clouds stayed hovering above a peak and I spent most of the day walking in sunshine.

The day followed a simple pattern—uphill, downhill, uphill, downhill—as I weaved my way along the valley. I walked uphill, knowing I would have to walk down again. I walked downhill to where the path eventually levelled out, hoping that it would stay that way, only to have to walk uphill again. But it was beautiful. Castles dotted the valley. The sky was ever-changing as clouds gathered then dispersed. I passed old churches with fading painted frescoes on their external walls and giant ornate wooden doors. I stuck my head inside the old church at Nus, and Moses stared down at me, holding a tablet bearing five of the Ten Commandments. I walked past vineyards of moscato and petit rouge, while hundreds of grasshoppers jumped ahead of my feet. Butterflies flitted alongside me, as if to encourage me along the way. I ate my lunch sitting on the grass in the sun, leaning up against an old stone wall, watching the clouds float above the mountains. I passed mountain streams and rivers that bubbled over rocks, and I found myself once again walking beside the ancient aqueducts. In the villages, there were dogs that barked as I passed, and one fierce tan chihuahua that blocked my way, barking ferociously, daring me to come near. I shooed him off with a Rodney. All along the way, there was that *bella vista*, the valley lined by snow-capped mountains, glistening in the sun.

I accepted the constant climbing and descending until I lost the signs and followed the GPS route 100 metres up a steep hill, only to realise I was now on the longer, alternative route to Châtillon. I was annoyed. I didn't want to climb and walk the longer way, but I wasn't about to climb back down again and waste more time trying to find the other route. I continued walking, feeling irritated, until the path showed me that I was walking the right way for me. First, I came upon a large extended family, sitting on the ground and on wooden crates across the path, as they took a break from picking grapes. I wished them *buongiorno* and smiled as I weaved my way through them and continued on. Then further along, I approached a man cutting down trees with a chainsaw. He turned the saw off and stopped to chat, inviting me to stay at his house with his family and share a meal. I declined and continued walking happily, arriving in Châtillon much later than I had hoped, in light rain, hungry, tired and cold.

The snow-covered mountains were as freezing cold as they were beautiful, and my hotel in Châtillon had not switched on the heating. It was only halfway through autumn, so perhaps it wasn't cold enough by local standards. After I stopped walking and my body cooled, I began to shiver. Unusually, my room had a shower over a half-sized bath. I filled the bath with hot water and curled up awkwardly on my side to submerge as much of my body as I could. I stayed like that for thirty minutes: the first fifteen minutes to get warm and the last fifteen minutes because I didn't want to go back into the cold bedroom. Even with all my layers on—long-sleeved merino top, fleece, and the synthetic-fill jacket—I was still uncomfortably cold. I resorted to eating my emergency supply of chocolate so the sugar would kick in and warm me from the inside and curled up beneath the bedcovers until dinnertime, when I forced myself to leave the room in search of food.

In the morning, I left the hotel expecting that I would have to walk to the next town to find somewhere to eat breakfast as it was Sunday, but the town's bar was open. I sat down at a table to enjoy my cappuccino and *cornetto al cioccolato,* a croissant-like pastry filled with chocolate cream, as I watched the Formula One news on the television. The church of St Pietro was perched on top of the hill opposite the piazza. I climbed the steps and stood on the terrace, taking in the sunlit snow-capped mountain peaks with their indigo hillsides still in shadow and the cream and tan houses with their grey slate tiles gleaming in the sun. In the past, I would never have described myself as a morning person, but on this journey, it wasn't a chore to wake up early when it was still dark, no matter how sore and tired I was, especially in the Valle d'Aosta. It was only the cold that deterred me.

I entered the church through its giant wooden front door, guarded by statues of St Peter and St Paul standing on either side of it. The church was empty and filled with a holy silence. The marble floors, polished to a mirror-like sheen, reflected the two arched stained glass windows. I lit a candle for my mum at the shrine of St Thérèse. I thought of Mum as I watched the flame flicker. It was often the same images of her that came to my mind. She would be sitting up, cross-legged on her bed, concentrating on her craftwork in front of her, decorating baskets with lace and ribbon and fake flowers, or working on another long-stitch tapestry with a picture of a cottage or landscape, or knitting pale pink or blue or white booties for her future grandchildren. Even if she was in pain, she seemed content and fulfilled and happy in these images.

The steep climbing began as soon as I left town. I took step after burning step until I finally reached a plateau and a clearing with a sunlit misty view back over Châtillon. The path levelled out but was littered with rocks hidden by soggy leaves. I stepped carefully and emerged from the enchanted woods to walk along a wooden boardwalk that protruded over the edge of the mountain. I stayed close to the mountainside but stopped regularly to look back at Châtillon, with the Alps towering above it, and towards the misty, winding valley between the two ranges in front of me. I was alone with that view and blessed morning light. Tears warmed my cool cheeks as I walked and sang Ben Harper's 'Blessed to Be A Witness'. When I reached the chorus, the words caught in my throat; my lungs compressed and I sobbed as I started to feel within every cell of my body that I was blessed too, not only to be here on this path witnessing all this beauty, but also to have experienced all the joy, wonder, love, grief and pain throughout my life. I felt again all those years of believing I wasn't good enough, that there was something wrong with me, and that I wasn't worthy of being loved because I wasn't perfect, because I made mistakes, because I couldn't please someone else, and somehow all the blame I had placed on myself started to dissolve as I sang. With it came grief for having forgotten how blessed and loved I am in the first place. And so I walked and cried while this remembering and blessing was mapped within my body to stay with me always. I kept on trying to sing the words of that song until I could finally sing them without faltering.

Twenty-one—Lakeside detour

Berriaz to Viverone

I arrived in Berriaz at lunchtime and started crossing the bridge over the slow blue waters of the Dora Baltea, but suspecting that there might not be any other towns in which to stop for lunch, I turned back to the Irish pub and restaurant next to the bridge. The blonde-haired waitress spoke fluent English and she offered to show me a quicker way through the valley to Pont-Saint-Martin. I ate pork cooked in spices and drizzled with a little olive oil and drank a glass of the local Valle d'Aosta red wine, but the highlight was the *millefoglie,* one of the most delicious desserts I had ever eaten, with its crisp layers of pastry alternated with thick, sweet pale toffee-coloured cream and a layer of mascarpone. As I sipped my espresso, the waitress showed me on my map the shorter way that would take me along the valley beside the river then on quiet roads. I left the restaurant with a mild buzz from the wine, a burst of energy from the sugar and the caffeine, and a bounce in my step from the kindness of the waitress. I almost started sprinting towards Pont-Saint-Martin, 18 kilometres away.

Over the course of an hour, the sprint reduced to a fast walk and then from my usual pace to a plod as fatigue slowed me down. It was beautiful walking beside the Dora Baltea, past old

Roman bridges, but I misunderstood the waitress's directions and ended up walking along a busy road with no shoulder. I looked down at my feet and marched on, relieved when I escaped onto the entry ramp of a quiet country road. I arrived into Bard in the middle of Marché au Fort, the Fort Market. Sunday strollers filled the narrow streets of the old town, where there was lots of local produce to buy and try. It was a wonderful thing to stumble upon, but I was overwhelmed at being among so many people and I just wanted to get out of there. It was no easy feat on those narrow streets filled with a meandering crowd. I summoned patience when my way was completely blocked, but also mustered some skilful overtaking as soon as the smallest gap opened up. I paused in the Piazza Camillo Cavour in the centre of the town to listen to a folk band and watch the children dance in their traditional dress, and then I finally escaped along the quiet back street and made it into Pont-Saint-Martin. This was my second consecutive 30 kilometre day, hiking up and down hills as I worked my way along the east side of the Valle d'Aosta. I learned again that walking 30 kilometres over flat ground and 30 kilometres in hilly terrain are two different things. I was wiped out.

I left the town around nine o'clock the next morning and immediately climbed back up into the hills and vineyard terraces. I climbed steadily and quietly, and when I emerged into a small clearing, I was surprised to see a fox eating grapes that had fallen from the vines. He looked over his shoulder, saw me then and dashed over the terrace wall, disappearing into the undergrowth. The vine terraces were pretty and peaceful to walk through, but the constant up and down on the rocky and uneven paths was hard work. I decided to be kind to myself and walk the alternate route through the flat valley rather than spend the afternoon climbing more hills. The guidebook said it followed quiet roads and tracks along the western side of the river. That sounded nice and easy, and so it was until I reached a stream, three metres wide, bubbling over its rocky bed. I picked the place where it looked the shallowest and stepped on the exposed rocks, using both Rodneys to keep my balance. At the final gap, with no rock to step on, I took three quick steps through the water and onto the bank. The coldness of the water permeated my boots but my feet stayed dry. It seemed the waterproofing worked on the Red Beasts version 2.

As I walked out of the village of Quassolo after lunch, I realised I was leaving the mountains behind. They had previously towered either side of me, but now the valley was getting wider and slowly the mountains were dwindling into large rolling hills. I turned to look back at the peaks and the valley from where I had walked. It felt like a pretty incredible feat that I had walked across the Alps. I made my final approach into Ivrea through the village of Baio Dora. As I walked along the quiet street, a *nonna* wearing a blue apron stood on the edge of the footpath next to her apartment block, staring at me as I approached. The Italians liked to stare at me even more than the French. I looked at her and smiled then looked away and looked back as I got closer.

"*Camminando da sola! Sei brava!*" she said, congratulating me for walking alone.

My face lit up at her encouraging words. "*Sì! Grazie,*" I replied.

I felt like she was my own private cheerleader, divinely placed there to encourage me on, just when I needed it. I wasn't feeling especially *brava*. As usual, I was tired and sore. I made it to my hotel in Ivrea and rested, only walking back into the old town for dinner.

The next stage to Santhià was 32 kilometres. I didn't have it in me to walk that far in one day. It was 16 October and I had been walking for 44 days with only two rest days. It was taking its toll on my body and energy levels. I knew that after four hours, the walking would be painful and unenjoyable. In France, I would have sucked it up and walked, but now that I was on track to make it to Rome in time, I didn't have to be so adamant. For the first time, I decided to split a stage into two days and slow it down by walking to Viverone, to stay by the lake, walking on to Santhià the following day. Before I checked out of my hotel and left town, I walked back up to the historic town centre that I had only seen in the fuzzy light of dusk on my way to dinner. I stopped in the Cattedrale di Santa Maria Assunta and lit a candle then passed the old red brick castle, once a prison but now used for exhibitions. *Liberi tutti*, 'free all', was written in red paint on the base of one tower. I descended the stairs back into town. In front of me, two church spires rose above the sea of red and auburn roofs bordered by a ribbon of fog.

The quiet country road out of Ivrea passed between over-grown fields of golden weeds, and the snow-capped mountains slowly receded into the background. Lago Campagna perfectly mirrored the mountains, clouds and the thick stand of trees and shrubs lining its shore. I walked past cultivated woodlands of tall, pencil-thin poplars in perfect lines that were haunting in their symmetry and stillness. In the town of Bollengo, I sat on a bench in the sunshine eating my ciabatta roll and soon had company. A tabby cat came over and rubbed against my legs, covering my black pants with her ginger fur. I fed her some pecorino cheese but she left most of it untouched and was more interested in being patted.

Walking alone, I had a lot of time to think about my purpose in life and what I would make of myself when I returned home. I never had a clear vision of exactly what I wanted to do for a career or with my life. Initially I chose to complete a Bachelor of Commerce at the University of Melbourne because my dad and two of my sisters had long careers in banking and finance. It seemed like a safe choice for a secure job and a way of earning a good living. At the end of first year, I chose accounting as my major by default because I didn't like any of the other majors, but by the second half of my second year, I started to skip a lot of classes, as I wasn't enjoying my studies. It was at the end of that year when Mum died. Disillusioned with my course and now grieving, I deferred my studies for a year and completed a traineeship with a credit union. At the end of the year, I accepted a permanent position with them and returned to university part-time but decided the course wasn't for me and dropped out.

I knew I was intelligent and should complete some kind of tertiary studies, so I started asking myself what I wanted to do with my life. The answer, I discovered quite quickly, was to help people using my gifts and talents. I was good with numbers and problem-solving and had strong analytical skills. I felt that these were my most useful strengths. It was after talking with Lynne— the financial planner who came to our branch of the credit union every Friday to conduct appointments with our members—that I felt I had found my answer. I decided that becoming a financial planner to help people achieve their financial dreams was the best fit. Over the next several years, I completed a Diploma in Financial Planning, my certified financial planner studies and then finished my Bachelor of Commerce, majoring in financial planning. Eventually, I worked with Lynne in the business she had started, commencing my employment just before it listed on the Australian Securities Exchange. I started as a client services officer before quickly moving on to be a paraplanner, preparing projections and writing financial plans. The next step would be to become a financial planner.

In my role as a paraplanner, I attended the financial planners' sales meetings but was very quickly deterred by their focus on sales targets and the pressure the sales manager put on the financial planners to get clients to invest more money into our investment products, especially during a prolonged downturn in the investment market. His approach was ruthless. Financial planners who failed to meet targets were bullied and shamed, and some were even fired. I was in my mid twenties and just starting to learn about the commercial realities of the business world. I was scared by what I witnessed. I wanted to help people, not sell to them, and I never wanted to experience that kind of pressure or treatment if for some reason I didn't meet sales targets, so I decided that I didn't want to be a financial planner anymore. Instead, I discovered I had an aptitude for designing and improving processes, as well as a natural tendency to lead, so I went down the management path.

First I built and managed the paraplanning team and was then promoted to manage all of the back office operations. I became part of the executive management team, heavily involved in due diligence and integration of our business acquisitions, and I loved it. However, the rapid growth of our business necessitated a restructure for continued growth, so I moved into a project role, reviewing our client segmentation and product offer. As part of that project, I wrote the position description for my new role as executive manager of product. That was the role I discovered I didn't like and that resulted in me leaving the company. I felt like I had detoured so far away from my initial intention of wanting to help people with my gifts and talents, so I took a detour and went on my yearlong sabbatical to explore my passion for scuba diving and to be free for a while. That detour inadvertently led me to where I stood now, walking an ancient pilgrimage path, seeking the answers to my life's purpose. The paths we walk in life are never straight lines, and the detours we make aren't mistakes.

There was a part of me that wanted to hear very clear and

specific instructions about my purpose in life and what I should do next. Right then, I would have welcomed instructions from a great voice, booming out "Thou shalt...", Ten Commandments-style, as I was standing on top of the mountain. But there was no great booming voice. There were no specific instructions. There were only the whispers and glimpses that came to me as I walked.

"Your purpose is not a problem to be solved."

"Teach what you know."

"Help others grow into their own fullness."

"Write."

I understood these whispers but I didn't trust them as final answers. They weren't clear enough. I wanted specifics. I wanted to know how I should help people, what I should teach, what I should write about, and where I should get it published. I wanted to know what, where and how I needed to study to do all of this, where I should live, and how I should support myself financially while I worked towards it. So I kept walking and trusted that if I kept asking the questions and was open to the answers, then in time they would come.

Viverone combined some of my most favourite things in this world: water, sunset, tiramisu and wine. The town was quiet, with only a few tourists strolling along the lake's shores. It had been too long since I had been able to sit and watch the sun set over water, but I did so that night, sitting alone on the step of a jetty by the calm glossy lake. As the sun dipped towards the horizon, the clouds teased the outcome, and the light and colours were ever-changing. Watching the sunset is a meditation for me and a prayer that calls me into a deeper presence with myself. Sitting by the lake, I remembered how important and soothing water is to my soul. I'd spent school holidays playing joyfully in the shallows of Port Phillip Bay with my brother as my Nana watched us from the shore, and there were weekends visiting the local indoor heated pool with my Dad, where I left my earthly troubles poolside and transformed into a dolphin, ducking and diving and moving freely through the warm water. Most especially, there was the joy of scuba diving in the sea, submerged in a magical world in which my body was neutrally buoyant and my spirit would meld with the ocean that held me. My heart tugged with longing. I missed scuba diving and the sea.

Twenty-two—The gold and the lonely

Viverone to Vercelli

In the morning I woke to find my immediate world shrouded in silver. I meditated facing the lake that I couldn't see behind the thick fog. Halfway through my journal writing, I glanced outside to see the fog had almost cleared. I grabbed my camera and dashed out barefoot onto the balcony, wearing only my black leggings and singlet, not caring about the cold. The lake was a hazy, ice blue. A single marshmallow cloud of the palest rose hovered above its centre. I took some photos then went back inside to finish my writing. By the time I had repositioned myself comfortably on the bed, the fog had stolen the lake from view once more.

After checking out from my hotel, I lingered by the lake, not wanting to leave its peace and stillness. I lay on the boardwalk's stone wall, basking in the sun and enjoying the view of the distant, snow-capped, rocky peaks of the Alps. The town was even quieter than when I had arrived. Most of the sunset strollers were still sleeping and the bars were not yet open for business. Two men worked on the roof of the restaurant opposite my hotel. A couple strolled by the lake. A man wearing an orange wetsuit waded into the water to fix a mooring buoy, as his three-year old son and his elderly mother watched from the boardwalk. I could have stayed there for days. It would have been the perfect place to rest and reflect and write, but I still had a long way to walk, and I hoped to use some rest days to finally visit Cinque Terre and to slow down and meander my way through Tuscany. Besides, these shorter walking days—by which I mean 20 kilometres or less—were a kind of rest day, just because they were shorter and less strenuous. Reluctantly I walked away from the lake and up the long hill to the main village to buy lunch. In the local supermarket, I bought a panino with *prosciutto crudo* and a sweet pecorino cheese, recommended by the young woman that served me. I visited the *pasticceria,* intending only to look at the pastries and cakes, but I walked out with a custard tart in hand. I ate the panino and tart at my own private picnic lunch in the middle of the countryside, lying on Kermit in the sunshine, looking at the Alps on the horizon.

I arrived in Santhià and easily found my way to the café in the centre of the small town, opposite the main church. I waited for the young, dark-haired barman to finish making espressos so I could ask about staying in the town's pilgrim hostel, known as an *ostello.* Of his reply, I only understood the word *chiave,* but I got the gist that it would be okay. I just needed to wait for someone with the key. I ordered a beer and sat at a table by the front window to wait, looking up frequently from the book I was reading on my iPad to watch the other people in the bar. Outside, three old women drank espresso. Another couple of middle-aged women entered the bar and ordered espresso too.

A man entered the bar, spoke to the barman, and then walked straight over to me. He had the *chiave* for the *ostello.* I paid my bill and followed him out of the café and across the square to the *ostello.* It was a ground floor apartment with a bathroom, office and a bedroom with three bunk beds. He showed me the pilgrim guestbook, where to leave my donation, and explained where to leave the key, adding that the local restaurant offered a pilgrim menu for dinner. Then he left. I selected the bottom bunk against the far wall and set up my bed with sheets and my sleeping bag. After showering and dressing in cleaner clothes, I strolled the streets and found myself at a local park, sitting on a bench in the sunshine, eating a cup of *fior di latte* gelato and watching everyday life around me. A fifty-year-old man with dark wavy hair, greying at the temples and above his ears, walked hand in hand with his elderly mother, her shoulders hunched over and her upper back rounded. They sat side by side on the bench opposite me. From my left, I heard a young boy cry out.

"Lorenzo! Lorenzo!"

"*Arrivo*, Luciano!" another boy replied.

A woman wearing a black leather jacket with dark brunette hair pulled back in a long ponytail sat on a concrete statue of a soldier, smoking a cigarette while talking on her mobile phone.

"*No! No!*" she cried out, her voice high-pitched yet husky.

A man walked by, hand in hand with his three year old son.

"*Sì*," said the man.

"*No*," said the boy.

"*Sì.*"

"*No.*"

"*Sì.*"

"*No.*"

Eventually, the fifty-year-old man and his mother stood up to leave. They strolled off the same way they arrived, still hand in hand. I, too, walked away and back to the *ostello*. The sun had dipped below the buildings, leaving a chill in its wake, but I felt warmed by so much richness in just being present in the one, tiny place.

Walking from Santhià to Vercelli was golden from start to end. As I paced along the paved Corso Nuova Italia, the sun struck the side of the terraced buildings, and was slowly rising skyward as a shimmering golden diamond. I crossed the railway line and walked along a quiet road that stretched straight towards the sun's underbelly, hovering just above the horizon. After a short stroll beside a busy road, I crossed the tree-lined bridge over the railway line, all the while trying to glimpse the misty fields and golden apricot horizon through every gap in the foliage. The bitumen became gravel and I passed between farm buildings, feeling like I was trespassing. At first the surrounding fields were thick with dry, golden grass and huge round hay bales and then I reached the sunken rice fields, glowing lime and yellow with fiery tips. The colours were hypnotic next to the terracotta gravel road bordered by lush green grass. Over one hundred varieties of rice grow around Vercelli, but the most popular are short-grains, including arborio, which is the most well-known outside Italy.

In the town of San Germano Vercellese, I took a cappuccino at a bar near the Piazza Giuseppe Mazzini. Four old guys sat in a booth at the front window, chatting and laughing. I heard them call me *la nuova donna*, the new woman.

"*Non freddo?*" one of the men asked me. They all wore jackets while I had only my long-sleeved t-shirt on.

"No, *non freddo*," I told them, shaking my head and assuring them I was not cold. I had walked eight kilometres in the sunshine. I was pleasantly warm.

I walked back into the countryside among the golden fields of rice. On the far side of some farm buildings, I glimpsed two figures with backpacks, a male and a female, a hundred metres ahead of me, walking slowly side by side. My heart soared then sank. I was excited to see pilgrims on the road but my solitude was important to me. I was in love with that golden land and the silence of my own company, and I didn't want to walk with other pilgrims that day and maybe not any day, but there was no way of avoiding them. They walked too slowly, and if I kept my distance behind them I wouldn't arrive in Vercelli until after dark. I took a breath, relaxed my shoulders and walked on.

They had stopped in the shade of a tree on the side of the track between rice fields when I caught up to them. Both had grey hair covered by round straw sunhats. She drank from an aluminium water bottle while he checked a map.

"*Buongiorno,*" I greeted them, assuming they were Italian.

They looked at me without smiling and didn't greet me back.

"*Sei pellegrini?*" I asked.

Silence.

"*Italiani? Non Italiani?*" I asked.

"No," he answered in English with an accent.

I switched to English too. "Where are you from?"

"Switzerland," the man replied.

"You walk Via Francigena?" I asked.

"Yes," he nodded.

"Today, you walk to Vercelli?" I asked.

"Yes."

"You are walking to Rome?"

"We will walk some while the weather here is good. Home is getting cold," he explained.

We stood in silence for a few moments, but as they didn't try to make conversation, I took it as a sign to leave and wished them *buon cammino,* a good walk. When I turned the corner of the rice field, I glanced back. They were a hundred metres behind me, ambling beside the rice field. I looked back a few more times before turning onto the road and never saw them again.

I crossed a small bridge into a rice field, where the guide-book directed me to skirt the field on my right. I wasn't sure if 'skirt' meant I should walk around the perimeter of the field by turning right immediately parallel with the road or if I should walk straight ahead then turn right at the end of the field. There were no signs, and after checking my map, I decided to turn right immediately. I followed the dirt embankment away from the road, with the canal to my right and the sunken rice field to my left. The overgrown reeds in the canal rustled as a grey cat crouched in their midst, stalking frogs. When the embankment became completely overgrown with grass and weeds, I suspected I had walked the wrong way but I had come too far to turn back. I continued through the overgrown grass, picking my feet up so as not to trip over, until there was no way forward. Then I stepped down into the harvested rice field and walked along the edge of it with the cracked mud squelching beneath my boots until I climbed back out onto a clear path. There were only two more obstacles for me to overcome before I reached my destination: the busy highway I had to cross to get into Vercelli and a big red truck carrying harvested rice that blocked the raised path between the sunken rice fields. I averaged five kilometres per hour that day. Maybe it was the fields of gold or maybe it was the music I listened to in the morning, but I had found my rhythm and didn't want to stop.

Vercelli was one of those places that I felt I wanted to explore soon after arriving. I walked into the town centre without an agenda, just letting my feet follow my eyes. The day had started out golden and it was ending golden too, as the afternoon sun cast a gold sheen on the terrace houses, the cream walls of the cathedral and the red brick churches. Eventually I found myself in Piazza Cavour, a wide, pebbled square bordered by four-storey terraces and medieval arcades. In one corner stood the red brick Angel Tower, which was part of a private home. I sat down at one of the outdoor tables of a bar and ordered an aperol spritz just as the sun dipped behind the apartments opposite me. The locals took their evening *passeggiata*, strolling around the square in small groups, stopping to greet others they knew, while the teenagers gathered around the white stone monument of Camillo Benso, Count of Cavour. Around me, other customers drank beer, aperol and even tea while smoking endless cigarettes. I was part of the scene but I felt separate from it; perhaps I had become too engulfed by my own solitude. I was an outsider in a town that had its own rhythm and connection, a foreigner just passing through.

I enjoyed experiencing new towns and scenery every day, as well as my solitude during the day, but I was starting to yearn for a deeper and longer connection to place. The constant movement left me feeling like I was skimming the surface. I was moving too often and too quickly, even at four kilometres per hour. I also felt homesick for the familiarity of being able to fully understand what was said to me, to communicate and be understood. I missed having that intrinsic understanding of how things work that we take for granted in our homelands. My sense of being separate and not belonging to any place I passed through was growing. I accepted that being a stranger was a necessary part of pilgrimage, but I still felt sad. Around me, I witnessed the strong social connections that are typical of Italian communities, and I missed being able to share with my own loved ones. I was alone, feeling a little obvious in the city in a way I never felt when I was in the middle of the countryside. Just as I was transient, passing through those places and through time, I understood that my emotions were too. I knew that if I stayed with it and just kept taking one step after the other, those feelings of disconnection would pass.

Twenty-three—The Certosa and the key
Vercelli to Orio Litta

I woke up in slow mode once again and didn't leave Vercelli until eight o'clock. The streets were busy with cars and pedestrians as locals made their way to work and school. In between the multi-storey apartment buildings, I glimpsed the rising sun, a giant ball of flaming pink hanging in the hazy sky. The only way out of town to the quiet tracks beside the river Sesia was along the peak hour SP11. There was no footpath and barely an edge to walk on. As I marched, I prayed over and over, "Please don't let me die today", until I was safely amongst the fields of corn and rice. The track meandered through a farm surrounded by neat and orderly rows of tall, pencil-like young poplar trees then back out to golden rice fields on my left and the sunken riverbed to my right. There were no mosquitoes, just the usual entourage of midges hovering around my head like a moving black halo. I felt joyful walking through those fields, in love with the colours of the landscape: the bright green of grass and new seedlings; the fields of ripe rice, glowing gold; and the green and gold of the young rice with its flaming orange tips against the muted blue of the hazy sky. Everything was a soft shade of bright. I drank it in with my eyes and quenched my thirst for beauty.

Signs in the town of Nicorvo claimed to welcome pilgrims,

but I felt anything but welcome as I walked by the front of the bar of a basic pilgrim hotel, where an old man, a middle-aged man and two teenagers all stared intensely at me without returning my *buongiorno*. My sense of aloneness was exacerbated so I put on some music to help me put a bounce in my step. I had turned onto a rocky track between rice fields and was taking off my long-sleeved top while still walking, when I glanced down and saw a metre long snake with its body reared upright in striking position less than a few paces away from me.

"Farrrrrrrk," I swore, as I instinctively sprinted faster than I ever thought possible with the Devil on my back. After twenty steps, I kept running but looked back over my left shoulder, expecting to see the snake lunging after me. This was only the second time in my life I had seen one outside a zoo or a reptile park. Once when I was around four years old, strolling along a dirt road in the country with my Nana and Papa, helping them collect dry native grass to take home for the budgerigars and parrots they kept in aviaries, I turned around to see a snake slithering stealthily behind us through the wiry grass in the middle of the road.

"Papa, look!" I stood and pointed at it as it coasted towards me. Papa quickly picked up the nearest stick, clobbered the snake then flung it towards the paddock. It landed on the wire fence and hung there for a few seconds before it wriggled free and fell into the grass, never to be seen again.

Alarmed by this second encounter with a serpent, I ran twenty more steps through the rice field before I slowed to a fast march with my heart pounding and adrenaline still coursing through my veins. I had a strong urge to get the hell out of those rice fields but I had another three and a half kilometres of them to walk through. From then on, every rustle and movement I caught out of the corner of my eye made me jump with the expectation of seeing another snake, but there were only tiny bronze frogs, and grasshoppers jumping in front of my feet. I passed the rest of the day without any further confrontations.

The Saturday morning markets were setting up as I left Mortara the following morning. Trestle tables were covered with tablecloths and laid out with second-hand trinkets, bric-a-brac and books. I took the subway under the main road then climbed up and out onto a gravel track and walked down to the Abbazia Sant'Albino. The church with an old monastery attached to it had been a resting place for many French and English pilgrims since the Middle Ages. I was standing and looking at it when a car drove out of a farm along the gravel path to my right and stopped in front of me. The window wound down and a lady with thick brunette hair told me that it was possible to visit the church if I went to the main door and rang the bell.

"*Cammini verso Roma da sola?*" she asked, wondering if I were walking alone to Rome.

"*Sì,*" I nodded and smiled.

"*Mamma mia! Sei brava signorina. Brava!*"

She wound up the window and drove off and I walked towards the church with tears in my eyes. I was tired after sleeping poorly above a noisy restaurant, but mostly I was pining for familiarity and company. Her kindness cut through my loneliness but she left and I was alone again.

At the door to the church, I rang the bell and a man answered through the intercom. In Italian, I announced that I was a pilgrim and asked if I could visit the church. The intercom went silent. I heard heavy footsteps approach then the brown wooden-slatted door opened. A silver-haired man wearing dark blue overalls gestured for me to enter. I followed him through the hall to the church, repulsed by the pungent stench of cigarettes. Once inside the church, which was built in the second half of the 4th century, I walked to the altar and paused, looking up at the frescoes painted on the red brick wall. The caretaker stood watching me from the back. I stood for only a minute then turned to leave, dropping some coins through a slot in the wall as a donation as I left.

As we walked back out through the hall to the front door, I noticed there were four fold-up beds against one wall and asked the caretaker if pilgrims slept here.

"Sì," he nodded.

Then I remembered having seen the church listed as an accommodation by donation option in the guidebook. However, I was glad I had chosen not to say there. The cigarette smell was unpleasant and overpowering.

I spent the day meandering through more rice fields. There was no sunshine, just a silver haze that hugged the earth. Most of the fields had already been harvested and some had been ploughed into clumps of moist brown soil. The canals that lined the fields were empty of water but were thick with mud and sludge and at times rubbish. They smelled foul and at one point I started retching. Gunshots fired frequently, near and far, as hunters scavenged the tufts of woodland for pheasants. I still found it unsettling to come across men with guns in the middle of nowhere. At one point, a group of four idled along in front of me with their two hunting hounds at their heels. One hunter carried their catch of three pheasants slung over the side of his leather waist satchel. As I caught up to them, we exchanged greetings and the man carrying the dead pheasants volunteered directions around the military zone. I thanked him for his help although I didn't really need it as I had my maps and guidebook.

I wanted to leave the smelly, hunted fields behind me and get to the town of Tromello as quickly as I could, so I marched for 19 kilometres without a rest break. After seven weeks of walking, I should have known better. I hobbled into town, my feet throbbing and sore. The final four kilometres after I stopped briefly for lunch were even more painful. My feet, knees and hips stiffened and rejected further walking. It took fifteen minutes for them to relax and the pain to ease after I started walking again. However, I made it to my hotel in Garlasco by early afternoon and had the remainder of the day to wander the town a little and then rest.

I checked out of the hotel at half past seven with the aim of arriving in Pavia by two o'clock. Before I left Melbourne, I emailed David and his father, Sergio, to ask if there were any places along the trail that I really should see. Sergio had always been a great source of travel advice. He didn't list many, but one of them was the Certosa di Pavia, one of the largest monasteries in Italy, which was situated only eight kilometres from Pavia. He described it as *molto bellissimo*, very beautiful, and said that I must see it. With that advice in mind, I wanted to arrive in Pavia early enough to take a train to visit the Certosa without staying an extra day in Pavia.

The rice fields outside Garlasco glowed gold against the morning's silver haze and drew my attention to the shape and form of the silhouetted poplar trees lining the fields. I stopped for second breakfast in Gropello Cairoli, where I was the centre of attention as usual, with the locals turning to stare at the strange, dishevelled woman with sunglass marks tanned onto her face who was walking through their town. Late in the morning, I passed through the village of Villanova d'Ardenghi and eventually arrived at the jade waters of the River Ticino. I sat at a dark green wooden table on a matching bench seat at a riverside *trattoria* that was closed for winter as I ate my homemade sandwich of prosciutto and pecorino on day old ciabatta bread.

As I walked towards the covered bridge to enter Pavia, it started to rain lightly. I was approached by a kind man who wanted to make sure I knew where the pilgrim *ostello* was. I did, but first I was heading straight to the train station to catch the train to Certosa. I wasn't going to walk eight kilometres there and back. At the train station, I bought a return ticket and boarded the train bound for Milan. It felt strange to be moving so fast after travelling slowly for so long. On the train, I covered eight kilometres in five minutes. When I walked, I covered eight kilometres in two hours. I watched the golden fields pass by too quickly, missing the detail and the opportunity to pause amongst it. As I crossed the station car park, I glimpsed the very top of the church spire peaking above the monastery's red brick walls that were covered by thick red ivy. I walked quickly, following the path beside the wall next to a canal filled with brackish brown water. The bounty of rich autumnal colours contrasting with the silver skies brought other visitors to a standstill as they stopped to take photos of the ivy on the walls and the trees. I stopped briefly too and then continued, eager to see the monastery.

The entrance to the complex was an understated gateway supported by two square concrete pillars, each topped with a cherub holding a scroll. I followed the path into a building painted with faded frescoes then to the inner gate where I paused.

"Holy wow," I whispered.

Through the gate's wrought iron rungs, I viewed the Certosa. It was majestic and elaborate like the Taj Mahal. I felt humbled and awed in its presence.

The church was built between 1396 and 1495 on a Latin cross plan and was inspired by the Duomo of Milan, although much smaller. The white façade of the church was completely decorated with marble and intricate sculptures, depicting different religious scenes. The monastery originally housed the Carthusians, an order of cloistered nuns and monks known for their seclusion and their preference for plain architecture, with the exception of the majestic Certosa. Over the years, different monastic orders had acquired and occupied the monastery. Some Cistercian monks have lived there since the 1960s and operate a gift shop that sells homemade produce including soap and wine.[5]

As I walked towards the building, tears burned my eyes. Humans are capable of such destruction and ugliness, but equally capable of creating objects of divine beauty too. The interior of the church was even more breathtaking. Each side was lined with chapels that were intricately decorated with marble, gold, and painted frescoes. The high ceiling was painted cobalt blue with gold stars and was supported by white ribs. I walked slowly from chapel to chapel, admiring the marble and the scriptural scenes that decorated recesses in the walls. I followed fifty Italian tourists through the black gates of the transept that were subsequently closed behind us. The apses housed huge elaborate tombs with reclining life-size statues of those who were interned there: Ludovico il Moro and Beatrice d'Este, the Duke and Duchess of Milan from 1494 to 1499 in the northern transept, and Gian Galeazzo Visconti, the first Duke of Milan in the southern transept.[5]

Back outside, I couldn't tear myself away from the church. I sat on a bench seat, staring at the adorned and adored church. I was awestruck by its intricate and elaborate detail. This building was a work of art created over one hundred years, painstakingly etched, chiselled and brushed to perfection. Its creation called for presence in each moment; no backing away from what might be hard or boring. The devotion was palpable. I sat for a long time, soaking in that devotion and thinking about what I would devote my life to. What would be the Certosa of my life?

After another quick train ride, I arrived back into Pavia. With a couple of hours to kill until I could check into the pilgrim *ostello*, I wandered the cobbled streets in the rain. By the time I checked in, I was so exhausted I couldn't even tell the receptionist where I had walked from that day. My mind was completely blank. I had walked for sixteen days straight and needed to rest. Although I had only intended to stay in Pavia for one night, it felt like the right place to stay and rest. I was enchanted by the town's vibrant undercurrent that mingled with the old world charm of its ancient university and cobblestoned streets. For me, it was just the right size. I could spend a few hours looking around and use the remainder of my time to rest my weary body.

I slept well in the *ostello* until eight o'clock, when I was called from my slumber by the church bells singing their sweet song loudly next door. I packed the Devil, as I was relocating to a hotel one kilometre away, heading north out of town, so that I could relax in a private room. I had a couple of hours until I could check in, so I crossed back over the Ponte Coperto, took breakfast in a quiet café then wandered around the streets, meandering without intending to go anywhere in particular. My feet continued to feel sore and tender until they relaxed into walking, but at least my blisters had healed and the Red Beasts version 2 hadn't caused any new ones.

I wandered into the Duomo di Pavia and found myself in the middle of mass. The singing and the chanting echoed and vibrated throughout the cathedral, seeming to be everywhere at once. I stood near a white, octagonal marble column listening to the service while looking up at the central dome, 97 metres above me. I understood little of what was said, except *Spirito Santo* and *hallelujah*, but I felt the vibration directly in my body of every word and every note sung, as the sound bypassed my rational mind and entered my heart. I will always remember that feeling, holy and sacred.

After dropping the Devil off at my hotel, I took myself out for a long and slow lunch at a *trattoria* in a piazza opposite the *duomo.* There, I enjoyed risotto with pumpkin, rosemary and pecorino, along with white wine, tiramisu, and espresso. I ate slowly and enjoyed each mouthful, as couples, families and fashionable women dined around me. With a contented belly, I continued to stroll the cobbled streets. I wandered past the Castello Visconteo, once a castle but now a civic museum, and was tempted to visit the Monet exhibition inside, except the ache in my feet reminded me I still had 700 kilometres to walk to Rome. Instead, I made my way to the supermarket, where I replenished my supply of snacks and bought a picnic supper I could eat in my hotel room. The rest of the day I spent resting on my bed, emailing family and friends, and writing a long blog with dozens of photos about my last two day's walking and my visit to the Certosa.

My exit from Pavia was beside a main road through suburbia. There was no soft morning light that day and nothing pretty to look at, just apartment buildings, shops and houses. I felt bland and unwell after eating what I suspected was a dodgy slice of cold pizza for dinner. There was a pain in my left shoulder blade that was constant and searing. I stretched my left arm across the front of my body and the pain subsided momentarily, but as I let it swing lightly by my side the pain returned. It took an hour and a half for me to find my rhythm. As I settled into my steps, the pain in my shoulder eased and I enjoyed walking again, feeling my feet on the earth and the energy moving through my body.

The day was filled with more intense colour and bursts of beauty: astonishing autumn-flamed trees, green and gold spotted woodlands, the bright gold of the rice fields, and ghostly silhouettes of trees against the hazy horizon. As I walked, I hummed 'The Long and Winding Road' by The Beatles. The way forward was never-ending, over bitumen, gravel, dirt and sand. The path went on and on. I walked the perimeter of a working quarry, hemmed by the main road and a dry dirt field being ploughed by a tractor. I crossed a bridge over a small river and sat at a picnic table beneath a shelter to rest and eat an apple. Near the river, three old men worked on their fishing rigs. A tall, gangly man smoking a cigarette wandered over and sat at the end of the picnic table without greeting me. I felt uneasy so I stood up, gave him a feeble smile and walked off along the gravel path. Another man stood next to the canal, holding a fishing rod with the line dangling in the brown water.

"*Da dove vieni?*" he asked me.

"Pavia. I walk to Santa Cristina," I replied, realising as I walked away that he was asking from which country I came and not from which town I had walked.

I emerged from the golden fields into Santa Cristina, comprising no more than a main road with some side streets, a few bars and pizzerias. As there were no hotels or guesthouse, I needed to find the priest to ask for accommodation. The church was easy to find but my timing was bad. Dozens of bicycles were lined up against its patchy rendered façade, as mass was about to commence. I sat on a step and waited. Thirty minutes later, when the parishioners walked back out, I stood at the left side of the door, waiting until I could enter and find the priest. The women filed out first, casting curious glances at me as they passed. Finally, a thin, white-haired gentleman exited then abruptly stopped and looked at me.

"*Pellegrina?*" he asked.

"*Sì,*" I replied.

"*Vieni,*" he invited.

He took me by the arm and led me down the driveway beside the church to a two-storey building. He chatted cheerfully and continuously, despite my limited comprehension, and asked the usual questions like where I was from and where I was going. We entered the side door and I was surprised to find myself in a bar containing two tables at which sat four old men playing a serious game of cards. My escort introduced me as an Australian *pellegrina*.

"Oh, Australiana!" cried one of the card-players in welcome.

"Ooh, *lontana!*" said another, noting that I had come from far away.

The white-haired man left me with the barman and wished me a cheerful *buon cammino*. The barman introduced himself as Enzo, as in Enzo Ferrari, and stamped my pilgrim passport, making sure I knew how to organise the river ferry to cross the River Po on my way into Piacenza. He showed me to my room, checked the hot water was working, turned on the heating, showed me how to lock and unlock the doors, and told me where I could go to eat dinner. All the things that mattered to me were taken care of without me having to ask, which was such a comfort and relief after the long walk. The accommodation was simple—just a room with two single beds and bathroom attached—but it was safe and warm. I had a heater, an actual working heater, which I hovered over before going out for dinner and hovered over again before going to bed. I was not cold that night.

Orio Litta was only 16 kilometres from Santa Cristina, so I was in no rush to leave the next day. I sipped my strong cappuccino in the corner of the café wine bar, pretending to read a book. Actually, I was listening to the dramatic-sounding conversation taking place at a nearby table. The women commenced each new topic or opinion with an emphasised *allora*, meaning *well* or *okay*. On my way out of town, I visited the *pasticceria* and purchased an apricot *crostatina* to eat later, except it looked so good that I couldn't wait and ate it as I strolled towards the main road. It was a delicious circle of crunchy buttery biscuit pastry, topped with a tart apricot jam.

The weather had turned cold. On the previous day, I walked in a t-shirt but now I wore my long-sleeved top, as well as my windproof jacket, beanie and gloves, and it rained for the first time in many days. It was mostly just a lot of spotting that didn't warrant putting Kermit on until lunchtime when thunder rumbled behind me and some big fat drops of rain started to fall. I stopped in a pizzeria in the village of Lambrinia and lingered over my pizza *prosciutto crudo*, drizzled with olive oil infused with chillies. I was only an hour from Orio Litta. I had read about a local man in the town who greets pilgrims as they arrive through the fields and then helps them find accommodation. I hoped he would see me arriving. He could hardly miss me in my bright green Kermit poncho, but he didn't appear.

The Cascina San Pietro, one of the religious accommodations, was in the midst of renovations. A workman in white overalls tried to direct me into town, but I didn't understand what he said to me. I was unsure of where I was going until I spotted a pilgrim sign pointing left. I found the pilgrim accommodation next to the municipal office, but it was closed and locked. I stood at the door, wondering what to do, when a municipal workman appeared. He tried to call the caretaker then went into the municipal office and returned with a mass of keys that he fumbled through until he found the right one and unlocked the door. Upstairs, opposite the gym hall, were two rooms, one with four beds the other with three, and a bathroom that had heavenly hot water. The workman and I searched the rooms for spare keys but didn't find them. When he left, I assumed that I was stuck in the building for the rest of the night and would have to eat my two-day-old ciabatta roll for dinner, but luckily there was a knock on the door twenty minutes later and the caretaker entered. He was a schoolteacher, and as I had arrived during school hours, he had not been able to greet me. We chatted for a while then he gave me the spare key and left.

For dinner, I walked to the *osteria*, a simple local restaurant around the corner from my accommodation. I stepped through the hanging beads in the doorway to find the restaurant void of customers. An auburn-haired Italian mamma, who stood watching the television above the bar, turned to look at me. I asked if the restaurant was open for dinner.

"*Sono una pellegrina*," I added, as explanation for my presence when she didn't respond immediately.

"*Ah, si!*" she replied, ushering me to a table then rushing off to the kitchen where I heard her put a pot on the stove.

I looked around the empty restaurant. On the apricot-beige walls was a painted mural of sights and towns along the Via Francigena: the Po River, the covered bridge in Pavia, and the cathedral in Reims. Also adorning the wall were some traditional pilgrim staffs carved from tree limbs.

Mamma returned with two bowls, one with spaghetti and one with bolognaise sauce, and put them on the table in front of me so I could serve myself. She didn't give me a menu, so I assumed that this was all that was on offer for dinner. I ate a modest serving and then had seconds, but as she cleared the dishes from the table she offered me *secondo*. I declined a main course, being already full from the two-servings of pasta. She had just returned to the bar after taking the dishes to the kitchen when a man walked through the beaded doorway. His hair was spiky and steel grey in colour with white tips. He spoke to Mamma, and I got the gist that he was her husband.

"*Pellegrina!*" he exclaimed with a broad smile, as he walked over and shook my hand. I told him my usual story: where I was from, that I had started my pilgrimage from Canterbury on 1 September, that I planned to walk to Rome, and yes, I was walking *da sola*. As we chatted, a lady with short brown hair and wearing glasses walked through the beaded entry.

"*Mia amica*," Mamma explained, introducing her friend, and they left to see a movie together.

The grey-haired man walked over to the bar and returned to my table, holding a wooden box. He opened it and took out a small bronze key that he threaded onto a piece of burgundy string. After tying the ends together, he held it out to me. I took it in my hand and looked at it. It was one of St Peter's keys. St Peter, one of the twelve apostles of Jesus, is buried beneath St Peter's Basilica in the Vatican. His tomb is one of the key sites in Rome that pilgrims visit, to pay homage to the saint and seek blessing. In the Book of Matthew, Jesus said that he would give Peter the keys to the kingdom of heaven and invested in him the divine authority to govern the church. The keys, one silver and one gold, crossed over each other, are a symbol of this authority, appearing on many coat of arms, including that of the Vatican City. They are also the symbol of those who make the pilgrimage to Rome.[6]

"*Per me?*" I asked the man.

"*Sì, per pellegrina*," he nodded.

I slipped the string over my head and the key hung right in front of my heart. I felt humbled and deeply touched to receive this token from a stranger. I rubbed the key between my fingers as I walked back to my accommodation in the dark. I had been given one of the keys to heaven. Now all I had to do was make it to Rome and perhaps I would find the other one too.

Twenty-four—Too many rivers

Orio Litta to Fidenza

I woke excited the following morning. This was the day I would cross the River Po by ferry, like pilgrims of old. While they probably crossed the river in some kind of punt or Roman boat, I would take the current day ferry, a small powerboat used as a river taxi. I left early, not wanting to rush or be late and keep the ferryman, Danilo, waiting. I had pre-arranged to meet him at the river landing in Corte Sant'Andrea at half past nine. As I walked down a dirt road away from Orio Litta, the palatial 17th century Villa Litta Carini made an impressive feature in the landscape. With three high stories plus attic space, the building sat in a U-shape on raised ground, towering over the surrounding ploughed fields. Once the home of a count, it is now used for weddings and conferences.

At the river, I walked down the metal steps to the landing slowly and carefully as they were wet and slippery and I had the added downward force of the Devil. The brown waters of the Po slipped by silently and the rowboat tied to the side of the landing snaked with the shifting current. The sound of high speed revving from my left warned me of the ferry's approach. Minutes later it appeared around the bend, a small white craft with its nose jutting slightly up out of the water. Danilo wore a faded fluorescent green jacket and had a blue canvas cap sitting back-to-front on his head. I was surprised to see he had already a passenger, a young lady sitting at the back of the boat with a black scarf wrapped thickly around her neck.

Danilo tied the boat to the landing then he and his passenger both stepped up onto the metal platform and I followed them back up the steep steps to the riverbank. The young lady, who I estimated to be in her late twenties, spoke only Italian. She was a journalist for a local news service and wanted to interview me for a project she was working on. Danilo held the microphone beneath my chin as she started talking, asking questions in Italian that I understood only a little. I felt like a deer caught in headlights. I was able to tell her my name, where I was from and that I had been walking for 54 days alone. Then she asked me why I was walking. I scanned my Italian vocabulary, trying to find the words to explain. I searched and I searched but couldn't come up with any. The journalist kept the camera running, and I felt the need to offer some kind of answer.

"Perche... mi piace cammino," I stuttered, intending to say it was because I like to walk. I could have slapped myself, firstly because this was too simple an answer that didn't really explain why I was walking, and secondly because I pronounced cammino the lazy Australian way, by saying ca-mino instead of cam-mi-no. What I actually told her was that I liked fireplaces. Neither Danilo nor the journalist appeared to notice my mistake. Both nodded as if they understood. The journalist then asked Danilo a few questions, and when had finished we packed up and walked back down to the landing to board the boat.

The ride on the river Po was only ten minutes long, but I loved every one of them, despite the cold wind. I loved being on the water. Through all my scuba diving adventures, the boat ride out and back to the dive site, even on an angry sea, was something

I always enjoyed. There was something magical about the feeling of being buoyed by an immense mass of molecules, about which I was infinitely curious and sometimes even fearful, due to its depth. Danilo brought the boat into a tiny landing and we climbed up the steep riverbank then up another steep embankment onto the path that led to Danilo's house. The journalist, wearing trendy sneakers, lost her footing and slipped, smearing her jeans and hands with mud.

"*Tutto bene?*" I asked, checking to see if she was okay.

"*Sì, sì,*" she laughed. I looked at her palms. They were muddy but there were no grazes or cuts.

At the riverside camp, Danilo showed us the imprint of what was said to be Archbishop Sigeric's footprint in the cement base of a red brick obelisk that honoured pilgrims. I put my foot beside it to compare the size. I was wearing size 43 boots, two sizes larger than normal so I had extra space for my toes, but if this really were Sigeric's footprint, then he was either a very short man or had very petite feet. The print was no more than two thirds the length of my foot.

Out the front of Danilo's house, we said goodbye to the journalist and I followed him inside. I sat at an old wooden table and wrote my name in the *Liber Peregrinorum*, a scratched red leather journal that the ferryman had specially made to record the names of all of the pilgrims he had helped cross the river since 1998. There were more than 2000 entries, but I wasn't surprised that the total number was so few. Compared to the camino to Santiago de Compostela, which attracts more than 200,000 pilgrims every year, only around 2000 pilgrims walk the Via Francigena all the way to Rome each year. Given the distance and time commitment it takes to travel so far, many pilgrims choose to walk specific sections only or break up the total journey over time, and not every pilgrim who arrives at the River

Po would cross with Danilo. Some walk the long way around to Piacenza.

Danilo stamped my pilgrim passport with his special stamp that was made from old-fashioned wax with red ink. Then he wandered off to the kitchen and returned, carrying a tray with a pot of freshly made coffee, two white espresso cups on tiny saucers, a small white ceramic bowl of sugar cubes, and a plate of biscotti. He sat down and poured me a coffee. As I stirred in a sugar cube, I heard tyres on gravel and looked through the window next to the front door to see a police car pull up. I assumed there was some trouble, but the three policemen in navy uniforms greeted Danilo with cheerful *ciaos* and hugs as they walked in and sat down. They had come for some of his home-made *salumi*. Danilo went back to the kitchen and returned with a huge platter of prosciutto and salami along with fresh ciabatta and olive oil. I stood up and announced that I was leaving.

"Non vuoi mangiare i salumi?" One of the policemen with black hair streaked silver asked me if I didn't want to eat some too. I was tempted to stay. The men were jovial and I enjoyed speaking Italian with them, but I really needed to keep walking to Piacenza. I thanked them and said goodbye.

The gravel path lead to a grass track where the thick mud clung to my boots and painted my trouser legs grey brown. It had been many days since I had walked through mud and I hadn't missed it. The dense clay clumped on the soles of my boots in uneven mounds and made walking slippery and uncomfortable. As I neared the entrance to the village of Calendasco, I found a solid stick and leaned up against a brick wall as I picked and flicked as much of it off as I could. The rest of the day was spent walking on bitumen roads. On the way out of Calendasco, a car honked at me as it sped past, a hand waving cheerily from the driver's window. It was Danilo. I waved back furiously, delighted to see him. For the last hour, I walked beside the crazy busy Via Emilia Pavese. As I approached the ramp that led up to the road, a concerned driver pulled over and offered me a ride. I declined and kept walking. A constant stream of traffic sped past in both directions as I walked along the narrow footpath and across the bridge over the river Po. There was nothing enjoyable about walking next to such frantic traffic, so I put on my headphones, turned up the volume on my favourite songs and marched into town.

Piacenza is a beautiful city with paved streets and towering basilicas and cathedrals. The *palazzo comunale,* the town hall, was a red brick second storey sitting on a white marble portico with five pointed arches. On each side of its white paved square stood life-size bronze statues of equestrians that were tributes to Alessandro Farnese, a 16th century Duke of Parma and Piacenza, and his son, Ranuccio, who became duke after Alessandra's death.[7] I sat in the Piazza del Duomo eating gelato then slowly walked two kilometres back to the suburban hostel, my accommodation for the night, arriving just after it opened for check-in.

After wandering the dark streets for thirty minutes, trying to find somewhere to eat dinner, I asked a barman for recommendations and he directed me to a pizzeria near the hospital. I ate pizza, again, drank some white wine, and then walked back to the hostel, wondering how I would feel when I arrived into St Peter's Square. Jubilant? Incredulous? Sad? At peace with my life? I was 690 kilometres away from Rome and I had many moments of kindness and tears still to experience before I got there.

I walked out of Piacenza along the Via Emilia. It was busy with traffic but there was enough of a shoulder for me to feel safe walking on it. In my gut there was a sense of desperation that I had 36 kilometres to walk that day, and a quiet voice was nagging at me, saying "I have to make it, I have to make it", like there was a possibility that I wouldn't. I walked swiftly, almost grabbing at the path for dear life as if I were clawing my way out of a hole, until I realised what I was doing. I felt my breath enter and leave my lungs as each foot connected with the ground. I walked with more presence in the here and now, rather than indulge in the desperation of the next step ahead. I still walked quickly, but the essence of my steps changed and I felt good to be in my body, exactly where I was, regardless of how many kilometres I still had to walk. I even put my headphones on and dance-walked my way out of town.

For most of the morning, the sun was like an opal moon behind the blanket of silver cloud. It broke through momentarily when I finally turned off the busy Via Emilia. Gone were the fields of gold. I was now surrounded by ploughed fields of chunky dirt. Five minutes out of the town of I Vaccari, an old gentleman walked his bicycle alongside me and we chatted. He was from Piacenza, ten kilometres away, and was out for his daily ride. He enjoyed riding for the exercise and the freedom it gave him. It made him feel alive, he said. He kept up a solid pace beside me as he pushed his bike and was neither puffed nor red-faced as we walked and talked.

"*Sono vecchio*," he said, telling me he was old.

"*No, non è vero. Qui*," I tapped my right hand against the centre of my chest, "*non vecchio*."

The man's body may have been old but his spirit wasn't. His friendliness, curiosity and daily forays out into the world on his bike demonstrated a vitality that made many a younger person seem older than him. He left me in I Vaccari, continuing straight on to San Paolo while I turned left toward the river.

The paths were once again comprised of slippery clay and thick mud. My boots were caked in it and clumped in the way that made me feel repulsed. I kept walking regardless and turned towards the first of three rivers and streams I would have to cross that day. The path came to an end at the exposed river-bed. Carefully, I stepped down, walking on clumps of grass and wood and tree litter to keep my feet out of the mud. I stood at the river's edge, scanning up and down for a place to cross. The river was seven metres wide and running rapidly over its rocky bottom. I couldn't tell how deep it was, but it looked a little too deep and it was running too fast for me to cross on foot. Sections of the far riverbank had collapsed and there were other sections that were vertical and too high to climb. Even if I could cross the river, there was no way up the riverbank on the other side.

"Fark!" I let out the tension I was feeling. "Now what?"

I checked the guidebook and the map. The only way around was to cut back to the main road and follow it to San Giorgio Piacentino, where there was a bridge, and then pick up the trail outside the town. That was going to add further distance to my day, but I had no choice. As I walked back towards the road, it started drizzling, so I stopped and put on Kermit. I was going to need it anyway to be seen on the road. There was no shoulder and the traffic was constant in both directions. I watched it forlornly as a spate of trucks passed.

"I am going to die," I said out loud.

At first I walked on the left side of the road, facing the on-coming traffic, but I came to a blind corner so I crossed to the other side and walked in the same direction as the traffic, pray-ing "Keep me safe, keep me safe". The cars and trucks passed within inches of me. It seemed like they would prefer to hit me rather than to slow down or stop. I had repeated visuals running through my mind of being clipped by a truck, faceplanting on the bitumen and picking my grazed and bruised body up, long after the truck had driven away none the wiser. Fortunately, I wasn't hit, although there was one really close call that made me swear and gesture rudely with my arms. I marched as quickly as I could to get myself off that road.

On the narrow country road out of San Giorgio, cars occasionally passed in both directions, and I stepped onto the muddy grass to get out of their way. I ignored the guidebook's directions and walked straight ahead to rejoin the GPS trail. In doing so, I made one seemingly small but consequently big error in judgment. I assumed that the GPS trail and the guidebook route matched. They didn't. The GPS trail was longer. I did the math and determined that I still had three hours of walking left. The frustration of it was too much and hot tears trickled down my dusty cheeks as I kept walking, one foot after the other. I would arrive eventually, as I always did, but I couldn't stay calm. My feet were sore, I had a mild temperature, my left shoulder was stabbing pain into me once again, and I couldn't get the Devil comfortable on my back. An hour later I was sobbing. I was sick of the cars and trucks passing so closely, sick of the dogs barking fiercely at me as I passed, and sick of not being there yet. As I passed a cluster of houses, a tan terrier ran straight towards me barking ferociously. I stood my ground, pointing Right Rodney at it.

"Go on, get!" I yelled.

I kept walking and it followed, lunging towards me as it growled. I turned quickly and pointed Rodney at it again.

"Go on, get you little shit!"

Eventually it tired or I passed out of its territory and it left me alone.

The afternoon improved before it worsened. Two little Indian kids playing in the backyard of their farmhouse ran down to the fence, waving and smiling at me. For a moment I was back in India on the Ganges River, with the village kids running down the riverbank, giggling and calling out for me to take a photo. I continued along the road then turned right onto a small country lane. The kids ran around the length of the property, waving at me, and I waved back at regular intervals until I couldn't see them any more.

I passed between a small cluster of houses then the road dipped down and in front of me was a stream, five metres wide and too deep for me to cross, even wearing the Red Beasts. My heart sank. I wasn't in the mood for a time delay or an obstacle, but there was no other way around. I took off the Devil then removed my boots. Standing up, I stuffed my socks inside them, put on the Devil again, picked up my Rodneys and stepped into the water on the concrete road. I usually hate cold water but this cool stream soothed my aching hot feet. I walked carefully, so that I wouldn't slip or step on a sharp and pointy stone, and paused in the middle to allow the water to ease my painful feet. At its deepest point, the water reached only one-third of the way up my shins. Once on the other side, I held onto a gate for balance as I put on my socks and boots again. I walked away on cold feet that stopped aching momentarily while they were numb, but I soon felt bits of dirt and grit rubbing against the soles of my feet.

I cut through private property to another bitumen road, where I walked behind two grey-haired gentlemen power-walking.

"*Torrente d'acqua,*" they warned me as I turned onto the pebbled road. It was littered with bright yellow leaves from the lime and lemon coloured trees that lined it. I could see the puddle of water the men had warned me about at the end of the path and watched it grow in size as I approached. It was only three meters wide but too deep to cross wearing boots if I wanted to keep them dry. I huffed and swore as I took off my boots and socks again. In the middle of the stream, I paused for a few moments to let the water chill and soothe my feet before continuing to the other side. Balancing on one numb foot at a time, I used a fallen leaf to wipe the grit and mud off then put the Red Beasts back on and continued.

I arrived in Fiorenzuola d'Arda one long hour later and walked straight to the church, where I asked the priest for accommodation. After I had shown him my credential and registered, he led me to a building out the back. The room had a bunk bed and a hospital bed. I was excited about the oil heater I saw, until I discovered that its plug didn't fit the socket. Resigned, I climbed into my sleeping bag for warmth and rested until dinnertime. My face was burning as my body fought off whatever was trying to attack it. All I really wanted was a hug and someone to bring me some chicken noodle soup so I could eat and go to sleep. Instead, I walked out into the dark and the cold and walked the streets for forty-five minutes without finding a single *ristorante* or *trattoria*, only bars. Reluctantly, I walked back to the only option I found. Takeaway pizza. Again.

It had been a long and hard day, but I woke to a fresh new morning. No matter how challenging and painful this journey could be, I knew there would be moments of beauty and kindness that made it worthwhile. That is what kept me going, along with the commitment I had made to myself to walk the trail from start to finish, completing all of it and not just the good bits. Packed and ready, I held my breath as I entered a café through the pungent cigarette smoke exhaled by a woman with a weathered face who was wearing jeans and standing near the door. I ordered a cappuccino and a *cornetto al cioccolato* then sat at a table studying my guidebook. An elegant woman entered the bar, dressed in a black pencil skirt and black fur jacket with red lipstick on her mouth. I watched her sip her macchiato, standing with poise at the bar, and guessed she had just come from Sunday mass.

I wandered the street and entered the Oratorio della Beata Vergine where I lit a candle. *This is for you, Mum*, I thought as the wick flamed. I stood quietly with my head bowed slightly, thinking of her as I watched the candle flicker and burn. I left when another woman came to light her own candle. As I walked away from the town, I was overwhelmed by tiredness and tears threatened to fall. I fought them at first as I passed a stream of people on their way to the cemetery, but once I made it onto the open country road, I allowed the sobs to come up and out. Ten minutes later, I was cried out and peaceful, accepting my tiredness and aloneness. I looked up to realise I was surrounded by the first blue sky I'd seen in a week.

Vietnamese Buddhist monk and mindfulness teacher Thich Nhat Hanh says that it is how we walk that matters most, and that this is the way to experience and spread peace and joy in life. Thinking of this, I remembered to walk mindfully, treading lightly and sending love down into the earth with each step I took. I put on my playlist of favourite New Age tunes and sang along to the mantras as I walked consciously, aware of the urge that kept pushing me to walk faster, to get there and to arrive. I remembered my friend Joey's instruction in yoga class: "There's nowhere to be." Although my intention was to arrive at the next town, right now there was nowhere to be but where I was, and all that mattered was my state of being in that moment and the weather of my heart. I pulled myself back into the present and slowed down. I sang and hummed as I walked, and I felt happy again.

White fluffy clouds drifted overhead as I passed fields of auburn dirt adorned with bright green seedlings. Beyond them lay golden trees and fields of pale, drying corn. A ladybug hitched a ride on my hand for a time. Later, a black and tan terrier trotted towards me. I braced for her barking, but she dropped down at my feet and rolled onto her back so I could pat her chest and belly. I happily obliged. The way could be hard at times, but I didn't come into this world to live a sleepy, comfortable existence, even if I occasionally wished that I did. Everything I experienced on that path and in my life was a divine opportunity to surrender or to grow. There was nowhere to be but where I was, and right then, it was walking this pilgrim path, step by step, with its joyous wonder, its pain and its many challenges.

Twenty-five—Into the Apennines

Fidenza to Pontremoli

I decided to ask for a bed at the Cappuccini convent on the other side of Fidenza. As I approached the convent, I saw a crowd was gathered in front of the bar next door while children played soccer on a field. Ignoring all the people who looked at me curiously, I walked to the main entrance and rang the bell. A friar with a curly beard that reached down to his chest opened the door. He was wearing the traditional long brown hooded robes with a white cord tied around his waist.

"*Hai un credenziali?*" he asked, checking to see if I had a pilgrim passport.

"*Sì.*" I pulled it out of my waist bag.

He asked me another question and I explained that I spoke little Italian.

"*Inglese?*" he asked.

"*Sì. Parli inglese?*" I asked, hopeful that he spoke English.

"*No.*"

He needed to speak to another friar and gestured for me to follow him. As we chatted, I told him I had walked many kilometres and that I was tired and didn't feel well. I hoped they would take pity on me and let me stay. I didn't want to walk anywhere else in search of accommodation. The locals who had gathered in front of the bar were talking and eating freshly roasted chestnuts from brown paper bags. It was *Festa della Castagna*, the festival of chestnuts. We weaved our way amid the crowd towards another friar. He was short, reaching only to my shoulder, and was clean-shaven with short dark-blonde hair.

"*Festa dei ragazzi,*" I heard him say and shake his head.

"*Lei è stanca,*" the bearded friar said, telling him I was tired.

The short friar turned to me and explained in English that the children were having a party in the hall and that they would be loud and it might not finish until midnight.

"No problem for me. I just need somewhere to sleep."

"But the accommodation is upstairs and you cannot use the communal area."

"No problem," I repeated. I would happily put up with some noise as long as I didn't have to walk anywhere else.

As I followed the bearded friar towards the main convent building, a bag of roasted chestnuts was thrust into my hands. I had never eaten chestnuts before. Eager to try, I put a whole one in my mouth and realised only after I bit down on it that I should have removed the outer shell. Not wanting to spit it out in front of the friar, I chewed a few times and swallowed, washing the remnants down with water.

I had a simple room to myself with cream painted walls, a parquetry floor partially covered by a worn rectangular rug, and a single bed. There was a bedside table, a desk and chair and a small shelf in the far corner next to the window. I was happy to have this small, private space to myself. After showering, I walked into town for an early dinner, intending to return to my room in the convent before the party started so I wouldn't interrupt. The evening *passeggiata* in the main piazza was at its peak, with the tables lining the perimeter of the square all occupied by people drinking wine and beer, and chatting while gesturing and laughing. Others strolled across the paved square that glowed gold beneath the streetlights. The upper floor of the terracotta-bricked *palazzo comunale* was spotlighted in fluorescent pink and green. The atmosphere was festive.

It was early and the *osterie* and *trattorie* were still closed, so I walked to a pizzeria, hoping that it might at least have pasta on the menu. It didn't. I ate pizza for the third time in four days. Back at the convent, the kids—around fifteen boys and girls in their early teenage years—sat around the long wooden table, eating crisps and drinking soft drinks as they chatted and laughed. I excused myself as I walked past them and went upstairs to my room. With the door closed, their laughter and chatter was muffled, and I was so tired that once I climbed into my sleeping bag and pulled the blanket over me, I quickly fell asleep.

I left Fidenza through an avenue of poplars that were turning gold and ghosted with a flimsy fog. The fog thickened as I walked out of town along a muddy path through a field of tall weeds adorned with dew-dotted spider webs. I waited five minutes for a safe gap to cross the busy road. Eventually, a silver Alfa Romeo sedan stopped to let me cross. I walked through the fog for almost two hours. It was only after I descended the hill and turned towards Costamezzana that the new landscape revealed itself. Before me were flat grassy fields, and beyond them I saw the Apennines rolling into high peaks in the distance. I was heading back into the mountains, but I wasn't daunted; I had walked through the Alps so I could handle these hills too.

I covered 36 kilometres over ten hours through the hills, walking in too much of my least favourite type of mud, which clumped to the bottom of the Red Beasts. I leaned up against a fence using a measly twig to ply it off, and five minutes later wondered why I bothered as I walked through more chunky clay. I scanned the way ahead looking, for the least muddy section, but eventually gave up and just walked through it. I used the two Rodneys all day. They stopped me from slipping on the mud and helped me settle into a walking rhythm that flowed and felt easier than if I had pushed through every step using only my legs.

Despite the mud, there was so much beauty. The grass was vivid green against an azure sky spotted with puffs of clouds that eventually gave way to sheets of thick grey. Sometimes the sun broke through and the silver rays caressed the ground or spotlighted a lone tree or abandoned farmhouse. All day, the sky kept changing, and I kept walking through the mud with my eyes continually drawn upwards. In the middle of the bridge over the Taro, I looked upstream in awe. The river was wide but shallow, rushing over its rocky bed and splitting off around islands. On the left bank was a thicket of trees, glowing gold and rust. Above the rolling, indigo hills, there hovered a thick sponge of creamy gold cloud. The landscape was all golden fire. My heart was on fire too. Despite the mud, my swollen feet, my painful shoulder, aching knees, hips and ankles, there in front of me was the reason I walked: to witness that landscape and beauty it contained without rushing by it.

As I walked into Fornovo di Taro, I hoped there would be a sign to direct me to my hotel. I had an address but I couldn't find it on my map, and all I knew was that it was on the way out of town. I just didn't know which way out of town. I asked a short, plump *nonna* plodding along the street, but she didn't understand my Italian and couldn't read the hotel's name without her glasses. I thanked her and then walked over to ask a couple as they dismounted from their touring motorbike, but they didn't know where it was. Finally, I went into the pharmacy and asked the spectacled male pharmacist with thinning white hair. He gave me specific directions in English and even showed me the exact location on my map.

The hotel was a three-storey ochre palazzo clad in ivy and nestled into the base of a pine-covered hill. In the middle of the paved foreyard stood a two-tiered fountain, supported by the sculpted heads of three white horses. I may have been covered in mud with wild hair, but I was about to enter a castle of simple comforts including a big double bed, wi-fi and heating. My feet were more swollen than usual, my temperature had returned, and I was feeling more tired than usual too. After eating steak for dinner in the hotel restaurant, I returned to my room, intending to get an early night but, anticipating that I might not have internet access for the next few days, I transferred photos from my phone to my Flickr account to free up space and caught up on my daily blog posts from the last few days. It was after eleven o'clock when I finally turned off the light and fell into a deep sleep.

I left Fornovo di Taro not sure of where I would end up that night. Maybe Cassio or maybe Berceto, if I thought I could make it that far. I wasn't sure how difficult the path over the hills would be or how long it would take me to walk uphill. I still had a temperature. My body wanted me to rest and give it a chance to properly fight off whatever was attacking it, but my heart was set on a detour to Cinque Terre after reaching Sarzana, so I kept walking. The bitumen road wound its way through the flattest part of the valley between rising fields of seedlings in neat rows. After a time, I turned onto another winding bitumen road, except this one climbed steeply. My legs burned and I breathed hard. I paused to look back often. I could see all the way back to Fornovo di Taro, where thick fog hovered over the river valley. Before me, the tree-covered mountains loomed.

I left the bitumen after the village of Bardone and climbed a steep path of broken rock that was scattered with tan and yellow leaves. I made it to the top and celebrated this minor victory, but I knew the climbing wasn't over yet. I continued on another narrow path of broken rock towards the silver sky then into yet another steep section in between the lime- and lemon-leaved trees. I emerged into a clearing surrounded by dense rolling hills with villages nestled into its curves, and later I walked on a path covered in tan-coloured pine needles between the thin pine trees that whistled, rocked and creaked in the breeze. Occasionally I heard a crack and looked up, wondering if a branch were about to fall. Like in the Alps, walking through the Apennines wasn't just one ascent to get to the top followed by a descent. I climbed up then down, up then down, on steep, narrow paths of broken rock that burned my knees while trees and bushes grabbed at my clothing. I was surprised to find the steep and broken hillside paths here were more difficult than those in the Alps. I was of course a lot farther into the journey, as well as being tired and fighting off an illness. That was probably making it harder than it might have been otherwise.

I arrived in Cassio in the early afternoon. It was a small village with one hotel that had a bar and *ristorante* attached. I sat on a step near the path and ate my two-day-old baguette and pondered only for a moment if I should stay or go. The decision was easy. It was too early in the day to stop just yet, so I kept walking to Berceto, where the guidebook indicated there were more accommodation options.

The sky ahead was dark and menacing, and I told myself I would be okay. The weather did the same thing as it had done yesterday and blew over. Clouds sprinkled a little from time to time, teasingly. The wind wrapping around my bones and shaking them hard was coldly fierce. On one particularly steep section, it took me twenty minutes to climb only 400 metres. "It will be okay," I told myself again, and put my head down, looking at my feet with each step I took, not wanting to see how much farther or higher I had to climb.

I thought Melbourne had beautiful autumns, but they were nothing compared to the Apennines. The colours were vivid and there were shades of autumn that I never knew existed. I wanted to drown in them all and remember it forever, but it was not my day for photos. The sun was always in the wrong place. The light was too bright. The angles were all wrong. I couldn't capture the beauty of the landscape in the way I saw it and how I wanted to remember it. As I climbed one last steep ridge before descending into Berceto, all of my frustrations evaporated. The sun pierced those menacing clouds as if to say, "I'm still king", casting a spotlight on the castle-like cemetery on the outskirts of the town below. It was the most amazing sky that I had seen on my entire journey. For the first time that day, I took a photo that was exactly how I wanted to remember that moment.

Descending into Berceto, I remembered it was Monday, when shops and restaurants were often closed. "It will be okay," I told myself. Near the centre of town, I passed an open grocer and picked up two rosy apples and two bananas from the table out the front. I watched as the grocer followed a customer outside, picking and packing her apples for her as directed. As I waited to pay, I saw the sign written in Italian confirming what I suspected. Customers shouldn't touch the fruit and vegetables.

"Scusa mi," I told the lady behind the counter, as I nodded towards the sign and put my fruit on the counter.

From the grocer, I found my way to the parish youth house that provided beds for pilgrims. The shutters were closed and the gate was locked. Summer was over and the youth house was closed for winter. I walked down the road and around the corner to the Santuario di Berceto. It was not only closed but also deserted. I had already walked past the town's expensive hotel on my way to the youth house, and it was closed too, although perhaps it would open later or if I called them.

I felt no rising panic as I might have done a few weeks ago. Instead, the thought of *uh-oh* bounced around my foggy head a few times, followed by a firm voice reminding me "it will be okay". I recalled a sign I had seen on my descent from the ridge where I viewed the amazing sky, advertising a bed and breakfast called La Casa dei Nonni. It turned out to be only a few doors down from the grocer. It too was closed, but there was a sign on the door with a number to call. I rang and spoke in Italian to the woman who answered, explaining my predicament. She replied to me in English, saying she would ring Mamma who would be there in five minutes. I sat down on a nearby bench seat and ate an apple as I waited. As promised, five minutes later, a black four-wheel drive pulled up opposite the building. Nonno had driven Nonna. She greeted me with a smile and showed me into the apartment, apologising that she couldn't provide breakfast.

"*Non problema,*" I told her. I just needed a roof over my head and a bed to sleep in.

My room had a double bed and a television as well as a heater. She turned it on for me and explained how to turn it off if it got too hot, although I doubted that would happen. She left and I sat on the edge of the bed, grateful to have arrived and to have a room. Just after half past seven, I went to find somewhere to eat. There were few places to dine in the small town, and all the ones I passed were closed. I still had the bananas and an apple and an emergency supply of chocolate that was being replenished regularly because I was having a lot of 'emergencies'. Finally, I spotted a bar and pizzeria that was open. I went in, not so excited to eat pizza for the fourth time in a week, but happy at the prospect of having something hot for dinner. The barman looked at me with raised eyebrows as I walked in.

"*Pizzeria è aperto?*" I asked him.

"*No.*" Of course the pizzeria was closed.

I frowned and was about to ask where I could eat when he offered to make me a panino. Without hesitating, I accepted. It was the best toasted ham and cheese sandwich I had ever eaten. I washed it down with my aperol spritz while I scanned the walls that were covered in caricatures of the locals and watched the old-timers play a round of cards at the table next to me. As I went to leave, the barman offered me a complimentary grappa that I swapped for a white sambuca. I stood at the bar, sipping the sweet clear spirit and chatting to the barman, an old timer and another guy wearing jeans. He had a thick scarf wrapped suavely around his neck and drank a glass of red wine while his small dog sat patiently at his feet. I told them that the Apennines had turned out to be much more challenging than the Alps. They assured me that once I reached the Cisa Pass, the walk down to Pontremoli would be easy. Perhaps 'easier' is what they really meant.

Twenty-six—To the sea

Pontremoli to Cinque Terre

Berceto was just waking up when I left. I walked back up to the bar, hoping to see a familiar and friendly face, but it was closed so I headed back into the town centre and went into the bar opposite the church. I took a cappuccino and *cornetto alla marmellata* while sitting at the bar, having the usual conversation with a few of the locals about being a *pellegrina da sola*. Breakfast over, I strolled on the deserted cobblestoned roads out of town. After crossing the main road, I immediately commenced the climb to Cisa Pass. At 1040 metres, the Pass is 600 metres lower than Bourg-Saint-Pierre, but climbing it would still be an achievement. It would also be the point where I crossed into Tuscany. The trail was steep and covered in more broken rocks. I placed my feet carefully, but my ankles still wobbled over the uneven ground. Upon reaching a grassed clearing, I stopped and watched the shadowed hills rolling out as far as I could see. The clouds' underbellies were dark grey and ominous, prompting me to wonder if it might rain. Sure enough, I continued along the path and reached the main road to the Pass just as it started to rain lightly. I put on Kermit, considering whether I should cross over and continue along more steep and broken trails or walk along the road instead. There was little traffic so I chose the road.

As I rounded the corner, I discovered a bar set back off the road. Although I had only walked for an hour, I decided to have a coffee break, knowing it could be my only chance to do so for the remainder of the day. A large man sat on a chair with his belly resting on his legs as he read the newspaper spread out on the table in front of him. I ordered my cappuccino and sat down at a table. Other than the lady serving at the bar, I was the only other female in the room. The men all seemed to be in their sixties and sat around talking and drinking espresso, although a couple of them were drinking what looked like red wine. I finished my coffee, and as I prepared to leave, the large man told me there would be rain at the Pass. I shrugged my shoulders.

"*Va bene. Ho camminare,*" I said, assuring him it would be okay and that I had to walk regardless.

Veils of silver cloud skimmed the road just ahead of me, blown in by the wind that battered me from my right. A white sedan pulled over and a workman in khaki uniform wound down the window to ask if I wanted a ride. I thanked him but declined. He drove away and I continued walking, watching the clouds sweep over the road not more than 50 metres ahead of me. I knew I might regret rejecting his offer. The wind rose, whipping Kermit into a frenzy. I was sure that if I held my arms out beside me parallel to the ground and started running, I could launch myself into the sky like an untethered kite, even with the weight of the Devil on my back. Five minutes later, the rain started to fall, lightly at first, but within a minute it was pelting down and thunder growled and rumbled to my right. I had walked through a lot of rain so far on my journey, but none of it was as heavy as that. Periodically, I lifted the sagging poncho up behind my neck so that the water pooled there could run off onto the ground. The rain came straight at my face and dripped off the end of my nose. I tried to wipe it away with the back of my gloved hand, but it continued to hit my face and my nose kept dripping rain-drops. I could barely see ahead. I hoped the storm would pass over quickly.

I made it to the *ostello* for pilgrims located just before the Pass. It was closed, but I took shelter under the meagre structure at the front gate. The rain poured, then eased off, poured again and finally eased to a light shower. I crossed my arms over my chest to keep warm and ate a muesli bar as I waited for it to stop. My pants were wet from the knees down and stuck to my calves and shins. The rain kept coming in bursts and I doubted it would stop completely. To get out of it, I needed to get off the Pass, so I decided to put my head down and march. The rain eased to a light drizzle for a while and I was able to take a few photos. Then it started pouring. Lightning flashed around me and thunder rattled my bones. I folded up the two Rodneys and tucked them into my waist belt beneath the Kermit because I feared they would attract the lightning. I saw the newspaper headlines in my mind: "Pellegrina hit by lightning, dies on side of road." Although the Rodneys were hidden under Kermit, I wondered if that were enough protection. I was sure lightning had an intelligence of its own and could find the metal rods beneath the flimsy green nylon.

I clasped my hands together at my chest in prayer but also to hug my own body warmth. As I walked, I chanted over and over, "Keep me safe. Keep me safe. Keep me safe". The fog came in and I could barely see in front of me, but I was only worried about being struck by lightning and not by cars, as I hadn't seen any since the workman in the white sedan stopped to offer me a lift. I approached some buildings and stood under an eave with my back against the wall. It kept me mostly dry, except for the occasional drip from the gutter and the spray blown in by the wind. I waited ten minutes, but when the rain didn't ease I resumed walking.

Twenty metres along the road, I passed a bar the fog had hidden from my view. Although it was tempting to have another coffee, to take some time out of the rain and warm up, I had already stopped long enough so I kept walking.

My pants were drenched glued to my shins. They felt like strips of ice. First my feet and then knees went numb, yet somehow I found all of this hilariously funny. A snowstorm had caught me at Bourg-Saint-Pierre and now I was stuck in this thunderstorm at Cisa Pass. I laughed out loud and wondered if maybe this was the day I could officially be deemed crazy. I intended to rejoin the trail just after the Pass, as it was more direct than the road that snaked its way down the mountain, but I decided against it. It would be too dangerous to walk through thick fog on broken ground streaming with water. I turned the corner and descended steeply. The rain eased and a few minutes later it stopped. I had been right. The storm was hovering around the Pass and I had now descended low enough to get out of it.

The winding road to Gravagna San Rocco passed between pines and lemon-hued autumn trees that were ghosted spectacularly by the fog. Catching glimpses in gaps between the trees, I marvelled at the motorway suspension bridge and how the road disappeared into the mountainside, its peak covered in thick cloud. There was no traffic and it was a peaceful and beautiful walk down the mountain, except for the cow that startled me when I walked too close to the bush in which it stood, eating the thick green foliage. I dreamed of finding a *trattoria* in Gravagna San Rocco where I could eat hot spaghetti bolognaise, drink a glass of red wine and enjoy the warmth that would dry out my cold, wet pants and feet. It was a nice fantasy. Gravagna was smaller than I expected. Terracotta-roofed houses gathered around a church with a stone bell tower rising visibly above them. I saw a sign for a *trattoria* pointing away from the road, but as the town was so small, I assumed it would be closed. I kept walking towards Gravagna Montale, still hopeful of my spaghetti and red wine, but it was a steep climb into the even smaller village and there was even less probability of finding an open *trattoria*. Instead, I sat on the safety rail on the side of the road and ate my cold prosciutto and pecorino panino. The first car I had seen since crossing the Cisa Pass drove by, followed by another and then two more. Their passengers started at me curiously as they passed. I suppose it was an unusual place to see someone taking a lunchbreak.

As I walked down the winding road, through the blazing yellow forest, I caught my first sight of Pontremoli nestled amongst the foothills. The city was all salmon, dusky pink and beige, with church spires rising above the terracotta roofs and the green roof of the *duomo*. I entered the old town through the Porta Parma, walking along its narrow, paved street between the terrace buildings. I stopped in at the cathedral to light a candle before attempting to find the Cappuccini convent. A barman guided me back upstairs to the street and pointed over the bridge to the hill, as he explained about the road to the sharp left and the bridge I should cross. I arrived at the convent just as mass was about to commence. I rang the doorbell and waited, hoping that not all the friars were attending and that someone would come and let me in so I didn't have to wait until the service was over. It had been a bad day for toilet stops, and I really needed to use the bathroom.

After waiting a couple of minutes, I rang the doorbell again pessimistically, but I heard quiet male voices approaching and eventually the door opened to reveal two elderly friars who greeted me. After explaining to them that I was a pilgrim and I had a credential, they led me inside to an office to complete the formalities of registering and making a donation. They were keen to tell me the history of the Convent and the Via Francigena, in Italian. I was always happy to listen and interact with these kind people who helped me on my way, but I had neither the heart nor words to interrupt what they were saying and explain that I was dying to pee. I crossed my legs and listened, saying *sì* in the appropriate gaps. Finally one of the friars rose to lead me to my room, but first he took me outside to show me the side gate and explain how to get in and out of the convent. I didn't understand his directions and hoped I could figure it out later when I went in search of dinner. As we walked back into the building and climbed the stairs, one excruciatingly slow step at a time, he paused and turned to ask me again which country I was from. I smelled the sweet fermented scent of wine on his breath. As soon as he left me alone in my single bedroom, I dropped the Devil then sprinted down the hall to the bathroom, reaching it just in time.

On my way to dinner, I used my head-torch for only the second time, to light the dark path and illuminate the gate of the convent while I figured out how to get out and made sure I could get back in again. Then I walked a long way to the other side of town, following signs to the Trattoria du Soleil, because I liked the sound of its name. Although everyone around me was eating pizza, I ordered the spaghetti bolognaise and small carafe of red wine that I had dreamed of as I walked away from the storm.

I was in no rush to leave Pontremoli. It's not that I didn't want to walk; I just didn't want to *start* walking. It had taken me a long time to fall asleep only to be woken from my beautiful slumber at 1.40 a.m. by the crack, rumble, flashes and downpour of another awesome thunderstorm. I lay snuggled in my sleeping bag, watching the lightning flash through my window, counting the seconds until the thunder cracked. I was grateful that it was happening at night and not during the day as I walked. I left the convent without seeing either of the two friars again and returned to the bar, hoping to see the familiar face of the man who directed me to the convent and to exchange some friendly banter with him, but he wasn't there. Instead, a plump, ginger-haired woman was behind the counter, making espressos and cappuccinos and serving pastries from the glass case. She served me without any greeting or even a smile as I ordered my cappuccino and *cornetto alla marmellata*, and offered me no *arrividerci* when I left.

It was Wednesday and almost the end of October. The mid-week market was set up in two piazzas, with stalls offering food and clothing for sale. The town was buzzing with slow activity as the locals shopped for their fruit and vegetables and stopped to chat. Pontremoli was one of the prettiest towns I had passed through so far and it was somewhere I would have liked to stay an extra day, but I had an aching desire to rest near the sea. I was only two days and one last mountain ridge away from reaching Sarzana, from where I would take the train to Cinque Terre and stay in Manarola by the Mediterranean Sea for three nights.

As I crossed the bridge at Via Antonino Siligato, I could smell the sea on the warm and salty breeze that brushed my face. Unexpectedly, tears welled. The sea is a sacred place of rest and healing for me, and I hadn't seen it since the third day of this journey. A few minutes later, an ambulance sped past me with its lights and sirens blaring, and to my surprise I started crying. My tiredness had made me hypersensitive. I needed rest. Eventually the tears ceased and dried and I found the sweet place in my walking again. That day, my walk was fuelled by the kindness of strangers. As I followed a sign away from the busy road, a man standing next to his parked car pointed me back towards the main road.

"No bridge," he told me.

Three drivers stopped to offer me lifts. In Barbarasco, an old-timer wearing a cap and blazer patted me on the shoulder in encouragement as we passed on the street. When I entered Aulla, one of the drivers who offered me a lift earlier in the day passed by again in his black Alfa Romeo.

"*Ciao! Piccolo mondo!*" I called out, grinning and waving at him. It was a small world. He grinned back at me and waved as he drove away. He felt like an old friend.

Later in the day, I approached the Abbazia di San Caprasio in Aulla to ask for accommodation for the night. A crowd of around fifty people, all wearing black, were gathered outside the church. Some stood chatting in small groups, while others sat silently on the steps. I walked inside and before I could open my mouth to explain who I was and what I wanted, I was ushered to a table, seated and given coffee and biscuits by a smiling, middle-aged lady. While she registered me, I sipped my espresso and chatted to a talkative old man who had once been a pilgrim too. Once my registration was complete, I followed the lady outside and through the funeral crowd.

"She was very young, only forty years old," she told me.

The accommodation was just around the corner. I followed my guide through a door and upstairs into a meeting room, where she walked over to the cupboard and pulled down the bed that was folded inside. There was a kitchenette, two new bathrooms with showers and hot water, and an outdoor terrace that was perfect for drying clothes. I showered and washed my t-shirt and my socks and hung them out to dry. It may have been 23°C during the day and warm in the sunshine, but by the time I hung my washing on the terrace, the sun had dropped behind the mountain ridge and the air was crisp. As the sky was cloud-free, I anticipated frost and realised my clothes were not going to dry overnight. It was no big deal. I had walked with them hanging from the Devil several times already. However, that was how I had lost one of my good merino socks in the forests above Cassio.

Now with only three left and two of them just washed, I would have to wear one dry and one damp sock.

I couldn't figure out how to turn on the stovetop or the power for the microwave in the kitchenette so I walked the streets looking for somewhere to eat, hoping for anything but pizza. I passed an expensive-looking restaurant and the only other one nearby was Chinese. I drank an aperol spritz sitting outside in the terrace of a bar as I caught up on some writing then walked around the corner and bought a doner kebab, salad and chips to take back to the room. At least it wasn't pizza.

I lay in bed with the cupboard doors open on either side of me, listening to the drumming and singing from a rehearsal downstairs. When it stopped, the people below chatted for another half an hour until I heard the door close and the final *buonanotte* called out by the stragglers on the street. A car engine revved and then faded into the distance. Finally I was alone in the silence.

In the morning, I was excited to start walking as I was only hours away from a rest break by the Mediterranean Sea. The town was golden in the rising sun and a feather boa of fog drifted over its auburn rooftops. I crossed the bridge over the River Magra and then walked alongside the peak hour road. Immediately, I started climbing up into the hills, first on bitumen and then onto a broken trail then on another bitumen road, where I was warned away by a small black dog barking ferociously as I skirted the perimeter of a house. After climbing a grass and mud path, I stopped to catch my breath. Fog completely filled the river valley below me and the sky was streaked with narrow white ribbons.

The guidebook described this section as being a "rugged segment over the final ridge". At times, it was rugged on steroids, made up of narrow mule tracks, broken surfaces, loose rocks, sodden leaves, deep and slippery crevices, and bushy blackberries that claimed space over the path, latching on to my clothing and scratching my skin. I paused often to catch my breath and kept my head down while moving, constantly looking at where I stepped for fear of losing my footing on the loose rocks. I slipped a few times but managed to stay on my feet. The climb was rewarded with views over the fog-covered valley and hilltop villages. The first of these was the neat, multi-coloured Bibola, with orange, lemon, pink and salmon hued terrace houses looking out over the valley. I walked through the small and ancient village of Vecchietto, whose concrete streets were so narrow they were inaccessible by car. I passed my first olive trees, laden with green olives. A few had begun to ripen and were dark crimson in colour.

Finally, after three hours of climbing, I reached the peak of the ridge. Beyond the rolling, dark-green forested mountains, I could see the hazy Mediterranean Sea. My heart buzzed happily, knowing I would soon be by the sea, although it was still far off and I had much walking to do to get there. I passed a hunter talking on a two-way radio. He said something about the *caccia di cinghiale,* the hunt for wild boar, and I assumed he was warning me about walking into the woodlands, but I kept on regardless. As far as I was concerned, they could make sure they didn't fire their guns near the public path. In hindsight, perhaps he wasn't warning me about the hunters but the *cinghiale.* I never saw one but I have heard they can be dangerous.

I passed through the mustard and dark salmon pink town of Ponzano Superiore, pausing to look again at the Mediterranean Sea shimmering in the distance, before continuing on past the archaeological site of Castello della Brina, with the brick belltower lying largely intact and exposed on the ground. From there, the descent became steep and pain seared my knees. My feet slipped on the precipitous gravel path and my heart pounded from the near fall. When I finally reached the bitumen road, I wanted to run to the sea but Sarzana train station was still three kilometres away. Instead I powered on, using the Rodneys and pushing the bitumen behind me for another forty minutes. I waited only ten minutes for a train to La Spezia, where I changed trains for Cinque Terre. When I disembarked at Manarola, I stood on the platform looking directly at the Mediterranean Sea, a rippled sheet of dark turquoise with a million sunlit stars dancing on its surface. I breathed in deeply and exhaled tiredness. It was time for two and half days of rest.

That afternoon I lay on top of the stone retaining wall, watching and listening to the waves lap against the rocky coastline as the sun kissed my wind-cooled skin. I watched the sea swallow the rosy sun whole and felt my weary spirit begin to restore. I can live my life away from the sea, but every time I come back to her, I realise just how much I have missed her and how healing she is in my life, and I never want to leave. I hoped the next two days would pass slowly. I had just over 500 kilometres left to walk to Rome and had walked three quarters of the Via Francigena. I lived and breathed the path every day, but it was only when I looked at what I was doing as if I were a stranger to my own life that I could see how incredible my journey was. Every day I witnessed my own grit and determination while surrendering to what I couldn't control. Strength and vulnerability are my two swords of power, and I was only just starting to appreciate how powerful I truly was.

Twenty-seven—Tired of lonely

Cinque Terre to Lucca

I was excited about being in the Cinque Terre, and at first I got caught up in the rush of tourism. I caught the train to Vernazza and Monterosso and strolled through the towns crowded with tourists, wondering what I was doing there when what I really wanted after two months of continuous movement was stillness. I returned to Manarola, where I relaxed in my apartment and wrote in my journal. I washed all of my clothes in a washing machine and converted my apartment into a drying room. I took myself out for a long slow lunch of fried anchovies, spaghetti with clams, and a large glass of the local white wine. I sat by the sea and dipped my feet in a little rock pool to feel the water on my skin. For dinner, I cooked myself a chicken and vegetable stir-fry in my kitchenette. I hadn't cooked a meal for myself in two months, and I enjoyed this simple act immensely. Every night, I watched the sunset over the sea and listened to the breathy rush of the waves.

After two whole days free of the Red Beasts, my feet were less painful. The blisters that had rubbed and re-rubbed themselves into the bottom of my toes had almost healed completely, but I still hobbled around the room on the morning of my departure as I packed and prepared to walk to Marina di Massa. I walked down to the train station full of energy and excited to be walking again. I had a bag of clean, machine-washed clothes so I smelled like flowers, and I had blow-dried my hair for the first time in weeks. It felt good to look a little more groomed and a touch less scruffy. I had to wait one hour for a train from La Spezia to Sarzana, so it was late in the morning when I started walking to Marina di Massa. After a slippery climb over a rocky pavement up to the fortress of Sarzanello, I walked on country roads through quiet villages surrounded by olive groves and vineyards with views to other hilltop settlements. I had a bounce in my step and was happily humming along to Katy Perry's 'Roar'. After reaching Luni, I had the choice to walk back up into the hills or beside the Mediterranean. I chose the sea. I had visions of walking along a promenade with the waves lapping the shore beside me, but that was not to be. Restaurants, hotels and beach clubs own most of the seaside land and the buildings blocked any view. I spent three hours walking beside the busy beach road on concrete paths and bitumen, pounding my feet with no view of the sea except for the few times when I cut down one of the access paths to the beach. The sand was brown and the water cloudy. There was too much development here and the cranes from the ports marred the landscape. I thought it would be pretty but it wasn't.

The walk was much longer than I expected. I hadn't properly checked the location of my hotel, which turned out to be four kilometres and two suburbs away on the other side of Marina di Massa in the middle of nowhere. Advertised as being on 4000 square metres of peaceful land, it appealed to my tired spirit when I booked it. However, not only was it Sunday so most of the shops were closed, but most hotels, bars and restaurants were also in a post-holiday season shutdown, including my hotel's restaurant. The owner directed me to a *trattoria*. It was another five minutes that I didn't really want to walk, but I was hungry and dreaming of lasagne or a penne *ragù* and a big glass of red wine. I followed his directions, but when I arrived there were no lights on and the front door was locked. I looped my way back to my hotel, hoping to stumble across any kind of eatery on my way, but there were no oases in the night. The residential streets were dark with few streetlights. A car stopped abruptly 30 metres after it passed me. I felt vulnerable and walked faster to get back to the safety of my hotel. I entered the lobby and the manager looked at me surprised to see me back so soon.

.   "*Chiuso*," I said, telling him they were closed. He seated me at a table then went to the kitchen and returned with a slice of pistachio cake, some crimson grapes and a cappuccino.

"*Gratis*," he told me as he sat it down in front of me. No charge.

Walking on hard concrete and bitumen after two days of little walking and no weight on my back was taking a painful toll on my body. My thighs and hamstrings kept cramping. I had constant lower back pain. The throbbing in my feet only died down to a tolerable level two hours after I stopped walking. I took some anti-inflammatory tablets before I went to sleep, knowing that if I didn't the pain would wake me. I was pissed off and over it that night. Surely after two months I should be able to walk for 27 kilometres free of pain! I thought I should but my body was telling me another story.

It started raining just as I left the hotel in the morning, but only lightly and not enough to dampen my spirits. I wasn't keen to wear Kermit into Forte dei Marmi, a wealthy, seaside town loved by the Italians in summer, but it was unavoidable if I wanted to stay dry. I walked on the footpath next to the rows of beach clubs. The rush of the waves up and down the shore soothed and lulled me into a meditative state. After an hour my feet started to hurt, so I put on my headphones and sang and dance-walked.

People were going to stare at me in my Kermit poncho anyway, so I decided they might as well see a crazy, green-cloaked pilgrim enjoying her journey.

In Forte dei Marmi, I walked out on the pier. White curdled waves rushed into the shore, littered with driftwood. Grey clouds hung thick and rain-laden over the Apennines that ran parallel to the coast. Twenty minutes later, not even the dance-walking could keep my spirits up. Rain, throbbing feet and tiredness engulfed me. I felt teary and I still had one more hour to walk to Pietrasanta. There was no point denying the sadness, it was there, but there was no point in giving in to it either. I kept walking, taking one step after the other along the autumn yellow street with cars passing by. A thin, old man, rode his bicycle along the bike track towards me. His silver blue eyes narrowed and his white bushy brows scrunched down as he stared not at my face but at my hunchbacked body draped in the bright green Kermit. I knew he was thinking *che cosa*, meaning 'what the?', and I giggled as he rode away.

The rain started to fall heavily as I arrived into Pietrasanta. I wandered past a busy *osteria* and a *trattoria*, feeling too wet and bedraggled to go inside. Instead, I huddled under the umbrellas of a bar in the Piazza di Duomo as I ate a panino with *prosciutto crudo*, tomato and *stracchino*, and indulged in a warming glass of red wine. My distress fluttered away. I had arranged to stay with a friend's parents, who lived nearby. I had met Valentina in Phuket, where she and her husband ran a *trattoria* overlooking Nai Harn Beach. David and I ate there often for the good food and the amazing view. Valentina's parents lived near Pietrasanta, and as they had walked 300 kilometres of the Via Francigena from Monteriggioni to Rome with friends twelve months earlier, they generously offered me a bed for the night in a gesture of pilgrim solidarity. I didn't want to put them out by arriving too early in the afternoon, so I killed some time by sitting and watching the locals walk through the piazza on their way to lunch. Some African men stood in the rain, waiting to sell their five euro umbrellas to those who had left home without one. They even tried to sell one to me when they saw my small travel umbrella. I shook my head and walked away.

Like in many towns, the shops were closed during the lunch break. I wandered the paved wet streets looking at the buildings before heading to the Coop supermarket. It started pouring with rain as I packed my supplies in the Devil out the front of the store. I waited and watched, but when there was no sign of the torrent easing, I called Valentina's mother, Patrizia, who came and drove me back to their two-bedroom home. I spent the afternoon wrapped in blankets on the couch, watching Hollywood movies dubbed into Italian while drinking tea and eating biscuits. Patrizia showed me their Via Francigena photos and pilgrim certificates, and it rekindled excitement for my own journey. In a week, I would be walking through those same places, and then all too soon I would be arriving in Rome and collecting my own certificate.

It rained all afternoon and all night without easing. Patrizia prepared a four-course meal, and when her husband, Paolo, arrived home from work at quarter to eight, their son emerged from his room and we all sat down at the table to eat. Our conversation was riddled with confusion and misunderstanding. They only spoke Italian and I had difficulty understanding Paolo's thick Tuscan drawl, but we muddled through, chatting and laughing. After dinner, I climbed under the covers of the foldout bed in the lounge room and listened to the rain pelting onto the roof, the ground and the trees. I was rested, but perhaps more importantly I felt cared for and nurtured, ready to continue and face the challenges ahead.

When I woke in the morning, everything was quiet. I pulled back the dark curtains to see what weather the new day had brought. There was nothing more depressing than the thought of having to walk 32 kilometres in pouring rain. Above the red tiled roof of the house next door, I saw blue sky and sunshine. I grinned and clasped my hands together at my chest in gratitude. Patrizia and Paolo drove me back into Pietrasanta and walked me to the *duomo*. We said goodbye and I searched my limited vocabulary in an effort to tell them how much I appreciated their hospitality and that it was exactly what I needed. Patrizia made me promise I would phone them if I needed any help. I did so, although I knew it was unlikely I would need to call. We embraced then I walked away feeling happier and more positive than I had for more than a week. I had thought I was just physically exhausted, but it seemed that what I really needed was company. I spent most of my days and nights alone. While I had frequent interactions with locals, they were mostly fleeting as we passed each other by. The last time I had shared a meal and conversation was with Veronique and her family in Nods, more than a month ago. Although I am introverted and like solitude, too much of it is not a good thing. I am human and need companionship too.

I left the town's narrow paved streets and after a short walk along the busy main thoroughfare I turned onto a quiet road past the cemetery. The sun made the road and trees and even me all bright and shiny. I veered onto a damp mulch-covered path between trees as ribbons of white light streamed through the darkened foliage. I knew I would walk through hills that day, but I expected them to be gentle and thought that my days of walking across mountains on challenging broken paths were well and truly over. I was wrong. The forest path led to a narrow crevice between stands of bamboo. It was too steep for me to walk down, so I crawled like a crab with my hands behind me and used the

Devil in front to stop me slipping forward. Later in the morning, I climbed up another steep cutting between two sections of winding road. The thorny creepers growing there grabbed at my clothes and scraped my arms, but the award for worst path of the day, and possibly the worst of the whole Via Francigena trail I had walked so far, was an 800-metre section from the cemetery in Piazzano back down to the road.

The guidebook warned cyclists to stay on the road because the path was unsuitable for bicycles, but there was no such warning for walkers. The descent was steep and the gravel path soon became smooth, slippery rock that was covered in lichen under a shallow stream of water. In places, I had to step down into deep crevices. Thinking of the Aussie hip-hop song 'Nosebleed Section' by the Hilltop Hoods, I named the path the Knee Bleed Section because of the pain it caused my knees. I could hear cars passing on the road below, and every time I rounded another corner I expected to see it just metres ahead, but instead there was just more knee-curdling, broken trail to walk down. It took me more than thirty minutes and a lot of swearing, but I finally made it down to the road, achieving another small victory on my journey.

After crossing Ponte San Pietro over the river Serchio, the main road into Lucca had a constant stream of traffic. There was no footpath or shoulder for me to walk on, so I had to follow the bike path beside the river in a wide arc before cutting back over to the main road closer to town. I wasn't happy about taking the longer way into town, because the sun was setting and I wanted to get off my feet. Nature may have challenged me that day, but it also knew how to lift my spirits. As I walked through the town of Sant'Angelo, I was welcomed by an amazing sky. The setting sun glowed apricot behind a thick plot of poplars while dark lavender clouds drifted above and silver fingers of light reached up into the pale sky. I stopped and said a silent thank you then followed that sky all the way to my *albergo* in San Donato, remembering the gratitude of witnessing it even when I misread my map and found myself on a no through road that required yet another detour. I was even more grateful when I arrived at the hotel and was shown to a room with my own private terrace and a beautiful four-poster bed hung with creamy chiffon curtains. I was glad I planned to stay here for the next two nights so I could have a full day to explore Lucca. I dropped the Devil on the ground and flopped down onto the bed. Despite the challenges I faced that day, I had made it here and was one day closer to Rome.

Twenty-eight—The art of staring

Lucca to Altopascio

I woke early to golden light streaming through the creamy curtains around my bed. I basked in the warmth, and with nowhere to arrive that day, there was no rush to get up. Later in the morning, I borrowed a rusty, brakeless bike from the guesthouse and rode slowly into Lucca, a little wobbly and conscious of the hard bitumen that would painfully break any falls. I had forgotten how fun and free it felt to roll along the ground and power my movement with the piston motion of my legs. I rode along the city's fortified walls among other cyclists, joggers, locals and strolling tourists, while admiring the terracotta buildings surrounded by green trees, the churches, the manicured gardens, and the Apennines rolling away in the distance. I enjoyed it so much I did a second lap before I rode down the path and off the wall in a zigzag pattern to compensate for the near non-existent brakes. After lunch, I lay down on a bench seat in the sun, peering into the private garden that was used in the movie *Portrait of a Lady*, but I soon found myself surrounded by an American tour group. Two ladies from the group apologised for disturbing my peace.

After the pale orange sun sank beyond the horizon to reveal the night sky, I stared at a lone bright star, feeling faith and hope, then rode back to my room. Later that night, I shared a meal with an Australian couple. I recognised their accents and struck up a conversation with them at the *trattoria* we were both dining. My energy was back and my loneliness gone. The next morning, I was once again in no rush to leave, as Altopascio was only five hours away. I enjoyed lying in the four-poster bed and the luxury of blow-drying my hair. After a simple but slow Italian breakfast, I walked into Lucca then out the other side. The azure sky was cloudless and the cool air brisk against my cheeks while the sun warmed my dark clothing. For the locals, it was perfect weather to dry the washing that they hung from their window shutters.

I took my first break for the day at a little café just outside Lucca. The cappuccino I had there was so amazing that I felt compelled to compliment the female barista. She looked surprised when I gushed that it was *molto buono* and then walked out the door. I set off towards Altopascio feeling even happier and more contented. Neither the throbbing in my right foot nor the dark clouds that threatened rain could dampen my spirits. I was pleased to see that they soon drifted away.

On a quiet suburban side street, I walked towards two old men and a woman who were standing on the nature strip, talking to a man in an old white Fiat. I tried to return their stares but couldn't hold them and glanced away then back again as I greeted them.

"*Pellegrina?*" the man with thinning white hair asked. I nodded. He walked over and told me that he had also walked the Via Francigena with a few friends, completing it in separate stages over seven years. He offered me water and use of his bathroom because he understood how hard it was to find a toilet when you needed one. Not needing either of his offers, I declined and thanked him for his kindness.

One hundred metres further down the road, I approached three men standing and talking. One was a young guy in his twenties, the next was an older man with a beard, who I presumed was his father, and the third was a workman with curly hair, wearing blue overalls. This time I stared back at them without flinching and greeted them with *buongiorno* as I approached.

"Australia!" they each said, almost in unison, when I told them where I was from. Enjoying the incredulity of their response, I volunteered the rest of my story, where I was going, where I had started from, and how far I had walked *da sola*. They looked at each other with raised eyebrows and shook their heads in disbelief. I was grateful to have these friendly interactions on what was not a picturesque day of walking through residential and industrial areas and along sections of busy road.

In Capannori, I stopped at a café for lunch and ate a caprese salad drizzled with olive oil, served with fresh white bread, and drank a cheeky glass of white wine. I left feeling extra happy to keep walking and wasn't even fazed by a message from my friend Viv, telling me that she had moved from London to Old Netley near Southampton and I couldn't stay with her as planned immediately after I finished my pilgrimage. I told her it was okay and not to worry. Maybe it was the wine or maybe after everything I had experienced I was just going with the flow, trusting that everything would work out as it always did. I took a short cut to Porcari, walking on the edge of the SP23. It saved me two kilometres but it had a constant stream of semitrailers and cars passing in both directions. I put in my headphones, cranked up the Black Keys and dance-walked all the way, returning the stares of the occupants in the passing vehicles with either equal intensity or a smile and a wave. I was finally mastering the art of staring. By the time I arrived in Altopascio, I was only 396 kilometres away from Rome. I was excited that another big number had ticked over and that the next day I would walk to San Miniato, where two years earlier I had taken my first steps along the Via Francigena.

I was woken at some ungodly hour by the television standby lights flashing blue and red, then again at six o'clock when the church bells rang out, melodic but loud. I dozed a little more before my alarm sounded at half past six then sat up in bed as I completed my morning meditation practice, noticing one thought floating in and out of my mind continuously: *I'm going back to San Miniato!* However, after my initial excitement, the day didn't start so well. At breakfast, I accidentally chose a small espresso cup for my coffee and the instant cappuccino from the machine poured over the sides, flooding the tray and the table. I flushed with embarrassment as I realised that a stylish couple and two businessmen at nearby tables had witnessed my mistake, but I pretended nothing happened. I maintained my composure and walked slowly back to my table with my espresso cup of cappuccino, as if that was exactly what I wanted. Later, as I harnessed myself into the Devil and left my room, I felt a sudden cold and familiar sensation on my butt. The water bladder had leaked again. I tried to ignore it but five minutes after leaving, I stopped in the Piazza Umberto to check the leakage. The seat of my pants was fully saturated, as was the base of the Devil. I had no way of soaking it up and started walking again with water dripping down my legs. Cold, soggy fabric clung to my butt, which I knew would dry eventually from wind or sun.

For the first four kilometres, I walked on the edge of the busy SP3 with a constant stream of peak hour trucks and cars speeding past me less than a metre away. I made it more fun by dance-walking... fast! Behind me, dark grey clouds threatened rain, but I walked towards a patchy pale grey sky with pools of golden apricot that whispered of sunshine to come. When I finally turned off the road fifty minutes later, I found myself on Roman road made of fist-sized grey stones covered in moss with weeds, clover and short tufts of grass growing in between. I stood still for a moment and looked at my red boots standing on this ancient road that had been here for two thousand years. Again, I was conscious of following in the invisible steps of pilgrims who had walked before me. I felt the timelessness of that place, the blessings of their steps, and the energy that called me forward to Rome.

The path led into woodlands, littered with leaves of mottled brown and tan then through the town of Galeno. I missed a sign and almost walked through someone's backyard, except it felt wrong so I backtracked and found the obscure sign at the beginning of their driveway, pointing to an equally obscure path that ran along the perimeter of the property. The woodlands and pine plantations were riddled with puddles in the aftermath of the rain two days earlier. I couldn't avoid them and often walked at the edges of the muddy paths, stepping on the small grassy embankments to stay out of the mud as much as I could. Sometimes I had no choice but to grimace and walk through it.

At Ponte a Cappiano, I passed through the covered bridge that spans the Usciano canal and past the 16th century *ostello* where pilgrims still stay today. I walked beside the canal on wet grassy embankments to Fucecchio. The wet grass was like a car wash for my muddy boots, and the Red Beasts were soon clean but soaked through. My wet feet proved that the Red Beasts II had officially failed the waterproof test as well. It was a hard climb up steep steps to the hilltop village of Fucecchio, but I rewarded myself with a delicious lunch of gnocchi in a creamy pumpkin and saffron sauce and a glass of white wine at a small café. Then there were only eight kilometres further to go to reach San Miniato. As I trudged through the wet grass of a paddock beside rows of dead grapevines, I could see the town in the distance, perched on what looked like a minor hill, except I knew better. After re-stocking my supplies from the supermarket at the base of the hill, I started the 800-metre climb to the top. I used the Rodneys and found my rhythm, pushing the hill down and away from me. I felt strong. I felt like I could keep going and going, but I stopped to take in the panorama. Giant marshmallow clouds hovered above lines of conifers that created prickly ridges on the gently rolling hills. I was in Tuscany, the land of hilltop villages.

I stayed in the same hotel as I had done on my first visit to San Miniato, although I was in a different room this time. It smelled musty and the window was high and offered no view of the outside world. I wandered into the heart of the town, busy with people setting up stalls for the *Festa de la Tartufo Bianco*, the festival of the white truffle, and found my way to the bar where David and I had drunk aperol spritzes together. This time I sipped my aperol spritz alone on the back terrace, watching dusk descend over San Miniato Basso, the village at the base of San Miniato. I was back in the place where this journey had started for me two years earlier. I remembered feeling unsure then of what I was doing and where I was going, questioning why I thought it would be a good idea to walk 120 kilometres through Tuscany alone. I didn't know how to find my starting point on the trail, and the directions and compass headings in the guide-book I had received only a few days earlier made me nervous. That was when I knew it wasn't going to be just a stroll through the Tuscan countryside. I was glad that David was there with me then, distracting me from my impending aloneness, reminding me that I was *brava, Amore, bravissima*, and that I would be just fine. I had been too.

In some ways, I hadn't changed. I was still unsure of what I was doing and where I was going. This, after all, was the main reason I was walking—to make a decision about my purpose, career and future—but I wasn't scared now to walk alone into the unknown. I enjoyed my solitude and was fascinated by the mystery of what lay beyond the realms of the known. I was proud of myself, this courageous and deep woman I had become. Even if I still doubted and faltered at times, I always found my faith and kept going. I had stayed on this path through rain, thunder, snowstorms and persistent mud. Pain, tiredness and frustration didn't stop me either. I had taken brave steps to venture into the unknown in my life, quitting secure employment to follow my passions for scuba diving and travel in search of a new path. I had found the courage to face what was painful in my life and to allow it to heal. Although fears about financial security had prompted me to return to corporate life when I really wanted to be free, I refused to go back to that kind of life permanently and only accepted temporary contracts while I continued to find a new way forward. Most importantly, I had never given up on myself or my belief that I was here to serve a greater purpose, and I knew that I would keep on walking until I could see clearly what that purpose was.

Twenty-nine—Crying Rivers

Altopascio to Monteriggioni

I woke early and walked up to Rocca di Federico II, the 37-metre-high red brick belltower that sits on the highest part of San Miniato, some 192 metres above sea level.[8] With views over the surrounding Arno Valley, it was the perfect place to watch the sunrise. I was so captivated by the flower of yellow and pink light reflected in the thick grey clouds that hung in the sky to the southwest of the town that I almost missed the moment the sun appeared, piercing the broken cloud in ripples of golden yellow and tangerine. Back in town, I expected that the streets would be empty as it was Saturday and only seven o'clock, but with the festival starting, the streets were a hive of activity with stalls being set up and stocked, rubbish getting collected and streets being cleaned.

After breakfast, I meandered my way out of town, stopping frequently to look back at Rocca di Federico and the terracotta terrace houses that stretched out along the hill, surrounded by tall dark green trees. I hoped to retrace my steps and understand how I got so lost when I walked this section last time, back when I was a city walker who naïvely thought she was going for a lovely long stroll through Tuscany. Even with the guidebook, I had struggled to find my starting point. David spoke to the locals in Italian, and once we found it, he kissed me goodbye and drove back to his hometown of Fabriano, leaving me alone to walk. I had felt vulnerable without him, a lone female in a foreign land, only able to speak a little Italian, but I was happy to be walking alone. He wanted a week with his friends without me and I wanted my adventure. I almost lost my way only an hour after David left me, when I kept walking along a broad path through a farm when I should have gone up a hill and past the ruins. Fortunately, there just happened to be a young man working on the engine of his car nearby and he whistled to get my attention and pointed up the hill, but I wasn't saved for long. A couple of hours later, I became well and truly lost on another hill. Unable to match the guidebook's directions to my surroundings or find the next Via Francigena sign, I spent an hour walking clockwise then anti-clockwise while consulting my guidebook, trying to find the correct way off the hill without success.

When I eventually accepted that I was lost and needed to find my own way, creative, problem-solving Kym came to the rescue and the adventure really began. I walked away from the hill then through a grassy paddock down to a road and over to another hilltop town to ask for help, only to find it was deserted because it was afternoon siesta. I didn't give up. I knew that Gambassi Terme, the town I was staying in that night, was located roughly south of San Miniato, so I took a southerly heading on the tiny compass I had attached to my watch with a hairband, and then tentatively walked down a gravel path, unsure if I was going to reach a dead end. I emerged onto a bitumen road and kept walking, following road signs until I arrived at Gambassi Terme. I felt victorious but exhausted. I found my own way, but I had walked ten extra kilometres in the process.

This time, I recognised the road, the houses and the scenery for the first few kilometres on the way out of San Miniato, but after I passed a bar, it all became unfamiliar. At first, I thought my memory was failing, but as I stopped to take a photo of the rolling hills, I recognised the ruins of a farmhouse and two intersecting paths in the valley below. That was where I almost got lost for the first time two years ago and was where I was saved by the guy fixing his car. Now as I stood looking down at the valley, I checked the directions in my guidebook to see if I had missed a turn and should have been down there instead of up here, but I was where I should be. The European Association of Via Francigena that coordinates the development and promotion of the route must have changed the direction so it no longer passed through the valley, perhaps to avoid the private farmland. This time I would walk a different way, which meant that I wouldn't find out why I got so lost. I shrugged it off. The days never turned out how I expected anyway.

Away from traffic, the loudest sound I heard was the wind roaring past my ears and rushing through the fir trees. An eagle cried somewhere ahead of me, unseen. Hidden birds chirped. Free-range roosters crowed. A cow bellowed from within a barn. Dogs barked, locked away in their separate pens. On the air drifted the scents of summer: jasmine, rose, and the moist, exposed earth. The warm breeze wrapped around me welcomingly. Olive trees were laden with fruit ripening in colour from green to currant to black. Their leaves shimmered silver green. Grapevines died a yellow death while the freshly ploughed earth sat in giant brown clumps. Fluorescent grass snaked and swayed under the wind's forceful breath. I passed terracotta farmhouses that were deserted and crumbling. Giant oblong clouds hovered above the green rolling hills, and the paths of white gravel, grass, and grey-brown clay led on and on towards Gambassi Terme.

There was so much beauty in Tuscany that called to all my senses. I loved how it felt to be out in those hills. Perhaps it was just the familiarity of the landscape and the nostalgia, but it felt like home. Tuscany is earthy, peaceful and real. I wanted to remember that day forever, to hold on to the beauty and the peace that was with me at almost every step, interrupted only by the thick clay mud that clumped to the bottom of my boots. There was no rush, no counting of kilometres, no constant checking of the guidebook, and no awareness of pain in my feet or anywhere else in my body. My day ended with a long uphill hike into Gambassi Terme. Last time I had cried and stopped halfway to eat some emergency chocolate, but this time I had no need for that. I kept walking and watched the giant clouds reflect the setting sun in pools of golden cream, rippled pink.

In the morning, I knew it was raining before I even got up. I lay in bed and heard water splashing beneath car tyres as they drove past. I left the cheap hotel and headed straight to the bar for breakfast. It was spitting rain but not heavily enough to justify putting on Kermit. By the time I left the bar, it was drizzling. One of the dozen local men drinking coffee out the front of the bar stood up and helped pull Kermit over the Devil. As I buttoned it closed, we chatted and I told the men I was walking to San Gimignano. A few commented that a lot of rain was forecast for the day. I shrugged and I told them I had walked many days in the rain then put up my umbrella and set off.

Golden rays of sun poured through a few holes in the grey blanket of cloud clinging to the horizon. The rolling green hills were a vivid contrast to the grey. Just as I started to descend downhill to leave the old town behind, the rain began to pelt down and the wind picked up, blowing in frenzied gusts. I sheltered as much as I could on a doorstep, hiding behind my umbrella, but the rain blew in against my lower body and my pants were soon wet from the knees down. I didn't think the rain would stop, so I continued downhill and turned back towards a café in town. At least I could stay warm and out of the rain there until it stopped. Just as I reached the café, the rain subsided to a light drizzle and the clouds parted, revealing some blue, so I turned around and started walking towards San Gimignano.

The road was a stream of water. I avoided most of the current by walking in the centre of the road. Ten minutes later, the rain stopped completely and I pulled Kermit off. For the next six kilometres, I feasted my eyes on green and gold and grey as I walked through classic Tuscan countryside, along the cream gravel road that stretched towards the indigo clouds skimming the hills, past the neat rows of yellowing grapevines running down the sloping hills and surrounding farmhouses, and on through more olive trees with ripening fruit. I arrived at the church in Pancole just as mass was beginning. I walked down the steps, past statues of shepherds and sheep, to see the nativity that had been set up in the grotto for Christmas and emerged to discover it had started drizzling again. I put Kermit back on and kept walking, pausing just past the church to listen to the congregation sing the first hymn.

It continued to drizzle as I walked along the road beside rows of lemon-leafed grapevines parallel to the walled city of San Gimignano, still some five kilometres away. The town, shrouded by low-lying rain cloud, was instantly recognisable by its tower houses poking up towards the grey sky. San Gimignano once had 72 towers, some reaching as high as 50 metres, built into the houses by rich families as a symbol of their wealth. Only fourteen of the towers now remain.[9] It started raining heavily when I was only four kilometres away. I put my head down to stop the rain from hitting my face and kept walking. The rain eased off before rolling in again in another heavy wave that kept on pouring. There was nowhere to stop and nowhere to shelter. I was wearing only a t-shirt beneath Kermit and my wet clothing was chilled by the constant wind. My hands were purple and pruned as they held the handles of the Rodneys in the rain. My arms were covered in goosebumps and my teeth chattered. I walked swiftly but I couldn't get warm.

I stopped at a bus shelter only 800 metres from the town centre. I couldn't face walking for another ten minutes in the rain while feeling so cold. I ripped off Kermit and put on all the extra clothes I could easily access from the Devil, including my beanie and my gloves, shook the water off the Kermit then sat down and hoped it would stop raining. A man parked a car 20 metres away, and when he opened his car door I could smell fresh pizza. My stomach grumbled. I wanted to get out of the rain and eat something hot. I sat in the bus stop for half an hour, waiting for the rain to stop. It didn't so I decided to keep going.

I marched uphill past the small grocery store. It looked the same as I remembered it from last time, with fruit and vegetables to the left and other non-perishable foods on the right of the store. The same owner was in it, a solid man with a balding head. I entered the walled city through Porta San Matteo, where the paved road was unusually free of tourists, then walked straight up to the main square and into a café opposite the *duomo*, leaving my dripping umbrella and Kermit at the front door. I lingered over my lunch of papardelle with wild boar *ragù* and a quart of chianti, as I watched the few people who had ventured out in the rain cross the square in front of the church. I had an hour to kill until I could check into my hotel and I had no interest in walking in more rain with the Devil on my back. The pasta and the wine warmed me. The owner of the café brought Kermit over and hung it over the spare chair, telling me in Italian the poncho would be too cold for me to put on later. My heart warmed even more at her kindness.

It rained in fierce bursts for the rest of the day. The wild wind swept in sudden downpours and turned even the strongest of umbrellas inside out. The paved streets became streams. I braved the rain, borrowing a large, sturdy umbrella from my hotel, and strolled the waterlogged streets, taking shelter when the rain became too heavy. My canvas shoes were no match for the streams and my feet were soon cold and wet. During one downpour, I sheltered in the gelato shop, licking the cold and creamy dessert from a cone as I watched the rain torrent outside. It was the price of shelter. I was grateful to experience San Gimignano without the hordes of summer tourists. At times the streets and piazzas were deserted and I had them to myself, even if only for a few moments. I had loved Tuscany when I had been here in summer and I loved it even more this time in autumn, with all her vivid colours and amazing light. I loved her despite the rain she poured over me and the icy wind she whipped across my skin. Although I was cold and wet from walking in the constant rain, I was grateful that the wild weather was on that short walking day and not the next when I had 30 kilometres to walk to Monteriggioni. I was grateful for my warm hotel room and its heating that was switched on so I could dry the Red Beasts on top of the radiator.

I left San Gimignano through the gateway Porta San Giovanni and walked back into the golden-vined countryside beneath pale grey but rainless clouds, looking back often at the medieval town, sitting like a grand princess on the hill. The landscape changed noticeably as rolling woodlands soon replaced the grassy rolling hills. The track seemed innocent at first, just dirt and gravel, until I passed behind a house onto the muddy banks of a stream. It was three metres wide and the brown waters flowed steadily. I had to cross it but I had no way of knowing how deep it was in the middle. The only way to avoid it was by walking an hour back to San Gimignano then taking the long way to Monteriggioni on main roads. I sat down on a damp, moss-covered tree stump, took off my boots, tucked my socks inside, tied the boots together and rolled up my pants above my knees. Holding my boots up by the tied laces with Left Rodney in my left hand, I put Right Rodney in the water to test its depth then stepped carefully down onto the rocky bed as the freezing water rushed my calves.

I tested each step with a Rodney, moving slowly and carefully, hoping that I wouldn't cut my foot on a sharp rock or piece of glass. The water numbed my feet, but each step was still painful as the pebbles pressed into every tender spot. In the middle of the stream, the water lapped just beneath my knees. I stepped onto the muddy far bank to find it more painful to stand on its scattered stones than the pebbles on the creek bed. Sitting on another mossy rock, I used a leaf to wipe the mud and tiny bits of gravel off the bottom of my feet before putting my socks and shoes back on. As I turned to leave, a dog ran towards the water eagerly but was called back and put on its leash by two ladies who stood looking at the flooded creek for a moment before they turned and walked away. Perhaps a few days ago there had been exposed stepping-stones to assist the crossing. If so, they were now well and truly submerged after the heavy rain.

I skirted the perimeter of a private property where the grapevines were turning crimson and followed the path that had become thick terracotta clay. I walked near the vines on thin patches of grass for traction, but the soles of my boots were caked in mud and I slipped and skated most of the way up the hill. When I emerged on the property's gravel driveway, I picked up a twig and scraped and flicked the mud from the soles so I could walk without the icky clumped feeling beneath my feet. The road became gravel again and I continued along it, enchanted by San Gimignano and the rows of yellow grapevines to my right, until I realised I was walking the wrong way. Annoyed with myself for adding almost one and a half kilometres and an extra twenty minutes to my long walking day, I trudged back to the turning and saw the sign I had missed, partially obscured by a tree. I walked down the path and rounded a corner only to be confronted with another stream.

"Fuck!" I swore out loud. I wasn't expecting the first stream or this second stream. I had walked this way before, but it was at the beginning of summer and the streams must have been dry. This one was only two metres wide, but its brown waters flowed swiftly and there was no way to cross without taking off my boots again. The riverbank was clay with only a few patches of wild grass and wiry shrubs, so I took off the Red Beasts while standing up using one Rodney to keep my balance. Once more, I stepped tentatively, testing the depth of the stream with right Rodney. In the middle, it swirled halfway up my calves. There was nowhere to sit on the other side, so I put my socks and shoes back on again while standing up and holding onto Rodney. I didn't even bother to take the Devil off my back. Boots on, I started walking again. The whole process had taken another fifteen minutes.

With the streams behind me, I walked on a flat gravel track that eventually turned into an uphill mudslide. There was no way to avoid the mud and I burst into tears. Then after a few steps, I discovered one strip of dry mud amid the bog and walked on it, amused by my premature tears. At the top of the hill, I emerged from the woodlands into a clearing where the path split right and left around a farmhouse. I misread the guidebook and walked right, between the house and a large metal shed. Two dogs came towards me, barking. The golden retriever wagged its tail happily and walked straight to my side so I could pat her. The other, a black-faced, brown boxer blocked my way and started to snarl. A man working in the backyard of the house stopped what he was doing and held the boxer up with his arms around the dog's chest so he stood up on his hind legs. I patted the golden retriever on her head, thanked the man and kept walking. Five minutes later, as I walked happily down the gravel road, I heard barking coming from behind me. It was getting louder. I spun around, surprised to see the brown boxer with his head down and back hunched threateningly as he bared his teeth and snarled at me.

"No! Go!" I yelled, pointing a Rodney back towards the farm. He kept coming towards me, running a few steps then stopping and snarling. My heart pounded. "Go on! Go home!" I yelled again as I poked Rodney towards him and backed away slowly, wanting to put distance between the beast and me. He lunged again. I wondered where his owner was. Couldn't he hear the dog barking and snarling like a crazy beast?

"Fuck off, you fucker!" I yelled, stabbing the air between us with a Rodney as I continued to back away.

The dog stood his ground and barked until I was sufficiently out of his territory or he had tired of menacing me. Then he turned and walked back to the farm. I continued on, looking back over my shoulder every few steps to make sure that he was not sneaking up to surprise me again. Instead, there was a different surprise in store for me. Two hundred metres along the clay and puddled track, I stopped and burst into tears. In front of me was a third stream, five metres wide and rushing with water.

"No, no, no!" I sobbed.

The shock of the dog's attack and now having to go through another fifteen minute process of removing my socks and boots and putting them on again while balancing on one leg up was more than I could bear, but I had no choice. There was no other way around. I sobbed as I took off my boots and shoes, standing on the damp clay bank. I sobbed as I stepped slowly and carefully across the rushing stream. I sobbed as I sat down in the mud on the other side, no longer caring about getting dirty. I sobbed as

I wiped the mud and grit off my feet with a tattered leaf and put my socks and boots back on. I sobbed as I calculated that I had advanced only 6.7 kilometres in two and a half hours and I still had 23 kilometres to walk to reach Monteriggioni. Eventually the sobs ceased and I stood up to keep going.

The trail became friendlier for a while, first as a pale orange sandy path and then as a pebbled Roman road that led past fields of corn with blackened cobs and past dilapidated farmhouses that were spotlighted in the ten minutes of sun that managed to break through the silver clouds that day. I lost my way again. Confused by the guidebook directions and the signs painted on the road, I walked up a long steep hill, past a farm building made from red bricks and various stones with an antique wooden door painted a watery but vivid turquoise, then past a chapel to a path overgrown with tall grass and blackberries. It wasn't the right way, so I backtracked to the bitumen road.

In Quartaia, I ate my panino while sitting on a wooden bench exposed to the wind and cold, then went inside the bar to take an espresso and warm up for a few minutes. A white-haired old man with a tanned and deeply lined face stood at the bar to my right. He asked me a question in Italian and stood waiting for my response with his bushy white eyebrows raised. I didn't understand his Tuscan accent so I looked at the ruddy-cheeked bar lady for help.

"Where do you come from?" she asked me in English.

"*Sono Australiana,*" I answered, and told them I was walking the Via Francigena from Canterbury all the way to Rome. The old man misunderstood my words and was incredulous that I had walked across the sea all the way from Australia. Everyone in the bar laughed, including me.

I wore my beanie and gloves the whole day. It was really cold and the wind was gale-force at times. Out the front of the Etrusca company building, three flags flapped wildly in the wind: the European Union, Italian and the company's own. Their ends were as ripped and as tattered as I felt. I continued on a long track that led into open country with golden grapevines to my right and a steep grassy embankment to my left. The track became partially flooded so I walked on the strip of thick green grass running through the middle until I was stopped in my tracks. The path ahead was completely flooded and thick with mud. I managed to walk along the raised grass at the edge of the path by sticking Right Rodney into the puddle for balance and to keep my feet out of the water. I almost made it to the other side unscathed, but three feet from the end I slipped and my left foot landed in the muddy pool. I cursed as I stepped back onto the grassy edge and took two more steps to the end and back onto dry path.

Ten metres along, I stopped again and burst into tears. Before me lay 30 metres of flooded and muddy track. To my right, the steep embankment was overgrown with blackberries. To my left, the path was lined with thorny bushes. At first I thought I would have to take off my boots and socks and wade through it. I hated the feeling of mud beneath the soles of my boots and had zero interest in feeling it cold and squishy between my toes. The thought of walking for the rest of the day with dirty feet in my socks was not remotely appealing either. I stood looking for a way around and found a small clearing on the embankment where the incline looked less steep. I climbed, using the Rodneys to push my way up and keep me stable. The field had been ploughed and was a mass of clay clumps, but it was the better option of the two. I walked on the thick mud to the end of the field where it tapered down to rejoin the dirt and grass path that was no longer flooded.

Fortunately the rest of the walk to Monteriggioni was uneventful and even pleasant, except for the searing pain in my left buttock and hip. I stopped and stretched often, which eased the pain but only ever temporarily. I walked past more golden grape-vines and along the cream gravel path parallel to Monteriggioni. The towers and circular wall of the town were visible on top of the low hill that I knew was much steeper than it appeared from the distance. I took tiny steps and grimaced in pain as I climbed the winding path up to the town. When I reached it, I found the piazza was deserted. Unlike in summer, there were no tourists drinking wine and eating early dinner at the tables outside the bar and restaurants. I was cold and tired and all I wanted was a hot shower and to lie down. Instead I walked over to the bar, ordered a glass of red wine and sat outside in the Piazza Roma, watching the clouds above the old stone church flare pink as I waited for the caretaker of the *ostello*. The young man was apologetic for keeping me waiting when he arrived thirty minutes later, explaining that he had a day job.

"È *non problema*," I told him.

The difficult day was now over, and I was relaxed and warmed from the red wine. The caretaker showed me around the accommodation, pointing out my bedroom and the bathroom I should use. He even showed me where there was a secret stash of coffee in the cupboard so I could make my own espresso in the morning. I was especially grateful for this, as I planned to leave before the bar opened at nine o'clock. I never knew exactly what each day would bring, but that day had been much harder than I ever expected. Last time I was here, it was just a long, hot slog and the streams were all dry. This time, navigating the mud and fording three running streams and flooded paths had made for slow progress. I cried five times that day, but I kept going because I had to and because I refused to let mud or cold or rushing streams or pain stop me.

Thirty—The end of solitude

Monteriggioni to Ponte d'Arbia

In the morning I emerged from my room into the kitchen that was bathed in sunlight. I looked out the window to see blue sky patched with white cloud. The sun was back after four days of being mostly veiled by thick silver. I clapped my hands together and smiled. After visiting the church and lighting a candle, I approached the only bar in town. It had already opened, although it was not yet nine o'clock. I drank a cappuccino while standing at a wooden bench with my back to the surly, non-talkative barman. When I had finished, I stood in the piazza, drenched in sunshine, as a busload of Japanese tourists arrived, the first ones for the day. I strolled a lap of the small, circular castle town then left through Porta Senese towards the fields of auburn-coloured soil, looking back regularly at the town on the hill and feeling grateful for where I had been and how far I had come.

Although I was happy to be walking in the sunshine, my body really started falling apart. My eyes bulged, my face throbbed and my throat was scratchy and sore as the cold I had been fighting off started to win. The pain in my left hip and buttock was constant. Only thirty minutes after leaving Monteriggioni, I became light-headed and thought I was going to faint. I sat on a rock by the side of the road and ate some crackers until it passed.

Despite my cold and the pain, the day's walking felt peaceful and meditative. I liked the stillness I felt inside when everything was quiet. My walking pace was slow because of my physical state. I focused on each step, present in my body, in a beautiful rhythm. The landscape was familiar but I looked at it with fresh eyes, happy to be walking there again. The paths were either bitumen or gravel and mostly mud-free. I felt like the universe was being kind to me, given my poor physical state. I decided to be kind to myself too and walk my own version of the alternative route that shortened the day by four and a half kilometres and enabled me to avoid the busy Via Cassia.

The pain in my hip and buttock became almost unbearable only five kilometres from Siena. I tried to ignore it until I couldn't take it anymore. Having walked this way before, I knew that I was about to descend a steep hill beneath the freeway and then walk up another long and steep hill on the other side. I wasn't sure I could make it and I sat down and cried. As a car passed, I hid my face in case it stopped and I had to attempt to explain in Italian what was wrong. Crying was not going to help me but it relieved some of the stress. I stretched then swallowed two anti-inflammatory tablets and continued on my way. I was barely able to walk. I shuffled down the steep hill, one slow, tiny slow step after the other, stopping regularly. At the bottom, I looked up at the steep hill ahead, took a breath and resumed shuffling. I kept my head down, looking at my feet and not how much farther I had to go. It was better not to know. Halfway up the hill, the pain in my buttock started to ease. I was surprised that a tough, steep walk like this would make it feel better, until I remembered that I had taken the tablets. It had taken only twenty minutes for them to kick in. I made it to the top of that hill and I raised my arms in a V-shape. Of all the hills I had climbed and all the challenges I had faced, this was one of my larger victories.

I walked for another hour until I finally entered Siena through Porta Camollia and walked straight to a *trattoria* for a slow lunch. My hotel was love at first sight. Built in the late 13th century, it was originally the convent of barefoot Carmelite monks. I entered the hotel along the red brick cloister next to the paved courtyard. The hotel retained the building's existing architecture with exposed wooden ceiling beams and brick arches. Inside some of the walls were still adorned with frescoes of the Madonna. An old rug ran up the length of the steps to the second floor, weighted with metal rods on each step. The whole place was quiet and peaceful.

I hadn't loved Siena last time I was there. I had a lot of pain in my feet and didn't want to walk around. It was also the beginning of summer and the town was full of tourists. I dislike crowds. There were still tourists here this time around, although not as many, and I had this feeling for Siena, a desire just to stroll her streets and explore her in my own intuitive way, to feel the place by roaming and finding my own way around. I took my *passeggiata* in Piazza del Campo, the city's grand main square, where the famous bareback horserace, Palio di Siena, is held twice a year. After walking a lap of the shell-shaped piazza, paved with red bricks, past the *palazzo comunale* and the 102-metre-high tower, Torre del Mangia, I strolled into the narrow streets of the town and found a quiet *trattoria* where I could eat dinner. Another big number had ticked over that day. I had only 284 kilometres over eleven days left to walk to Rome. I felt a mix of disbelief and pending victory. I was not wishing the days away, but I was looking forward to arriving, to stillness and even buying a new outfit to wear. I could hear the trumpets herald faintly. I was starting my victory march.

My rest day in Siena was slow. I didn't do much and I didn't try to. I visited the cathedral and sat for a while, just feeling the sacredness in that old and holy, high-ceilinged space while trying to ignore the tourists wandering around, chatting and taking photos nearby. I climbed up to the roof of the Museo dell'Opera del Duomo and stood mesmerised by the sweeping views over Il Campo, the whole terracotta town and the rolling hills of the countryside. I could have stayed there all afternoon, except the wind was cold and I was hungry. The remainder of the day was all about eating and drinking: my favourite caprese salad with white wine for lunch, gelato in the cool afternoon sunshine, an aperol spritz on a terrace overlooking the golden-glowing Il Campo in the evening, and a three course meal at a small *osteria*. My dinner consisted of oven-baked crostini with mozzarella and pancetta, ravioli filled with pecorino from Pienza and pinenuts in a broccoli cream sauce, and a pear tart with a vanilla and Vin Santo sauce, all washed down with a tangy Vernaccia wine.

Back at my hotel, I enlisted the help of the handsome, English-speaking receptionist with dark hair and dark brown eyes, to ring the caretaker of the *ostello* in Ponte d'Arbia. As it was the only place to stay in the town, I wanted to avoid any potential misunderstandings in my Italian communication and ensure that I had somewhere to stay. The receptionist dialled the phone number that I pointed to in the guidebook on my iPad, and a few seconds later he started speaking in rapid Italian. All I understood was 'tomorrow', 'pilgrim' and 'room'.

"What time will you arrive?" he asked me.

"I'm not sure, maybe four o'clock. Five o'clock at the latest."

He started talking in Italian again on the phone.

"*Sì, sì, grazie,*" he said and hung up. "It is arranged," he told me. "There has been a flood so you cannot use the kitchen downstairs but upstairs is okay. The key will be under the doormat."

"*Grazie. Grazie mille,*" I thanked him a thousand times.

It was such a relief to avoid another awkward telephone call and to know that all I had to do the next day was walk and that my accommodation would be available for me when I arrived. I didn't know then there would be more waiting for me than just a key.

I was pulled out of bed the next morning by an urge to go to the window and draw back the heavy gold drapes. Beyond the terracotta roofs, the sky was streaked with cottonwool clouds of deep lavender-grey, their bellies brushed with electric pink. It was an omen for the miraculous day ahead. After one last meander through Siena's streets, I was soon walking through quiet villages, leaving the town behind. A local man walked with me for a while before he powered off and left me on my own. I passed farmers harvesting and trimming their olive trees. Large nets lay on the ground to collect the pruned tips of the branches that they cut with rotary trimmers. I also passed an old couple, strolling hand in hand, pointing out features of the landscape to each other. Tears welled in my eyes to witness such an old and enduring love.

I was traversing the final error-riddled section I had walked last time before I quit, thanks to my injured toe and swollen feet that I couldn't fit back into my runners. This time, I was able to retrace my steps and understand where I went wrong. The first time, I forked left instead of right. The second time, I missed the left turning onto a country track. I walked down the white gravel driveway of the *agriturismo* tentatively, looking around for a large white dog. Last time, it had barked at me ferociously as I approached the farmhouse, and then lunged at me, biting a hole in my pants as I tried to march past him. I didn't want a repeat of that experience. As I approached the two-storey villa, the same white dog was there, off the lead and barking fiercely. I braced myself for another attack, but his owner stuck his head out of the second floor window of the farmhouse and called him off, allowing me to pass by safely. I turned onto a farm track then spent all but the last hour of the afternoon walking along a ridge with views over the rolling green hills of the Val d'Orcia with rows of soldier-like conifers standing at attention on top of distant ridges. All day, the sun streamed golden warmth through powder puff clouds. And all day, I could see Siena slowly getting smaller and smaller behind me.

I was back in the mud again, but I decided that I was going to make peace with it or try to at least. I thought about why I hated mud so much and I put it down to three things. First, although I couldn't remember a specific example, when I was a little girl my mum probably told me not to get dirty when I was playing outside and scolded me if I did, as getting dirty created more washing and could ruin good clothes. As the daughter of a church minister, my mum was taught to be properly presented at all times in both her appearance and her behaviour, and she passed this on to me. While she was physically able, she always ensured that I had nice clothes to wear and my hair was done, mostly pulled back in a neat and tight ponytail. Second, there is a natural feminine tendency to want to be beautiful, to groom one's hair, to highlight eyes and lips and cheeks with makeup, and to wear pretty clothes and jewellery and gorgeous perfumes. Being covered in mud, even if it is a special mud facemask, isn't exactly beautiful. And third, this external mud was like a metaphor of my own internal mud. Sometimes we have to experience things that feel icky and uncomfortable before we make it out the other side.

In my endeavour to make peace with the mud that day, I chanted every time I walked through it. "It's only mud, it washes off. It's only mud, it washes off. It's only mud, it washes off" became my mantra as I exhaled the tension in my belly. It started to work. I still felt a little repulsed, but I grimaced less and I didn't cry. I even laughed a few times when I slipped although I still had a long way to go before I learned to love mud. After an hour-long walk beside the railway line through more mud, I finally arrived in the small town of Ponte d'Arbia with its one bar, one tobacco shop, one *alimentari* (a small grocery store) and one pizzeria, which was closed on Thursdays, and of course it was Thursday when I arrived. I easily found the commune's pilgrim accommodation and retrieved the key from under the mat as instructed.

Inside, the brick floors were covered in a thick layer of dirt that was the aftermath of the flood I had been warned about. I walked upstairs to find a bed. The hallway light was on, which I thought was a little strange. I turned to my left and opened a door. The dark room had three single beds. I closed the door and walked to the next room.

"Hello," a male voice called out.

I was startled. "Hello?" I called back then walked in the direction of the voice.

In the last bedroom on the right, I discovered a man with short, shaved white hair, sitting at a small table next to the wall, facing the doorway. Although he was sitting down, I could tell he was tall by the way his legs extended beneath the table. At first I thought he was the caretaker, waiting for me to arrive, but as I scanned the room I noticed a sleeping bag rolled out on the bed, and on the sill of the open window were mud-spattered leather hiking boots with the linings pulled out, some socks and a pair of denim pants. I realised he was a fellow pilgrim. I hadn't seen one in the month since I had passed the couple on the way to Vercelli.

"*Sei pellegrino? Mi chiamo Kym*," I said. I had assumed he was Italian, but when he didn't understand me, I asked him in English if he were a pilgrim and introduced myself.

"Ah, Kym Wilson?" he asked.

I jerked backwards, surprised that he knew my surname. "Um, yes. How did you know?"

"I saw your name in the book in Monteriggioni and I say 'I catch up to Kym Wilson', but I think you a man."

"No, I am not a man," I shook my head and smiled.

His name was Paulius. He was a fifty-four-year-old Lithuanian and he had left Canterbury eight days after me on 9 September. He had seen my name written in pilgrim registers along the way, and after his last companion left him in Siena to walk to his hometown, Paulius decided that he would try to catch up to me, and here he was. He told me that he had walked only two weeks alone. Just hours after leaving Canterbury, a Danish man named Peter, the same age as Paulius, caught up with him and they walked all the way down into the Valle d'Aosta together. Peter got sick and needed to rest, but Paulius was keen to keep walking, so they separated.

"Rest and then we talk," Paulius told me.

He showed me a room away from the main road where it would be quieter. I brushed the thin layer of dirt and dust off the far mattress with my hand then laid out my sleeping bag. In the bathroom, I tiptoed over the pool of water on the bathroom floor from Paulius' shower. He assured me the water was hot and it was. After I dressed, I joined him at the table in his room and we spoke about our journeys. I was surprised to learn that he didn't use a guidebook but relied only on a list of the towns and a compass to find his way.

"No map?" I asked him.

"No map," he confirmed.

As we talked, the doorbell rang. Before we could stand up, the front door opened and we heard footsteps coming up the brick stairs.

"*Permesso?*" a male voice called out.

"*Sì*, hello," I called back.

The man with grey curly hair walked into our room. He was

Giuseppe, the caretaker. I stood up, shook his hand and introduced myself.

"*Tutto bene?*" he asked.

"*Sì, grazie, tutto bene,*" I assured him everything was okay.

He prattled away in Italian and I listened intently.

"*Due pellegrini... lontana ...più tardi,*" I heard.

"Oh, okay. *Non problema,*" I told him then turned to translate for Paulius who spoke not one word of Italian. "Two pilgrims might arrive later. They are far away."

After Giuseppe left, Paulius and I put on our shoes and jackets and walked into town to the *alimentari*, where we played charades with the man at the deli to explain what it was we wanted to buy: eggplant parmigiana, roast rabbit and pheasant. Paulius selected a bottle of red wine for dinner before deciding one wouldn't be enough. He grabbed a second one, as well as a jar of pickled vegetables. I picked up some bread and replenished my supply of chocolate biscuits. Back at the *ostello*, we laid out our feast on the small table in his room and had just started grazing when the doorbell rang. Paulius stood up to go downstairs, but as he did so the front door opened. We could hear two male voices and the sound of footsteps coming up the stairs.

"It is Peter," Paulius told me. "He has been trying to catch up to me so we walk into Rome together as Peter and Paul."

I raised my eyebrows, surprised by his comment then turned around as two males appeared at our door, wearing packs on their backs. Peter had short grey hair and wore a bright blue polar fleece jacket and tattered pants. Paulius and Peter shook hands then hugged. Standing next to Peter was Roberto, an Italian man, wearing a navy blue beanie pulled over his short, curly brown hair. Peter had met Roberto not long after Paulius left him, and they had been walking together for almost two weeks. Peter told us how they had thought the *ostello* was in Monteroni d'Arbia, the previous village, and they had to walk eight kilometres in the dark to arrive here. Paulius poured Roberto a glass of wine but not for Peter, as he didn't drink alcohol. They both sat down on the spare bed.

"Life is good, thanks to God," said Paulius.

"Yes, life is good, thanks to God," echoed Peter.

In just two hours I had gone from having zero to three pilgrim friends. I had walked alone for 75 days and assumed that I would walk the rest of the way to Rome alone. I knew from the outset that this scenario was highly possible, and it was one of the things that attracted me to this route, but it seemed the universe had different ideas. There was an unspoken assumption between us that we would walk together the next day, and I didn't object although I was concerned. Would it change the rhythm of my walk or my experience of the landscape around me to have companions? Would I feel compelled to walk at their pace or could I walk at my own? Would they walk fast or slow, stop often or keep going? The guys had a good energy about them. Peter was very funny, and it felt good to laugh and have company, to speak English and talk about my journey with people who understood because they were walking it too. I surrendered my aloneness, at least for the time being, to have the experience of sharing this pilgrimage with others.

Thirty-one—Pilgrims

Ponte d'Arbia to Radicofani

My alarm went off at seven o'clock. I was enjoying the warmth of my sleeping bag and was in no rush to leave it and feel the frigid air wrap against my skin and the cold stone floor beneath my bare feet, but I could hear Paulius and Peter talking and moving around as they prepared to leave. Five minutes later, I heard Roberto as well so I reluctantly got out of my sleeping bag and started to dress and pack. I didn't want to keep them waiting. By the time I walked out into the hallway, Paulius was already standing with his pack on his back, ready to leave.

"I go downstairs," he told me.

Down the hall, Peter was dressed and had his hiking shoes on. He was almost ready to leave too and was just signing the guestbook. In the end, I was the last to leave the building, but only because I had to wait for Roberto to finish in the bathroom. We walked back into town over the bridge in single file, facing the oncoming traffic. We ate breakfast at the only bar then walked back over the bridge, again in single file, on our way to Buonconvento. Giuseppe had advised us to follow the Via Cassia out of town then take the second road to the left and follow the trail because the official way added unnecessary distance. Paulius walked in front of me at first and then behind me. He also used walking poles, but whereas I used them on every step, Paulius had a lackadaisical rhythm where he swung the poles forward on every third step and tapped the ground lightly without propelling himself forward. His step-step-step-tap was annoyingly close, so I tried to walk faster to gain some personal space. When I did, he matched my pace and stayed exactly the same distance behind me.

The path became a long stretch of clay mud. We walked on small patches of dead and dry grass on the side of the track where we could, but mostly we walked through it, the mud clinging to our boots and squishing up around the sides. I groaned.

"I am trying to make friends with mud but I still hate it," I told the guys.

I found it easier somehow to endure the mud when I wasn't the only one slipping and sliding in it. Eventually the path became gravel again and it continued that way for the rest of our journey into Buonconvento.

"I stop. I take five minutes break every hour," Roberto announced as we arrived in the town. "But you don't have to wait."

"It doesn't bother me," I said and looked at Peter and Paulius to see what they wanted to do.

"We will wait," Peter announced.

We walked into town and took coffee in a sports bar. Then as we left town, I finally picked up a signal on my iPad and was able to check my email. In my inbox was a message with the subject "Did we find the lost sock?" I read the message and laughed. A Canadian couple who had been reading my blog said they had found the sock I lost in the Apennines near Cassio. They offered to post it to me.

It was a golden day for walking in the hills to San Quirico d'Orcia. In the distance, we could see Montalcino, famous for its Brunello wine. Rows and rows of grapevines—some muted gold, some bright yellow flecked with rusty orange—stretched between the hilltop town and us. We walked for hours, surrounded by the vines. Occasionally, Roberto would take some of the leaves between his fingers and bend down so his face was inches away as he inspected them then took photos. He had a keen interest in grapevines and winemaking, as he had his own vineyard in the north of Italy.

"It is the best wine in the world," Roberto told us. "Maybe second best after Brunello," he conceded.

We stopped for lunch at a bar in Torrenieri, where Roberto ordered us each a panino with *prosciutto crudo*. Ravenous, we devoured the sandwiches within minutes. Roberto ordered us another round. It was handy having an Italian speaker with us. I was relieved to have a break from awkward conversations. After coffees, we continued on out of town. At first I led the way, but then Peter picked up speed and marched past to take the lead. I had no desire to walk as fast as he was and ended up lagging far behind the group as I stopped to take photos. I was in love with the colours of the landscape. The hills to my right were striped green and dark orange. A tiny house was perched on top of a hill in front of the bruised sky and a giant puff of thick white cloud hovered above it. I rounded another corner and descended down the hill into the valley to find that Paulius had stopped to wait for me at the next bend. A few hundred metres farther down the valley, Peter walked beside Roberto. They stopped and waited for us to catch up.

We arrived in San Quirico d'Orcia at the church of Santi Quirico è Giulitta. Roberto marched off into town to find the priest and I followed behind him. We literally ran into the priest walking out of the church of San Francesco. He told Roberto that he would meet us back at the other church in fifteen minutes. Paulius and Peter were sitting on the marble step of the wishing well in the piazza when we returned. I sat down beside them but began to shiver. The buildings blocked what little sun was left and the breeze was cold. I put on my beanie, gloves and polar fleece and hugged my knees against my chest, but I still felt like ice water was running down my spine. I stood back up and jumped around trying to get warm.

It was thirty minutes before the priest strolled back down and let us into our accommodation. I had no qualms about sharing a room with the three men. We had an instant camaraderie and they felt like safe and trustworthy friends after only one day. Although our dorm room was on the top floor, it was still very cold and the priest wouldn't turn on the heating. He told us it was too early in the season. I went to take the first shower so I could get warm, leaving Roberto to talk to the priest about where we could find the best *bistecca alla fiorentina* in town. This Tuscan specialty is a large and thickly cut T-bone steak, cooked rare on a wood or charcoal fire and seasoned with olive oil and salt. Roberto raved about it and we agreed that we must try it, but first we had to visit the priest after mass so that we could register, get our credentials stamped and pay the donation.

We met the priest at the church and followed him back to his office. He had stamped only a couple of our passports when three teenage boys walked in. The priest called them over and they stood side-by-side to the right of his desk as he spoke to them sternly. The tallest boy raised his voice occasionally and threw his arms around when he spoke. I didn't need to understand what he said to know he was arguing back and disrespectfully too. Peter, Paulius and I started talking amongst ourselves, but Roberto glanced at us with a serious look and gestured with his hand for us to stop. The conversation between the priest and the boys continued for another ten minutes before the boys finally left and the priest stamped the rest of our books. We paid our donations, but before we left he briefed us about the next day's route to Radicofani. He told us where the road was dangerous, where to stop for lunch, how to bypass streams, and said that the last nine kilometres into Radicofani was all uphill but that this would be the last hard section on the way to Rome. He warned us about avoiding two Maremma dogs that were guarding sheep without any human supervision. He also told us that snow was forecast at 400 metres. Radicofani sits at an altitude of 800 metres, so there was a chance we could encounter snow. It sounded like it was going to be a challenging day.

As we walked out into the cold, I asked Roberto why the boys were in trouble.

"The tall boy hit one of the smaller boys and the priest wanted them to share a meal together to be friends again but the tall boy didn't want to."

"We must eat," Paulius interrupted as we strolled across the piazza.

"It is too early," I replied. "The *trattorie* won't be open yet."

Paulius shrugged. Roberto led us into the *trattoria* recommended by the priest anyway. A young boy and girl sat at a table with plates of spaghetti in front of them. A plump, black-haired woman emerged from the kitchen and told Roberto they didn't open until half past seven. That was still thirty minutes away.

"Let's go to the bar," I suggested. "I don't want to go back to the cold room to wait."

We entered a bar a few doors down, ordered drinks and sat at a table. There was red wine for Roberto, an aperol spritz for me, a coke for Peter, and grappa for Paulius. We chatted and ordered another round of drinks then took our party to the *trattoria* where we shared two tender and delicious *bistecca alla fiorentina*, red wine, more conversation and laughter. We were a motley crew but we were all pilgrims on our own journeys, and this coming together somehow worked despite our differences. After more than two months of walking by myself, I was enjoying the company. We travelled in a group but also as individuals with the freedom to walk our own way. There was conversation and laughter between us, as well as silence and solitude. Our walking rhythms complemented each other. We had stopped every hour for Roberto's five-minute break and we had arrived in San Quirico d'Orcia together. I was happy and grateful that I had the opportunity to experience part of my pilgrimage with others.

I slept badly that night. I wasn't the only one. Peter had a sleeping disorder that meant there were times when he couldn't sleep and he warned me that Paulius was prone to snoring loudly. It was one of those nights for both of them. I woke up to hear Paulius snoring. At least it wasn't one of those harsh back-of-the-throat sounds that grated on my nerves. Peter went to the bathroom then returned to bed where he tossed and turned. I woke at four o'clock and tried to count myself back to sleep but gave up after half an hour and went downstairs to the kitchen. I made a cup of sweet black tea and wrote in my journal for an hour then went back to bed and fell asleep just after six o'clock. An hour later, I stirred as Peter sat up in his bed. A few minutes after that, Paulius sat up too. I could have slept longer but I needed to start packing straight away so I wouldn't keep them waiting.

Peter carried very little with him. He had posted many items home after the first two weeks of walking: his tent, his cooking stove, and even his sleeping bag. He had only one pair of pants that he wore day and night, tattered at the ankles and starting to fall apart at the crotch. He hoped they would last until Rome. He carried a silk sleeping bag liner, a thick polar fleece and a pair of leggings, but little else. His bag weighed only five kilograms. Paulius' bag was larger than mine but was still lighter at only eight kilograms, despite the heavy clothing and other items he carried, including a full grey fleece tracksuit, a thick woollen jumper, a pair of denim jeans, a sleeping bag, and a sleeping mat strapped to the outside of his bag.

"Whoa, you strong woman!" he exclaimed when he picked up the Devil during one of our rest breaks.

All three guys were astounded that I had walked so far carrying thirteen kilograms. I knew the Devil was heavy. I felt its weight and the pain of having carried it all those days and kilometres from Canterbury, but I could think of very little to send ahead to Rome or post home. It would have been nothing more than 300 grams combined. The weather was getting colder and the layers I carried were barely enough to keep me warm at night. I wasn't sure I could be as minimalist as Peter. I had carried thirteen kilograms for 76 days. I could carry it for another nine days to Rome.

The morning started with blue skies and scattered cloud, through which the sun stroked my cold cheek. By the time we turned off the bitumen and onto the gravel path towards Bagno Vignoni, a thick sheet of dark grey cloud had blanketed the sky and I expected rain. After an hour, we took a five-minute break, sitting on the stone wall bordering a farmhouse. When we stood to leave, the sun streamed in silver fingers through the last of the grey cloud. As we arrived in Bagno Vignoni, the heavy cloud had vanished, leaving only sunshine and white puffs drifting across the pale sky. The small town was built around the Square of Sources, the original thermal water that looked like a stone-walled swimming pool. These days, it is no longer open for bathing; there are luxury day spas instead. We took our second coffee for the day standing in the local bar, watching the day spa customers eat breakfast in their white bathrobes. Then we continued on towards Radicofani.

We walked along a quiet section of the Via Cassia through more picture-postcard vistas: lone farmhouses surrounded by gentle hills with green seedlings in neat rows; freshly ploughed fields striped with remnants of harvested, golden crops; oblong clouds hovering over the ridged hills lined with spiky rows of conifers. I put on my headphones and dance-walked and sang for almost an hour because I felt so happy and I had to express it somehow or I would burst. I couldn't feel anything but joyful walking through the Val d'Orica with new friends.

The bar in Gallina that the priest from San Quirico d'Orcia recommended had closed permanently. The guys kept walking, but I went back to check a metal sign we had passed. It had a picture of a trolley pointing left into the town. I called my companions back and we walked down the road, hoping to find a supermarket. Instead we found a plant nursery and a shop selling artisanal items. Roberto went in to check if they had any food. A minute later he walked back out and waved for us to come inside. Peter was tired and irritable and sat outside the shop in the sun playing chess on his iPad. There was only salami, cheese and bread on offer, but we agreed it was good enough fare to share for a simple lunch. I walked away to browse the aisles, leaving Roberto to discuss with the young lady behind the counter which cheese would best match the salami. When he laid our picnic outside in the sun, I discovered he had selected the best panino for himself and left us with one baguette that was too small for three people. I went back inside and bought another roll. We sat in the intermittent sunshine for twenty minutes as we ate. When we started walking again, Peter was still quiet and irritable and walked off ahead, needing to be alone.

The traffic on Via Cassia was sporadic and the road was wide enough that the few passing cars and motorbikes didn't bother us. This meant we avoided crossing the two streams and meeting the unsupervised Maremma sheepdogs we'd heard about. Perhaps this was a good thing, given the four separate warnings we had received back in San Quirico d'Orcia, but it left me with unsatisfied curiosity. The nine kilometre climb to Radicofani was steady and tiring. It didn't snow, but it was very cold and becoming even colder as the sun began to set. The four of us spread out, each walking on our own. I lagged behind the others, slowed by my constantly aching hip. We could see the castle town perched on top of its camel-humped hill getting bigger as we approached, yet it seemed like we would never arrive. At my recommendation, we veered off the road and followed a track the rest of the way up the hill. I thought it would be a shorter and quicker way, but instead the slippery mud slick at the end slowed us down. The final road into the town was steep. I was done, exhausted and crippled by my hip pain. I stopped and looked at the hill then started shuffling along, one tiny step at a time. I felt the weight on my back lessen as Roberto walked behind me taking some of the heaviness of the Devil in his hands. When I made it to the top, I could barely whisper a thank you to him.

Thirty-two—The fallout

Radicofani to Acquapendente

Some locals directed us to the *ostello* caretaker's house. We rang the doorbell and a grey-haired woman stuck her head out the window on the second floor. Roberto spoke to her and we waited for her to come down stairs. The door opened and the petite *signora* appeared, wearing a black skirt and a cardigan. As we followed her, she told us that one French man had already arrived that day. I wondered if we would start meeting more pilgrims as we neared Rome. In the small office in the *ostello*, I leaned up against the wall with my arms crossed tightly across my chest to hug my own warmth. I felt my shoulders slump in tiredness while waiting for my turn to complete the registration card.

"*Sei stanca?*" the *signora* asked.

"*Sì, è molto freddo.*" I was tired and very cold.

"I'm having first shower," I declared to the guys. "I need to get warm."

As we walked out of the office and back to a small room that was furnished with three bunk beds, the *signora* fiddled with the thermostat. While I fetched my toiletries and a change of clothes from my bag, Roberto and Paulius disappeared without a word. By the time I had showered and dressed, they had returned and were sitting at the end of the long wooden dining table with a large carafe of white wine, some cheese and salami. I also discovered that the radiators were billowing warm air into the cold rooms. I was so happy. I joined them and they poured me a glass of wine. As we chatted, the front door opened and the French man walked in. He had chin-length blonde hair and a white beard and wore a fedora on his head. He was either very skinny or his pants were too large and baggy around his legs or both. He spoke only French and Spanish, no English or Italian. Roberto spoke some Spanish and chatted to him, but he offered only infrequent and brief translations to us. The Frenchman's name was Jimberto and he was sixty years old. He was walking north to Santiago de Compostela in Spain and had been walking this camino continuously for eight years. Eight years of continuous walking to Santiago de Compostela then back to Rome then back to Santiago de Compostela again! I was incredulous. Being a pilgrim was not an easy life, but maybe it gets easier as you let go of the things that you don't need and as you learn the way. Perhaps one day you just wake up and your body embraces the long and arduous walking without any pain… or maybe not. Jimberto's face was tanned and deeply lined, and I don't think he had many teeth. I suspected he had lived a hard life, one spent mostly outdoors in the sun. I never learned exactly how many times he had walked the camino, but he showed us many stamped pilgrim credentials that he carried with humble pride in a clear plastic bag.

Just before eight o'clock, we left Jimberto eating his pasta alone at the dining table and went to find somewhere we could eat dinner. The only open restaurant in town was full and we were sent away with a carafe of white wine for *aperitivi*, pre-meal drinks, and told to come back in thirty minutes. We didn't really need more wine, just food and sleep, but we walked back to the *ostello*, dutifully drank the wine then returned to the restaurant. It was still busy, and although we were seated, we had to wait another thirty minutes just for our orders to be taken. Roberto, Peter and I ordered the Tuscan soup. Paulius didn't open the menu that he couldn't read. He wanted meat and vegetables. Peter suggested a steak and I suggested *verdure cotte*, cooked vegetables, for his vegetable dish. The waitress took our orders and came back with another carafe of wine and a coke for Peter.

As we waited for our meals, I questioned Roberto to find out more about Jimberto.

"So does he have a home?" I asked.

"No, he just walks," Roberto replied.

"He never goes home?"

"No."

"But how does he pay for food and accommodation?" I asked.

"People give him money and food."

"So he is like a vagabond; he just keeps moving from place to place and he doesn't go home or ever intend to go back home but just keeps walking."

"You shouldn't say that. Jimberto is a good man. He is more pilgrim than any of us," Roberto said angrily. He stared directly at me, his face like stone.

"I don't call him vagabond in a bad way. It is just that he doesn't have a home and he wanders along the camino to Santiago and back to Rome. My understanding of pilgrimage is that the pilgrim eventually returns home and takes their experiences with them. Jimberto will never go home."

"Who are you to say this? You are judgmental and I don't like it!" Roberto yelled at me. He crossed his arms and looked away. I was shocked by the sharpness of his attack and upset that I was being misunderstood. I looked away, not wanting to make eye contact with Roberto who was sitting directly opposite me.

Our food arrived just after the awkward silence began, but it didn't help to break it. The soup was delicious but my appetite had died. When the waitress returned, I passed on *secondo*, Roberto ordered more soup, Peter ordered steak and *verdure cotte,* and we asked for Paulius' vegetables that never arrived with his steak.

"It must be steak and vegetable together!" Paulius said as the waitress walked away.

Roberto went out for a cigarette and I broke my silence.

"I didn't say vagabond in a bad way or mean that what he is doing is good or bad," I explained to Peter and Paulius. "I think he is incredible."

"I know. I understand what you meant," said Peter. "I don't understand why Roberto reacted like that."

"It was horrible," I said and started crying. "I didn't come on this pilgrimage to be attacked. I would prefer to walk alone than experience that again. Right now, I don't want to talk to him. I don't want to be near him and I don't want to walk with him!"

"Just wait until tomorrow," said Peter.

"Yes, I will sleep on it…" I didn't finish the sentence because Roberto walked back in. I wiped the tears from my cheeks and looked down at my lap, hoping to hide the fact that I had been crying and because I didn't want to look at him. I sat quietly as they ate their next meals. By dessert, I had recovered a little and even became chirpy when the waitress told us that they had *millefoglie.*

"It is the best dessert in the world!" I exclaimed then went on to describe the vanilla-slice-style dessert to Peter and Paulius, who both ordered one.

Roberto went out to smoke again while we ate. Several cigarettes later, he returned. "I am just paying my bill and then I will go back," he announced.

"We are finished," said Peter, "so we may as well all pay."

After we paid and left the restaurant, Roberto walked off ahead of us. We hadn't spoken one word to each other since the altercation. I was still upset about it. It was an unexpected attack that caught me off guard, and now Roberto wasn't talking to me either. It was reminiscent of how my mum used to treat me. Just like I had done in my childhood, I started to blame myself. If I hadn't said anything about Jimberto, if I hadn't used the word vagabond, then I wouldn't have upset Roberto and we'd all be happily walking back to the *ostello* after another delicious meal. Even so, I knew it wasn't just my fault. Relationships are two-sided. There had been a misunderstanding and I had tried to restore the balance by explaining exactly what I meant, but Roberto didn't want to understand because he was too overtaken by his anger. I had enjoyed walking with the three guys for the past two days but I was now unsure whether or not I wanted to continue walking with them. I would prefer to walk by myself and eat alone than to experience the night's events again, but Peter was right. I was tired and a little drunk and feeling overly emotional. I needed to sleep on it and make a decision in the morning.

At half past six, I heard movement in the bed below me. Roberto stood up and left the room. This was the first time since I'd met him three nights earlier that he was the first one out of bed. I lay warm in my sleeping bag, waiting for Paulius and Peter to wake. From the dining area, I heard muffled voices, footsteps, and a light thumping on the wooden table. I guessed Roberto was having coffee with Jimberto. I was still upset over Roberto's attack and part of me had no desire to walk with him, but I also knew that I had capacity to forgive and move on. I wasn't sure that Roberto could; he was a proud man. I doubted that I would need to make a decision anyway. I suspected that he was going to leave us and walk on his own.

Twenty minutes later, Roberto entered the room quietly, dragged his sleeping bag and backpack into the hallway and started to pack. I wondered if he was going to leave without even saying goodbye. This would upset Peter, who had walked with him for two weeks. I felt sick and sad that two days of fun had to end like this, but I also felt relieved that he was going. I couldn't see any non-awkward way to move past what had happened. The camaraderie in our small group would be forever changed.

Like clockwork and without alarms, Peter and Paulius woke at seven o'clock. Paulius left the room and greeted Roberto as he crossed the small stone corridor to use the bathroom. Once Peter had sat up, I unzipped myself from my sleeping bag and sat up too.

"Good morning," Peter said.

"Did you sleep better last night?" I asked.

"No, not really," he replied.

I climbed down from the top bunk and started packing my sleeping bag. Paulius walked back in and went over to his bed to start packing. Moments later, Roberto came in with his bag on his back.

"I am sorry about last night," he said looking at me. "I was tired."

"Okay." I accepted the unexpected apology and said nothing more. There was no point.

"I am leaving now," he announced. "Today, I walk to Bolsena. I want to arrive in Rome." He had said this several times over the last two days. He needed to reach Rome by 22 November so he could make it home in time for a party.

"Okay." Peter was the only one to respond to this announcement. "I am sad that you are leaving. I enjoyed walking with you."

They shook hands then hugged and patted each other on the back.

"Stay in touch," Peter added.

Paulius and Roberto shook hands. "Nice walking with you," Roberto told him.

"*Ciao, ragazzi,*" he said. Then he turned and left the room without saying anything further to me.

I returned to my packing, feeling hollow. Our group of four was now down to three, and I continued to blame myself. If I had never used the word vagabond then maybe Roberto would still be walking with us. I began to see that he was right. I had been judgmental in forming an opinion of Jimberto as a vagabond and calling him something other than a pilgrim just because he never returned home. The irony in the situation was that I could also be called a vagabond instead of a pilgrim. I had been somewhat nomadic over the last five years. Although I stayed in places for periods of time, technically I did not have a permanent home either. My direction in life was uncertain and I followed my intuition, living carefree. However, Roberto had interpreted my use of the term vagabond negatively when I had not intended it to be understood so. I wondered if the outcome would have been different if I had simply described Jimberto as a wanderer. Adding further irony to the situation, Roberto had also been judgmental in judging me for judging Jimberto.

It was Peter I felt sorry for. I felt I owed him an apology. He and Roberto had become good friends after walking together for two weeks. I had only walked with them for three days. Perhaps it should have been me who left.

At the bar, we ordered our coffees and our pastries from the glass display case and sat down to eat.

"I am sorry," I said to Peter. He looked tired but sad too.

"It is not your fault. He needed to arrive in Rome to go home for his party," he replied.

"Yes, but it is because of me that he has left now, because of last night. I feel bad. You walked with him a long time. It could have been me who left instead."

"Don't worry. It is not your fault," Peter repeated.

As we stood to leave, Jimberto walked in and ordered a cappuccino at the bar and took a croissant. With the Devil on my back, I walked over to him to say goodbye as he ate his croissant, his white beard flecked with pastry.

"*Buon cammino. Sei molto bravo.*" I wished him a good journey and told him he was amazing and honestly meant it. Although I didn't know his reason for continuously walking the trail, I was fascinated and impressed. Walking like this is not just walking. It is physically, mentally, emotionally and spiritually challenging. Perhaps by walking the trail for so long, Jimberto had found a level of peace and faith that I hoped to experience in my own life.

Peter, Paulius and I walked out of Radicofani beneath grey skies. It soon started raining and we all stopped to put on our ponchos. The gravel path snaked its way down into sheep country and the land rolled away either side. Pale green grass was punctuated by a brown water dam and dilapidated stone farmhouse. We fell into our own walking rhythms. As usual, Peter led the way and Paulius waited for me to walk ahead of him, except I insisted that he walk ahead of me. I needed my own space and was in no mood to have him tapping away so close behind me. The gravel path on the low ridge was one of those paths that just seemed to keep going and going. I lagged behind, taking photos of the sloping countryside and of Radicofani, slowly getting smaller behind us. We were a little more than 160 kilometres from Rome. By now, I had walked 1800 kilometres, yet what I was doing still seemed surreal. All I did was wake up and pack and walk then do the same thing the next day and the next, and little by little I was getting closer to Rome. Soon I would be there and the walking would be over.

Halfway to Acquapendente, just before the intersection with the Via Cassia, we detoured 30 metres in search of coffee, only to find the bar was closed, of course. It was Sunday. Instead, we crossed the road and took shelter in the bus stop. I sat on the left side of the bench, dampened by the rain blowing in through the gap near the roof, while Peter and Paulius stayed dry. Another hour down the road, we took our next five-minute rest break, sitting on the safety barrier on the side of the road.

"Look who is coming," Paulius said, facing the direction from which we had walked.

Peter and I looked to our right. Roberto walked towards us with his wooden walking stick in his right hand. He must have taken the main road that wound its way down from Radicofani to the Via Cassia and would have just discovered he had walked the long way.

"*Ciao*," he said as he walked past us without stopping.

"Wow, that was awkward. He must be really pissed off," I said.

We kept walking and crossed out of Tuscany into Lazio. I paused with one foot on each side of the invisible border and looked back to say a silent thank you for Tuscany's beauty and deliciousness. I could have stayed longer in Tuscany, but the path led me on. I hoped one day it would lead me back. Twenty minutes later, we walked to a pizzeria on the side of the road to find Roberto sitting on a bench seat next to the front door, biting into a large crusty white panino.

"*Ciao*," Peter greeted him.

"*Ciao*," Roberto replied and kept eating.

We were in no rush to make it to Acquapendente and walked inside to order pizzas. Roberto stayed outside, not wanting to join us, and awkwardness hung heavy in the air. Yesterday we had all been the best of pilgrim friends and now he didn't want to come anywhere near us, except to say goodbye. As we waited for our pizzas and sipped our soft drinks, Roberto stepped inside the restaurant.

"Ciao, ragazzi," he called out and waved.

That was the last time we saw him. He messaged Peter later to tell him that he had made it to Bolsena and to explain his behaviour, saying he was tired, he wasn't good at walking in a group and he needed to be alone. I still felt sad that we had parted without resolving what had taken place between us, but I was also glad that he had decided to walk on his own, given how he had reacted when we crossed paths during the day. Acceptance of what I could not change alone would eventually come.

Thirty-three—Unplanning

Acquapendente to Viterbo

We arrived in Acquapendente just as it was getting dark. The signs led us down into a small valley and then back up a steep hill, past chicken coops and dog pens, through what must have been the original gateway into the town. Peter and Paulius walked ahead. My hip was sore so I lagged behind. We found our way to the Casa del Pellegrino to find beds for the night, but it was closed. I rang the number listed in the guidebook. The woman spoke in rapid Italian that I didn't understand.

"*Okay, grazie*," I said and hung up. "I'm not sure, but I think someone is coming. I guess we just wait and see," I told Peter and Paulius.

We sat down on a bench seat. Five minutes later, a small black jeep pulled up and a fifty-year-old man wearing a khaki hunter's uniform jumped out and walked over to the door with key in hand. We followed him through the front courtyard to another door at the back, and then upstairs into the basic kitchen. It had a table and four chairs but no stove or fridge. We were shown into a room with four single beds then I followed him downstairs to the bathroom so he could show me how to turn the hot water on and off. After he left, we studied the heater on the wall, trying to find a way to rewire it so we could switch it on, but without success. Paulius found extra blankets stored in another room. It was still going to be another cold night for sleeping.

We left Acquapendente the following morning on streets shrouded by fog. It was warmer outside than it was in the Casa del Pellegrino, so we were happy to be walking again. Once we cleared the terrace buildings, the fog thickened and we could not see the cathedral until we were within 50 metres of it. We walked in single file on the side of the road, past an avenue of golden poplar trees with the fog held magnetically between them, past muddy fields sprouting seedlings, and past giant puddles that I was grateful we didn't have to walk through. The golden woodlands seemed even more beautiful and alive beneath the sun. As we walked towards San Lorenzo Nuovo, the fog began to clear and we could see Radicofani behind us, a small blip on its hill. The indigo-shadowed hills and lavender clouds looked like they had been painted on the horizon by the Divine's own hand. We stopped in a bar for our five-minute rest break. Peter and I took a second coffee while Paulius ate gelato, which is not such a strange thing to do in Italy, except that it was only ten o'clock in the morning. The bar lady raised her thin eyebrows as he pointed to the gelato in the freezer, and a table of three men wearing shirts and trousers drinking espresso stared at him as he walked back to our table, licking the frozen dessert.

As we left town, we caught our first glimpse of Lake Bolsena, a shimmering pool of silver surrounded by the low rising hills. The Via Cassia was narrow and winding with blind curves so we returned to the official trail, walking on gravel roads and woodland tracks surrounded by grassy fields and patches of woods. An hour later, Peter thought it might be nice to walk by the lake for a while, so we found a track that cut back down to the Via Cassia only to discover there was no lakeside path. Instead, we continued beside the Via Cassia with its consistent stream of cars and deluxe buses zooming past on the two narrow lanes. The gravel edging was being reconstructed and had holes and obstacles to navigate, so we walked on the white line on the edge of the bitumen, jumping into the soft gravel to get out of the way of traffic when we needed to.

Before I met Peter and Paulius, I planned to stay two nights in Bolsena in order to visit the cathedral in Orvieto that was 20 kilometres away. In the preceding two weeks, I had planned and often booked accommodation before I arrived in a town, staying more often in hotels than in pilgrim accommodation. I was tired and it was a way of comforting myself to know I just had to arrive and not worry about finding accommodation. With Peter and Paulius, there was no planning. We walked and we stopped where we felt like stopping and stayed wherever we could find a roof over our heads when we arrived in the next town. Their way of walking reminded me to let go of planning, to be more in the moment, and to trust that everything would work out. I decided to let go of my plan and would wait to see how I felt when I arrived.

Bolsena was a ghost town. Situated near the lake of the same name, it was a summer destination, and as autumn advanced towards winter, the tourists had all gone. We entered the deserted old town through the archway near Piazza Guglielmo Matteotti and continued along Corso della Repubblica, decorated with hanging snowflakes and stars and strings of lights. The restaurants, shops and hotels had signs in their windows saying *chiuso per ferie*, closed for holidays. We found only one pizzeria that was open for lunch. Peter and I ordered pizzas again for ourselves and steak and grilled vegetables for Paulius.

"It must be meat and vegetable," I teased him. We both ordered beers and made a toast.

"*Isveikata!*" he said in Lithuanian.

"*Salute!*" I responded in Italian.

I had mentioned the possibility that I might stay in Bolsena, but after lunch we just packed up and walked on towards Montefiascone, my decision communicated by my action. I needed some time alone so I walked at the back of the group. We passed through pretty woodlands of lime green and lemon, and our path was littered with tan and tangerine leaves. I stopped now and then to feel the woods and listen to their unique quietness. Eventually, we found our way back onto roads again with bursts of traffic speeding by. Peter dropped to the back of the group, playing chess on his iPad as he walked, so I took the lead. On a straight section of road, a truck sped towards us, staying close to the right side of the road.

It will move over, I thought, convinced that the driver had a clear view of the three of us on the straight road. I was right and wrong. The truck came to within a few feet of me and I jumped onto the grassy verge as it swerved.

"*Vaffanculo! Che cazzo fai!*" I yelled, pumping my right hand in the air and using all the Italian swear words I knew as the truck sped away.

Late in the afternoon, the thick clouds swallowed the sun whole. Paulius had been right that it would be dark when we arrived in Montefiascone, but I was right too because it didn't matter. I pulled my head-torch out of the Devil, put it on my forehead and switched it onto flashing mode. Some cars slowed down to look at us. Others put their high beams on to see what was flashing ahead of them and then slowed down and veered towards the centre of the road once they saw us. This may have been only the third time I used the torch on the whole trip—the first time when I was camping and the second to find my way out of the convent in Pontremoli—but it was worthwhile carrying all that way, as it kept us safe that night.

The next day, we followed a narrow paved road past the cathedral then exited Montefiascone through an arch and walked straight over to the viewpoint. I thought we had left Lake Bolsena behind us, but as we exited town on the south-west side, we had one last sighting of its silver blue waters. The land was a patchwork of light green fields and dark green woods all the way back to Bolsena. It was so beautiful. We stood there for several minutes, admiring the view and taking photos. I felt like I was standing exactly where I was meant to be standing. I had walked here, to this moment in my life. Everything I had experienced along the way—the challenges, the pain, the heartbreak, the joy, the love and the beauty—had shaped me into who I was right then. I stood there, receiving the beauty in front of me and knowing that although I was always in the midst of leaving and arriving, I belonged to this moment and to myself.

We followed farm tracks to Viterbo, some of which were muddy and some were white gravel. Peter and I joked that just around the next corner there would be a bar where we could stop for coffee and second breakfast, but there wasn't one. My energy waned and I walked slower and slower. We passed the thermal hot springs without stopping. It was overcast and the air was cold. Although there were a number of campervans parked nearby, only one man sat alone in a spring. It was lunchtime when we arrived in Viterbo and headed straight for the café on the other side of the Via Cassia. We stood in the middle of the road with cars passing within inches of us until a kind motorist slowed down and let us cross. I was relieved to sit down and rest in the warmth. I ate my *piadina* silently. I had neither the energy to speak nor desire to walk any farther. Peter was tired too. Although it was early and we had enough time to walk to Vetralla by sunset, we agreed unanimously that we would stay in Viterbo for the night and use the afternoon to rest.

We arrived at the Convento Cappuccini on the other side of town and were shown into a dormitory by a young friar. The small room had five bunk beds and one adjoining bathroom. I had hoped it would have single rooms like the other Cappuccini convents I had stayed in so I would have some privacy and space to myself, but at least we had a roof over our heads and a bed to sleep in, even if it was cold. I took the first shower so I could use the bathroom before Paulius flooded it as usual. I handwashed some clothes and hung them over the spare bunks to dry then went to bed and drifted off to sleep, only to wake as soon as Peter and Paulius returned from lunch an hour later. They went to bed too and we all slept for most of the afternoon. It was getting dark when I got out of bed to use the bathroom. I felt my clothes and discovered everything was still dripping water onto the floor. I suspected it was colder in the room than the 10°C it was outside and figured I would once again have to hang my belongings off the Devil the next day.

Before I met Peter and Paulius, I intended to stay an extra night in Viterbo, and now I contemplated staying behind to let them walk on without me so I would arrive in Rome the same way I started: alone. I realised, however, that I had nothing to prove. I had walked for 75 days by myself and I knew I could walk all the way to Rome alone if I had to. The thing was, I didn't want to. I wanted to arrive in Rome with Peter and Paulius, to celebrate our journeys and our arrival with them.

Thirty-four—Caught by cold

Viterbo to Campagnano di Roma

My clothes didn't dry overnight. I was half annoyed with my-self and half amused that I had thought there was any chance of them drying in the first place. After I packed, I hung my pants, t-shirt, long-sleeved top, socks and towel over different straps on the Devil and walked out into the day as a clothesline again. It was cool and there was patchy cloud but some soft sunshine too. As long as we walked through open countryside, my clothes would dry by lunchtime. We walked back through the town to the square of San Lorenzo. Viterbo Cathedral was directly in front of us, built from plain stone and unadorned. To the right, wide steps led up to the Palace of the Popes, home of the papal throne from the middle to the late 13th century, before it was moved to Avignon.[10] To its right was the Loggia of Blessings, an open gallery with seven arcades supported by double columns. We entered the church to pray and light candles. Peter and Paulius both kneeled at the altar. After leaving the cathedral, we climbed the grey, stone stairs up to the loggia and stood looking over Viterbo, with its terracotta and dark salmon buildings in-terspersed with dark green trees. I was still feeling tired, but the sunshine brightened my mood. We walked down the stairs and under the wide arch beneath the loggia then followed the path beside the wall until we exited through Porta Faul. In front of us, the Via San Paolo was busy with morning traffic. Opposite were three roads and I couldn't figure out from my map which one we should take.

"We must walk to Rome," said Paulius and started walking along Via San Paolo.

"That's not the way," I told him. That was the one thing I was sure of. "But if you want to walk that way go for it. I'm not. It's too dangerous."

He turned back and followed Peter and I across the road.

"I think it is this one," said Peter, leading the way down the road to the left.

We rounded a corner and walked along the narrow, traffic-free road cut through rock. On either side of us, the moss covered rock towered four meters upward and olive trees lined the cliff edge. We emerged from the cutting and continued along the quiet bitumen road until we turned back onto a farm track. There had been a lot of rain the previous afternoon and overnight, so we weaved around puddles and tiptoed through mud. One section of path was completely flooded and the only way to walk ahead was on a narrow embankment next to the barbed wire fence. I held on to the smooth wire in between the barbs to keep my balance. I had to admit that sometimes mud made the walking more interesting.

Despite eating and sleeping plenty, my tank was empty. Almost three months of walking had caught up with me. I had expected that after yesterday's short walk and the sleeping and resting I'd done in the afternoon I would be re-energised and able to walk effortlessly to Capranica, but I couldn't. By the time we arrived in Vetralla, I had nothing left to give. We walked into a *trattoria* and Paulius ordered us a carafe of white wine. I both needed and didn't need it at the same time. As we waited for the kitchen to open so we could order, we discussed accommodation in Capranica, still 16 kilometres away. There were few options and I wanted to phone ahead to ensure we had somewhere to stay when we arrived, except I couldn't find any of them on my map. Peter played chess on his iPad while Paulius, who never helped to find accommodation, sat drinking wine.

"We will walk," he shrugged, as if it were no problem, but it was a problem. They weren't helping me to find accommodation and I couldn't continue if I didn't know we had somewhere to stay when we arrived.

"We can stay here," Peter suggested, having sensed my distress.

"No, it's okay. We can walk but it will be slow for me. I'm so tired."

"No, we will stay here this afternoon and rest," Peter insisted.

"We will stay," Paulius agreed.

After lunch, we walked two kilometres out of town to a monastery, stopping at the supermarket on our way to buy some afternoon snacks. Peter selected some gorgonzola cheese. Paulius wanted grappa. I suggested wine. He compromised and bought a bottle of sambuca that he knew I liked, although I felt uncomfortable about taking a strong spirit into a religious house. We rang the buzzer at the monastery and a nun stuck her black-veiled head out of the second-floor window.

"*Aspettate,*" she told us, and we waited until she came downstairs and ushered us inside. We followed her down the corridor where she showed us into a dining room with a square wooden table.

"*Aspettate,*" she told us again then left the room and came back a few minutes later with the stamp for our pilgrim credentials. We followed her outside and into another building, where a lone tradesman painted the corridor wall white, then up another flight of stairs and down another corridor to the bedrooms. I wasn't allowed to sleep in the same room as the men and was shown into a room with three single beds made up with duvets and sheets. I felt a mix of relief and joy at the prospect of sleeping in a properly made bed instead of my sleeping bag. The nun showed Peter and Paulius into their room next door and I took off the Devil and started hanging my damp clothes over the chair and table and on the wall hooks. Another nun came in with an oil heater and my little seed of joy blossomed. Sheets, duvet and a heater! My definition of luxury had changed over the course of the walk.

Next door, I heard the water running for a shower.

"Agh! Good grief!" Peter cried out. I giggled. The water must have been cold.

I changed into my leggings and singlet and curled up in bed without showering. Right then, I needed to sleep. The phone rang and the nun said something about *freddo*, so I assumed she was talking about the water but that was all I understood. A few minutes later, she came in and flicked the switch on the wall to turn on the hot water then went to the guy's room to do the same, although too late for poor Peter. Paulius knocked on the door then walked in and put a small white plastic cup half-filled with sambuca on the table next to my bed. After he left, I rolled over and fell asleep for ninety minutes, waking up warm and cosy beneath the duvet in the heated room. Eventually I sat up, sipped some of the sweet anise liquor then showered beneath hot water and joined the guys in their room, sitting down on the spare bed. Paulius topped up my plastic cup with more sambuca and I saw that there was only one-third of the bottle left.

"Holy cow, man! You've drunk that much already?"

"Yes, that is Paulius," said Peter.

We spent the remainder of the late afternoon eating cheese and talking until it was time for dinner.

"Maybe there will be *dolce*," said Peter jokingly.

"Yes, *dolce*!" I agreed. "We are here early so maybe they will have time to make us dessert."

We knew there wouldn't be *dolce*, at least not the type of *dolce* we were thinking of. It was enough just to be fed so that we didn't have to walk two kilometres back down the hill into town. I had seen little of Viterbo and Vetralla, only walking in and out of the towns, but it didn't really matter. I was seeing and experiencing everything that I needed to. In our heated rooms in the convent, I felt comforted and comfortable, and I hoped that the rest I'd had was enough to get me through a long walk the next day. I didn't want to hold the guys back, but they really didn't seem to mind, not even Paulius with his incessant desire to keep walking. We were in no rush to arrive in Rome.

We left the monastery after breakfast and quickly veered off-road, walking through stunning woodlands, where the lemon-foliaged trees towered 20 metres high on either side of the dirt track. After that, we continued on through hazelnut groves all the way to the old town of Capranica, perched on a hill overlooking the Sutri valley. I felt much better than I had felt the previous day, but I still had a temperature and was still fighting off a cold. The weather started off sunny, but then it rained and there was a little hail. The sun came back out again until it started raining again within minutes of me taking Kermit off. That always seemed to trigger more rain. After entering Capranica, we found a café set back off the road and went inside to warm up.

As we sat at a small round table, drinking coffee and eating *cornetti*, a man walked in wearing tattered pants. His face was unshaven and his eyes red-rimmed. He walked to a table where three women sat drinking espressos and asked them for money. The bar lady faked a smile and spoke to him in Italian, repeating *ciao, ciao, ciao* to him over and over, insisting that he leave.

He was the first beggar I had seen since I started my journey. Although I was in Italy and the man was Italian, I could have easily have been back in Melbourne witnessing this scene. We're not as different as we sometimes think we are.

We walked into the heart of the old town through an archway so narrow that only one car could pass at a time then turned left through another stone arch beneath the clock tower and were soon walking up a narrow bitumen road cut into rock, past more stunning yellow trees. I stopped and turned around often for last glimpses of Capranica, high on its hill. The church of San Rocco towered above the clay pink buildings. By the time we reached the end of the cutting, the town was out of sight. We entered Sutri through Porta Vecchia. This was another town built on top of a hill, so we had yet another steep climb to reach it.

"We should go this way," Paulius suggested, gesturing to steep steps immediately to our right.

I looked at my map. "No, we should keep going this way," I pointed straight ahead. "That way winds back in the wrong direction."

Paulius must have gotten lost a lot and walked many extra kilometres during those two weeks that he had walked by himself with no guidebook and no map. Almost every time he tried to direct us, he either pointed us in the wrong direction or towards the longer or busier way. Despite this, he had managed to find his way on his own.

We indulged in a long lunch at a small *trattoria*. The next town was some 24 kilometres away. None of us wanted to walk 44 kilometres that day, so we decided to stay. We ate little Italian sausages grilled over the fireplace in the dining room. I ate mine with crispy potatoes while Paulius had his with cooked vegetables, because "it must be meat and vegetables." Peter and I both had *panna cotta* for dessert, thick and creamy and the right kind of sweet.

"Life is good, thanks to God," said Paulius when we finished eating.

Peter and I both agreed.

We paid a special pilgrim price for all that deliciousness, and my face glowed rosy red, partly from sunburn, partly from red wine and partly from the illness that had not yet beaten me. I felt happy and content in Italy with these two men who had become my friends. We finished our lunch just as the Monastero di Santissima Concezione opened to accept pilgrims. I had heard from other pilgrims that the Carmelite nuns were not very welcoming, but my experience was different. Although we never saw the nun who registered us because she was hidden behind the wooden grill of her office, she was bright, sweet and helpful. We sent our passports, pilgrim credentials and payment through to her via a countertop turntable, and she returned them with the key to our accommodation next door to the church.

Our rooms were on the third floor, clean and simple, although without any heating at all. I opted to have a room to myself again. I realised that part of the reason I felt so exhausted was because I was an introvert who had been in the company of others for almost 24 hours a day for the last six days, but it wasn't just this alone. We had walked a few long-distance days and my backpack really was five kilograms too heavy, despite my careful packing. I was fighting off a cold again, as I had done repeatedly over the last four weeks. And I felt emotional about the end of the journey approaching too quickly.

I turned on the hot water switch then lay down on my bed under a blanket to get warm while I waited until I could have a long, hot shower. The room was freezing cold. Winter was embracing Italy and snow was again forecast at 400 metres. Sutri was at 310 metres. I was glad I had carried my foldup water bottle that I had used more often as a hot water bottle than for drinking water. Cold beneath one blanket, I found another in the cupboard then curled up to keep my body heat close. I heard the shower running in the guy's room next door then Peter cried out and I giggled. The water must have turned cold on him again.

I went to bed with a sore throat and woke up with a full-blown cold. My face felt swollen. My head ached at my temples and behind my eyes. My body ached too. I had a temperature. It seemed the cold I had been avoiding for so long had finally caught me. I lay under the covers, not wanting to face the cold room or the task of packing. I heard the guys' door open at quarter past seven, as Paulius retrieved his stinky boots from the hallway. I knew they would be ready to leave soon, so I forced myself out of bed and started to dress and pack. It was just a cold, and although I felt dreadful I could keep going. Even if I were sick to the point of debilitation, I would have pressed on, if only to find somewhere warmer to stay.

Peter knocked on the door and announced that they were going to the bar. I replied I would meet them there and continued packing. By the time I reached the bar, they had finished breakfast. I dropped the Devil next to their table then walked to the pharmacy through the arch beneath the clock tower and past the stone fountain with its blackened water, only to find it closed. I sighed in resignation. I really needed something to get me through that morning but I was going to have to soldier on. Back at the bar, the guys were ready to leave. Peter played chess on his iPad and Paulius sat with his arms crossed, staring into space. He had told me how boring it was for him when Peter was on his iPad. I ate quickly and we left. My brain was fogged from illness and initially I led us north-west out of town. When I realised my mistake after 200 metres, I swore then apologised as we turned around and walked back into town then out the south-east exit, stopping to visit the ancient Roman amphitheatre on our way.

Thirty-five—Tutto il mondo

Campagnano di Roma to La Storta

For most of that day I walked alone, not wanting to match the guys' pace and risk making myself sicker. Although they were often out of sight, they stopped occasionally so I could catch up. I wasn't much company. I listened to music and spoke little. My well of humour was dry. I focused on taking one step after the other and making it to the next town, where I hoped to buy some cold and flu tablets. We arrived in Monterosi by lunchtime and headed straight to the pharmacy. I walked out with a packet of basic cold and flu tablets and the chunkiest paracetamol tablets I had ever seen. I swallowed two of the flu tablets as we walked back to a café for lunch.

It poured as we left town on a path beside the Via Cassia. The rain eventually stopped as we walked through farmland past the rusting hazelnut trees and golden poplars dropping their leaves to the ground. Around us were lush paddocks of green and ploughed fields of auburn dirt. As we approached Monte Gelato, I regained my sense of humour.

"Maybe there will be gelato?" I joked with the guys once I caught up to them.

There wasn't. Instead, there were many soldiers wearing army greens and carrying guns, marching past us in the opposite direction. They were followed by army trucks carrying soldiers in open trays. I assumed we had stumbled into some kind of training drill and was puzzled that the soldiers weren't bothered by our presence. Then we saw the cameramen following them and realised it was a television or movie set. They were moving to their next filming location and we kept walking towards Rome.

There were flooded trails for us to skirt, which required careful balancing on the edges, like on a tightrope, so we didn't slip into the puddles or mud troughs. Towards the end of the day, I had no energy to protest anymore. I just walked through it all without trying to avoid it. The mud and the puddles splashed over my boots and I didn't even grimace. One final steep climb was required up into Campagnano di Roma. A toddler could have crawled it faster than I walked. I was tired, my hip ached, and my face and body throbbed. I walked slowly and paused often, digging deep to find more energy to keep me going.

"Almost there, almost there," I chanted quietly to myself. I made it to the top of the path, past the rubbish and the graffiti. Paulius waited for me as I struggled up the hill.

"Life is good thanks to God," he said and smiled.

"Yeah," I growled as I walked past him. Although I knew he meant well, his favourite saying didn't encourage me in that moment.

We still had to walk downhill then over to the other side of the town and uphill again. Peter led the way, walking fast and ably. I lost sight of him as he rounded the corners, but Paulius stopped to make sure I could see him and knew where to turn. We arrived at the parish just as it started raining again. Out the front of the building, a few parents stood talking to the priest, who wore grey trousers and a white shirt. We followed him inside through a hall of screaming and laughing children then upstairs into our room for the night. Its everyday use was as a meeting room and it contained a number of tables that were pushed together to make a big square with twenty chairs on the outside facing in. At the back of the room were mattresses stacked on top of a table. The priest told us we could put them on the floor. I didn't care that the accommodation was so basic. I didn't want to walk any farther. I sat down on a hard plastic chair and took off my boots then lined up another two chairs and lay down.

"We will sleep on the tables," Peter said.

"Really?" I asked.

"Yes, we have slept on tables many times."

Peter dragged the mattresses off the table at the back, putting two on the tables in the middle of the room for him and Paulius. He then set up a mattress, pillow and blanket on the far table against the wall for me.

"You sleep here. You will be more comfortable," he told me.

I walked over and sat on the table's edge, but it started to tip. I grabbed a plastic chair and stepped onto it then sat in the centre of the table and lay down. I pulled a blanket over me and Peter threw an extra one on top.

"Thank you," I whispered.

I had just closed my eyes, ready for sleep to take me, when an oboe started squeaking next door. The kid must have been a complete beginner. Every note commenced with a high-pitched squeak. Every single note! The music lessons in the surrounding three rooms continued for the next two hours. Clarinets. Oboes. Saxophones. I couldn't help but laugh at our sleeping arrangements: in a meeting room, on mattresses on tables, surrounded by music lessons. Peter laughed too. At least we had heating and were out of the rain. It was pouring outside and it didn't sound like it was going to stop anytime soon.

After the music lessons ended and we had hot showers, we found our way first to the bar to use the internet and then through the rain to an *osteria* for dinner. Peter spent half of dinnertime obsessing over connecting his iPad to the wi-fi so he could Skype with a friend, only succeeding after our mains arrived. I ate tagliatelle *ragù* and saltimbocca with potatoes and drank a little red wine. We walked out into the freezing night air then back to our warm room to sleep on the tables. We were only two days away from Rome, but that night I was too sick and too tired to think about what that meant. All I hoped was that I wouldn't fall off the table while I slept.

I woke up feeling worse than I had the day before. I didn't want to walk into Rome feeling sick but there was nothing I could do about it. At least I had managed not to fall off the table during the night, although there were a couple of times when I rolled too close to the edge and the table started to tip. Instinctively, I rolled back to centre to save myself from disaster. Sleeping on a table hadn't worked well for Peter. Twenty minutes after going to bed, he got up and pulled his mattress onto the floor where he remained for the rest of the night. It was raining when we walked to the pilgrim café across the road, empty except for the barman, who was standing behind the counter and watching the small chunky television fixed on the wall. He looked over without greeting us as we walked to the back of the room to sit at a table. I took off the Devil and felt a familiar dribble of water down the back of my leg. I touched the back of my pants and the bottom of the Devil. They were both soggy. I wanted to cry. The water bladder had leaked yet again. I carried the Devil outside, pulled out the bladder and tipped what little water remained in it onto the road in angst. My fold-up water bottle would fulfil its intended purpose that day. It was 5°C at most and it would be a cold, uncomfortable walk in wet pants.

We walked four and a half hours in almost constant rain. We could have chosen to take shelter and wait for it to stop, but instead we covered up as best we could and took one step after the other. It was just rain. My cold was bearhugging me tighter and tighter. My head throbbed, my sinuses pounded, my nose dripped and my body was heavy and lethargic. The cold and flu tablets didn't help, so I took a double dose of the chunky paracetamol tablets and was grateful when the throbs and aches subsided for a few hours. The paths we travelled along were flooded and muddy. Sometimes we skirted them by walking on the raised edges of muddy grass, while other times we walked through it, stepping on the patches that looked least likely to swallow our boots.

"It's only mud, it washes off,'" I repeated my old mantra.

Too tired and sick to resist, I accepted it all—my physical state, the mud and the constant rain—and settled into a happy walking rhythm. This was my second last day of walking to Rome and I wanted to enjoy it. As we left a bar in Formello with our ponchos back on to keep off the light drizzle, a twelve-year-old boy with thick brown hair walked towards me.

"*Sei Australiana?*" he asked me and stopped in front of me.

"*Sì!*" I smiled but wrinkled my brows. I had no idea how he knew I was Australian. I had never seen him before and I couldn't remember telling anyone in the bar we had just left where I was from. The boy chatted excitedly about kangaroos and koalas. I nodded and laughed.

After my experience of crossing the three flooded streams on my way to Monteriggioni, I scanned the guidebook to identify the possibility of encountering any others. I didn't want any more surprises. I found one halfway between Formello and La Storta. The guidebook described it as potentially dangerous. Other pilgrim photos showed a steep descent from the bank and a number of square stepping stones to help with the crossing, but with so much rain over recent days, I expected the bank would be slippery and the stones would be covered by a raging torrent. I doubted I could cross safely in such conditions and I didn't want to risk walking all that way only to backtrack and add hours and kilometres to my day. I explained my concerns to Peter and Paulius.

"Is okay," Paulius said. "I will carry you on my back."

"No way! That would be dangerous too."

"I don't care. We can find another way," said Peter.

"We can take the road. It's shorter," I suggested.

"That is fine with me," said Peter.

"Okay. We walk," agreed Paulius.

With that plan, we left Formello along the Via Formellese. The road was busy with a constant stream of traffic in both directions. I don't know what clicked into place for me or why, but despite being sick, I found a strong walking rhythm, powered along by the two Rodneys and the desire to make it to La Storta quickly. Peter set off at his fastest pace and I kept up, staying only a metre behind him. There was no talking, only walking. I found that place within where I could keep going and we smashed out the ten kilometres on that road in only ninety minutes.

After passing through the centre of La Storta, we turned up a steep winding road to our chosen convent, the Istituto Palazzo Suore Povarelle. Peter pressed the intercom to the right of the heavy metal gate and I told the lady who answered that we were three pilgrims who wanted to stay the night. The gate opened automatically and we walked into the property along a brick-paved driveway lined with terracotta pots filled with pink and red geraniums. A nun wearing a habit comprising a blue-grey skirt and veil with a white shirt and navy blue cardigan walked towards us.

"*Buongiorno!*" she greeted us, smiling radiantly. "*Di dove venite?*" she asked, curious about where we came from.

"*Lituania, Australia, Danimarca,*" Peter answered pointing at each of us in turn.

"*Tutto il mondo!*" she exclaimed.

Peter and I laughed.

"*Sì, tutto il mondo!*" I agreed. We were all the world.

The nun took my left arm in her right one and led us to our accommodation, chatting away in Italian. I said *sì* frequently, although I didn't understand everything she said. We walked past a statue of the Madonna, wearing a blue-shawl and holding a baby Jesus, before descending some concrete steps and following the paved path to the front door of our dormitory.

"It's warm!" I exclaimed happily. "The heating must be on."

Our room had three bunk beds. I claimed the bed at the back, closest to the heater, but when I felt the radiator it was cold.

"Maybe it will come on later," I said, ever hopeful. It didn't, but we had an ample supply of thick woollen blankets that prickled but kept us warm.

By seven o'clock, tired of sitting in our cold room, we left in search of a bar for *aperitivi*. The only one we found had a plastic table and chairs outside with no indoor seating. We walked to a *trattoria*, where they let us sit at a table and have a drink until they opened. We enjoyed a long dinner comprised of carafes of red wine, pasta, chicken with potatoes, and cooked vegetables, followed by dessert. It was *tortino al cioccolato*, a small chocolate pudding with an oozing centre, for Paulius, while Peter and I had a type of smashed *panna cotta*. His was chocolate, mine mixed berry. We were only a few hours away from Rome, and this was our last walking night together. We saluted our journeys.

"Life is good, thanks to God," we all said in unison.

We laughed and talked and lost track of the time.

"Oh my goodness, it's almost eleven! Are we going to get back into the convent?" I asked in mild panic. The nun hadn't told us about a curfew, but I knew the hour was late for nuns. We paid our bill and rushed back. Peter pressed the intercom button on the gate and we stood waiting in the dark and the cold. After a few minutes, he rang the bell again.

"What if they don't answer? What are we going to do?" I asked.

"We will find a way in," said Paulius.

"Really? Where?" I asked. The gate and the walls were three metres high and appeared impossible to climb.

"I will find a way," insisted Paulius.

I didn't doubt he would. Peter pressed the intercom button again.

"*Pronto,*" a nun answered.

"*Très pellegrini,*" Peter told her. I added in Italian that we were sleeping there that evening.

"... *troppo tardi* ..." is all I understood of her response. Too late.

I explained in Italian that we had arrived two hours ago and had gone to eat dinner, returning just now. The intercom went silent and we waited for the gates to open. Except they didn't.

"I can't believe it. She's not letting us in. We're locked out of the convent," I said and laughed lightly.

It was funny but it wasn't. If we didn't get in, I had no idea where we would sleep. It was cold and my breath condensed on the night air in puffs when I spoke. Peter rang the bell again and after a few moments the gate opened. We walked down the paved drive to the dorm at the back. A short nun, wearing her habit and a veil that framed her wrinkled face, walked down the concrete path from their private building.

"*Scusa sorella,*" I apologised. Peter walked over to explain while Paulius and I walked to the dorm.

In the morning, we wrote notes apologising for our late

return from dinner in the pilgrim guestbook then left the convent and La Storta without eating breakfast. It was Sunday and the local bar was closed. At least it wasn't raining. Peter took the lead as we spread out along the Via Cassia. The road was quiet and we were too. Our journey was ending and we were all internally processing that in our own way. My sinuses still throbbed and my body was tired and aching. I wanted to sleep and rest, but I wanted to arrive in Rome as well.

Thirty-six—The arrival

La Storta to Roma

We walked for three kilometres on the footpath beside the Via Cassia to the next town, La Giustiniana, where we finally found an open café. We ordered our coffees and pastries and took them out to the glass-enclosed dining area. At the table in front of me, a petite old lady sat alone, sipping her cappuccino and taking dainty bites of a *cornetto* that she chewed slowly. She wore a navy blue skirt suit with matching high heel shoes, and her white hair was pulled back in a French twist. She exuded timeless grace. In comparison, I felt like a mess. I was wearing yesterday's hiking clothes and my hair was oily and scruffy beneath my pink and purple-striped beanie.

After we had eaten, we continued on the footpath beside the Via Cassia, hoping we might be able to enter the nearby nature reserve to escape the busy roadside, but as the guidebook warned, we found the gate was locked. We tried to find another entrance without success, so we continued on the footpath, passing apartment buildings, shops and Sunday worshippers as they left church. It was not a long walk into Rome, only 17 kilometres from La Storta through a suburban spread of apartments and shops, but being sick, it felt twice as long. I took more paracetamol and trudged along, focusing on one step after the other.

After a couple of hours, my energy waned and we took another break in a café, watching men and women dressed in dark suits of black, navy and grey, walk and gather on the street corner on their way home from mass. As usual, Paulius was the first to get up to leave, but for the first time I was quick to follow his lead. I left the bar feeling full and warm and with more energy as I started my final march into Rome.

We reached the River Tiber, spanned by old stone bridges, only four and a half kilometres from St Peter's Square, and walked beside it among Sunday strollers, joggers and cyclists. I caught a glimpse of the great dome of St Peter's Basilica, peeking above apartment buildings. Despite being sick, I expected that my first sighting of this would pierce my heart with exuberant joy and tears would well in my eyes as the magnitude of my journey and my final arrival in Rome became real. To my surprise, I didn't feel any great surge of emotion, just a flutter of excitement that spurred me on. We were almost there. I started walking faster.

We veered away from the river onto Viale Angelico, walking along the bike path down the middle of the road. Only one rider rode past us and we passed only one couple strolling along the path that led directly to St Peter's. I renamed it the Pilgrim Expressway. I checked our progress on the map regularly, and when were just over one kilometre away, I decided it was time to start celebrating our arrival in Rome. I played Daft Punk's 'Lose Yourself to Dance' on my iPhone and turned the volume up as loud as I could, dancing my way along the footpath. Peter joined in, but Paulius just laughed.

It was Sunday and Papa Francesco had just finished Sunday mass. A sea of people walked towards us and I danced my way among them. I didn't care if anyone stared at me or thought I was crazy. This was *my* celebration. I had walked 2020 kilometres and was arriving in Rome twelve weeks to the day since I left Canterbury. I had walked all that distance my own way and now I was arriving at my destination in my own joyful way too. The three of us weaved and dodged through the crowd, finally reaching the centre of the square. Behind the metal barrier and rows of plastic seats stood St Peter's Basilica. We had arrived. There was no fanfare. No welcome party. I didn't cry. I just stood there in a fog of sickness and tiredness, staring up at St Peter's cream and white Renaissance façade. I was looking at one of the largest and holiest churches in all of the world, trying to comprehend that we really had arrived and that I could stop walking now. It felt like last week but also a lifetime ago since I set off from Canterbury alone. Having walked that section of the path through Tuscany a couple of years earlier, I thought I knew what to expect this time around. In reality, I'd had little idea.

We three pilgrims took photos of each other and asked some tourists to take a photo of all of us together. Then we walked away from the barrier directly in front of the Basilica, where people kept gathering to take their own photos. Tired of standing, I took off the Devil and slumped down onto the travertine pavement.

"Now what?" I asked Peter and Paulius.

This journey had ended, but life went on. The Vatican office where we could obtain our final stamps in our pilgrim passports and collect our official pilgrim certificates was closed on Sunday. There was nothing else to do but find some lunch and somewhere to sleep for the next couple of nights. I was too tired and sick to spend any more energy trying to speak and understand Italian, so Peter rang a convent to ask about accommodation but he hung up without having any comprehension of what was said or if it was okay to stay. Near the River Tiber, we found an outdoor café drenched in sunshine. I sat down and slumped over the table.

"Life is good, thanks to God," Paulius said, smiling as he sat down opposite me.

"To arriving in Rome," Peter said, raising his glass of cola.

I joined in the toast with my glass of wine and then set about finding us some accommodation for the night. I announced my arrival into Rome on social media and read messages of congratulations from family and friends and people I had never met but who cheered me on along the way. My heart was full of gratitude and love, and my eyes filled with tears.

We walked along the promenade above the Tiber down to the convent in Trastevere. I lagged behind. The light was extraordinary. Everything glowed soft gold, and everywhere I looked I saw a postcard that I was walking within. We arrived at the convent, rang the intercom at the front door, waited then rang it again, waited then rang it once more. Eventually it opened and we stepped inside the courtyard where a lady with short hair, a wrinkled face and a beaming smile greeted us. Her name was Maria-Luisa and she was our volunteer hostess. We followed her inside through a maze of rooms and up two flights of stairs to a dorm room we were to share with a Frenchman who had already arrived. We showered and settled in. The Frenchman finally returned, telling us his name was Fabian and he had spent six months walking different trails from his home in Montpelier to Rome. He had stopped along the way to volunteer at many religious sites, helping with building and restoration projects, as he contemplated whether he would commence a monastic life. After all that time, he was now fluent in Italian. Fabian told us to be at the dining room for a special welcoming ceremony before dinner then he left us alone in the room to sleep.

We arrived at the dining room just before half past seven, as instructed, and sat down on the wooden stools lined up against the grey-tiled wall to wait for Maria-Luisa. She emerged from the dining room, wearing a short black cloak with a golden scalloped border, carrying a small silver bowl and jug of water. She introduced us to an American friend who spoke both Italian and English and would recite the pilgrim welcome prayer for us. Maria-Luisa then knelt down in front of me as I removed my left shoe and sock. She bathed my foot with water from the jug while the prayer was recited then she dried and kissed my bare foot. She repeated the short ceremony for Peter then Paulius. At that moment, our pilgrimages officially ended, or at least the walking part of it did. We had arrived and been received.

I passed the next few days in Rome in a shroud of sickness. We spent two nights at the convent, with Maria-Luisa fussing over us and laughing while riding her silver scooter between the kitchen and the entrance to save walking the long hallway. The radiators in our section of the convent were switched on for a few hours at night, so the rooms were warmer than in other places we had stayed. Outdoors, I was constantly cold despite the sunshine. I wore every layer of clothing I had, including fluffy socks with my canvas ballet shoes. My appearance may have offended Italian style and fashion, but I just wanted to be warm.

We returned to the Vatican on Monday morning to obtain our pilgrim certificates and presented ourselves to the Swiss guards next to St Peter's Basilica. They directed us around the colonnade to another entrance, but Peter and Paulius misunderstood their directions.

"This is the post office. It's not in here," I protested as they lead me inside.

Still, they joined a queue and I stood behind them, too tired to argue. The lady behind the counter redirected us outside and around the colonnade, giving the same directions as the Swiss guards had done. We spoke to more Swiss guards then walked through metal detectors as our bags were passed through an x-ray scanner. Inside the visitor's office, I handed over my passport and was given a security tag then we walked into the foyer of another building where we handed our pilgrim credentials to a young male clerk dressed in a smart black suit. He walked upstairs and returned ten minutes later, handing us our certificates without pomp or ceremony. We pulled our certificates out of their white envelopes and looked at them. My name was misspelled as Kim, a common error and something I often let go, but not on this occasion, after walking 2000 kilometres to get here. I handed the certificate back to the clerk. He went away and returned with a replacement one, on which my name was spelled correctly.

"Is it possible to go into St Peter's from here?" Peter asked the clerk. He was hoping we could bypass the public queues.

"No, you have to go back out and in through the main entrance, but I can take you to the crypt," he offered.

We followed him across a courtyard into another building and down into the crypt. St Peter's tomb was unreachable behind glass doors. St Peter was not the reason I walked this path, but he was but part of the reason I was there. The Via Francigena is the way on which pilgrims have travelled from Canterbury to Rome since at least the Middle Ages in order to pay homage to St Peter, here at his tomb, as well as to St Paul at his tomb in the Basilica of St Paul Outside the Walls. We stood silently for a while, each with our own thoughts, looking at the green and pink marble tomb lit by incandescent gold light. When we were ready, the clerk led us back to the other building then left us to find our own way out of the Vatican.

We lined up and passed through the security checkpoint to enter St Peter's Basilica. Once there, we walked through the giant open doors towards a sea of people. I moved forward into the beautiful gold and marble space, but my spirit pulled me back. Tourists held their cameras up, snapping photos and chatting, ignoring the signs that requested visitors respect the church as a sacred place of worship. Peter and I looked at each other, our grimaces expressing the same thing. I followed him to the prayer chapel entrance, but we lost Paulius along the way.

"We want to pray," Peter told the guard. He moved the barrier aside and let us in.

We sat down on a pew. It was a relief to be among the nuns, monks and laypeople sitting still in prayer and contemplation. I looked up at the altar then closed my eyes, thinking of my mum and about everyone who had helped me along the way: family, friends, past pilgrims and strangers. I prayed my gratitude for the journey, for the beauty, and for all the kindness shown to me. After we had concluded our prayers, Peter and I quietly left the chapel and were reunited with Paulius, who was waiting for us at the exit of the Basilica. None of us felt like visiting any tourist sites, so we walked away from the Vatican and over the river to find somewhere to eat lunch.

"Let's go to Via del Pellegrino. That sounds like the perfect street for us," I suggested after looking at my map.

The street was filled with restaurants, shops and bars.

"Best food in Rome!" said a white-aproned waiter, standing out the front of a *trattoria*.

"Of course," Peter replied with humour.

We went inside and ate pizza and pasta for lunch and drank more wine. It wasn't the best meal we had eaten, but our hunger was satisfied and we walked back along the Tiber to the convent. I was still sick and we were all tired and wanted to rest before one last dinner with Maria-Luisa.

On Wednesday morning we left the convent for the final time. Maria-Luisa took us to her favourite local café for coffees and pastries, introducing us to her barista, deli-man and the pastry chef, each of whom was *il migliore*, the best. She led the way as we walked behind the convent to the beautiful church of St Cecilia in Trastevere. Inside, Maria-Luisa pointed out the paintings, the altar and a sculpture of the martyrdom of St Cecilia, describing everything as *bellissima*. Soft light streamed in through the upper windows, spotlighting the ciborium above the altar. It was indeed beautiful. With a simple goodbye, she left us inside the church without looking back. We had already hugged and said farewell when we were at the convent, and Maria-Luisa told us that if we ever returned to Italy, we must come and stay with her in her home.

Paulius was flying back to Lithuania that afternoon. Peter had one more night in Rome, and I had two more, so I booked a hotel room in Trevi for us to share. Peter had never been to Rome before, and although we still didn't feel like being tourists, I decided he couldn't come to Rome without seeing some of the amazing city. I took the lead as we walked from Trastevere to our hotel, guiding Peter and Paulius past the Statua Equestre di Vittorio Emanuele II, the Roman Forum, the Palatine and Colosseum. We ate lunch at a *trattoria* near the hotel. It was our final meal as a trio. When we finished, we said goodbye to Paulius on the street.

"If you ever come to Lithuania, you have a place to stay," Paulius told me.

"You must come to Australia one day," I told him.

Peter and Paulius hugged.

"I don't do long goodbyes," said Peter, his blue eyes watery as he pulled away. Paulius walked towards the train station. The journey had ended and our trio was dissolving. We had come together and now we were drifting apart.

Later that afternoon, after resting in our hotel room, I took Peter to Trevi Fountain and the Spanish Steps, and we watched the sunset from the garden of Villa Medici, from where we could see St Peter's Basilica and the domes of many other cathedrals jutting up above the buildings. The horizon glowed apricot and lemon and an elongated heart-shaped cloud turned dusky pink. I experienced the first of what Peter called 'black sky', as the starlings flew in tight formation over Rome, zigzagging in black streaks beneath the rosy cloud. The next morning, it was time for Peter to go home. I walked him to Roma Termini station and kept him company until the train arrived to take him to the airport.

"Thank you. I am so glad I met you and walked into Rome with you," I told him.

"Me too," he said. "I don't do long goodbyes," he reminded me.

We hugged and we both had tears in our eyes as he pulled away. He stood at the door and waved then turned to find a seat. I walked away, with a few tears escaping down both cheeks. I was alone again. I felt out of place in my hiking clothes and was extremely cold. I walked to the closest department store but felt uncomfortable shopping among the well-groomed women and sales assistants and walked back out into the cold midday air. I wandered the streets and eventually bought a long down jacket, jeans and a red-knit jumper and changed into them back in the hotel. I felt warm and looked outwardly normal again, but inside I could not be cloaked or changed back.

For 85 days, I got up in the morning, packed and set off in the morning light, walking into unknown territory, always towards the next town, only to arrive for a while and then leave once again. It was as simple and as complex as that. In doing so, I had walked more than 2000 kilometres from Canterbury to Rome. That is how big things are accomplished, by taking little steps. I looked at the map of the path I walked and shook my head in disbelief. Had I really walked all that way? This journey exceeded anything I could have dreamed of in terms of its wonders and its challenges. I climbed the Alps and the Apennine mountains and crossed rushing streams. I weathered rain, thunderstorms and snow. I walked through copious amounts of mud. I cried. I laughed. I danced. I ate a lot of *dolce*. I walked into St Peter's Square with Peter and Paul. Yes, I really had walked from Canterbury to Rome, and in so doing I surpassed my own ideas of myself and what I am capable of.

I expected the first couple of weeks to be painful as my body adapted to walking long distances every day, carrying up to thirteen kilograms on my back, but I didn't expect to experience pain almost the whole way. It woke me during the night and forced me to walk gingerly on my feet, hunched over, when I first got out of bed and made my way slowly into each day. In the midst of this, I connected to something greater than myself, the great mystery that lives in the unknown, the Divine presence of this world. Although I noticed the pain and discomfort, I didn't allow it to consume me. If I had, I could have given in at any moment on the basis that it was all too hard and too painful. The call of the mystery was greater than the pain and I kept going. I discovered my inner strength and tenacity amid my vulnerability and consciously held these two swords of my power.

I cried a lot as I walked, sometimes because of pain and frustration, and sometimes because of the beauty and the intense freedom I experienced. For many years, I didn't understand my own highly sensitive nature in a world that hides its own tears. I thought that crying was a sign of weakness, that I cried too much and that there was something wrong with me. I believed that if I showed my feelings, I would be left vulnerable to attacks I didn't know how to defend. I now understand that our strength lies in being able to feel life deeply. Feeling is a superpower that can be used to serve and heal the world in immense ways. Our feelings of love and joy can fuel creative endeavours, while anger and injustice can fuel sacred activism and change. It is through opening to and sharing our feelings and inner worlds that we connect with others. I feel deeply and I'm no longer ashamed when I am moved to tears by watching a sunset or stumbling upon a field of purple flowers or just noticing the sunlight streaming through clouds. Allowing life to touch us deeply is what it means to be human and to be truly alive.

It was my most honest posts on my blog and social media that stirred the most heartfelt and supportive responses from those following my journey and enabled those who may never have the opportunity to undertake such a pilgrimage to experience it through me. This was important to me for many reasons: because there are many people who have disabilities like my mum's or their life situations prevent them from undertaking a journey like this; because I have been touched and changed by the journeys of those I have read about so I knew that my own journey and transformation could ripple out into the world to inspire and help others; and because I was grateful to be in a position to undertake such a journey.

As I walked, I was at the constant mercy of the weather, through heat, wind, rain, storms and even snow. I discovered that you could get sunburn walking in the rain. Although there were times I was annoyed and frustrated by the weather, I learned that I could be happy regardless of what was going on around me, especially that which I couldn't control. I stopped worrying about what others would think of me and walked into towns as a happy mess with wild hair, no makeup, looking like a lost skier, holding the Rodneys and wearing hiking clothes that were sometimes splattered with mud.

While I loved walking alone and in silence through the countryside, I also enjoyed interacting with locals when I arrived in towns. These residents are an important part of the spirit of any pilgrimage through foreign landscapes. To be a pilgrim is to be a stranger in a foreign land and the subject of curiosity. Locals want to know where you have come from, where you are going and why you are walking this way. Despite language barriers, the impetus of curiosity breaks through cultural differences and connects us as humans. For me, it offered the gift of being received for who I was, beyond my dishevelled hiker exterior and limited French and Italian, and beyond my role in society and what I did for a living. It also provided me with a deeper connection to place, because I will always remember the kind, encouraging and inquisitive human spirits who received me in each town.

Somewhere along the way, I surrendered my need to receive very clear and specific instructions about my purpose in life. I had wanted a great epiphany and indeed I received one, although it wasn't exactly what I hoped for. When I finally made it to the top of that very long hill into Siena, shuffling most of the way with excruciating hip and gluteal pain, I stopped and raised my arms in victory. Standing there, looking at the towers of Siena so small in the distance, I realised that I had walked all that friggin' way in order to learn that there is nothing I can't do. My response to this was probably predictable—*You're kidding me. That's what I needed to learn?*—but yes, that *was* what I needed to learn. That following and acting upon my heart's true yearnings might not be easy, and at times it may be really damn hard, but I had everything I needed within me to enable me to do it. It was time to stop searching and hovering in the unknown. It was time to make a decision and trust that it would be the right next step. Being unsure was a way of keeping myself safe and saying that I didn't know what I wanted to do gave me a wall to hide behind. It was time to come out from behind that wall and face the future despite my uncertainty.

Sometimes our greatest lessons come from subtle realisations. As I walked, my callings continued to flirt with me over and over again: to write, to teach, to coach. I wanted to write and create a body of work that came from my heart and felt like it was authentically infused with my truth and my unique essence. I wanted to coach and teach others to overcome their fears and walk their own unique paths in the world. I wanted to offer medicine to the world by sharing my light and inspiring others to do the same. Without knowing the specifics of what I was going to do and how I was going to do it, this felt too vague to be an answer, but I realised that this vision for my life is organic and will evolve, and that what is most important is the energy behind it, which is to infuse and serve and offer everything I have with love and joy. Like I discovered on those long and steep climbs, sometimes you have to stop looking at the big picture and just look down at your feet in order to take the next step.

My next step was to return home.

Thirty-seven—Returning home

I returned to Melbourne reluctantly. I had read that the most difficult part of returning from a pilgrimage was coming home changed and having those around you not able to accept or understand the new you. This was not so in my case. I have been blessed with a family that have supported me on all my adventures and with friends who have welcomed me back into their lives with open arms. What I struggled with most was trying to go back to an old life that I didn't want anymore. Although I was happy to see my family and friends, I wasn't overjoyed to be back. I felt guilty about that sometimes. I had met many people along the way whose dream was to visit or live in Australia, and there are others who risk their lives to come here by boat for the safety, freedom, opportunity and abundance it offers. Melbourne is a great city, but to me it is a sprawling mass of suburbia in which I feel disconnected from nature. Life makes more sense and feels better to me in wide open spaces, in mountains, forests and the sea. I longed to live in daily connection with nature, someplace where I could access these places easily without having to travel long distances and without feeling enclosed by sprawling suburbs. I didn't want to return to an office and the cycle of a working week that felt anything but natural to me now.

There is a point of no return when you start to wake up to your spirit and understand that you can't go back to your old way of being. It has been challenging for me to comprehend that I am not who I thought I was. Once I knew myself as corporate Kym, identified more with my work and career than who I truly am. Now I know myself as an adventurous free spirit. Practical Me struggles with that and is still learning to trust that security is to be found within myself rather than in external factors. I need to trust that I will always be supported when I follow my heart's dreams and to accept that my life might not always end up looking the way I think it should.

My first instinct when I came back to Melbourne was to run for my life, to be anywhere but here. Then, after accepting that I returned in order to integrate what I had learned into an ordinary life, my next instinct was to go back to everything that made me feel comfortable. But you cannot have a new life by going back to the old. I resisted the urge and spent weeks just breathing through it as best I could, crying when I needed to, retreating, watching, feeling, and inviting a new way of being to enter me. The one old comfort I allowed myself was to return to Melbourne's Royal Botanic Gardens, my little oasis of nature in the city, where waterbirds roamed near my feet and bellbirds called and replied. Curious turtles swam near to check me out, while sapphire dragonflies hovered on the grass near my bare feet. In the gardens, I relaxed and felt like I could breathe deeply once again. Then I went back to a favourite café, expecting to see familiar faces only to discover the entire staff had changed. Everything is always changing.

Returning to Melbourne, I felt certain I had answered my questions about the purpose of my life. I wanted to serve others by shining my spirit brightly and sharing my own humanness, strength and vulnerability. I intended to live uniquely and authentically and to help others do the same. As I walked the pilgrim path, the whispers and flirts told me to teach what I know and to help others. I wanted to help people find their own unique paths and step through the fears that held them back from living their dreams. Finding my own way and stepping through my own fear is what I have lived and breathed. I know the challenges and difficulties this can cause, but I also know its rewards. Living this way brings you alive, and this world needs more people living their unique dreaming. I wanted to establish myself in my own business, coaching and teaching others. Maybe I would even offer transformational experiences and lead small groups of women on the Via Francigena one day.

The whispers and flirts also told me to write. I had been writing regularly on my blog ever since my sabbatical. Writing is a natural way for me to express and share with others the way I experience life, and it brings me deep joy. I had considered freelance writing as a career option but it didn't feel right to me. There was something very specific and essential that I wanted to express in my life through my writing, and I didn't want writing to feel like work. I always loved reading travel memoirs, and after setting off on my sabbatical I dreamed of writing my own someday. When I returned to Melbourne after my relationship with David ended, I spent fifteen months writing a memoir inspired by my diving adventures, but after I finished the first draft and started to edit it, something didn't feel quite right; I wasn't telling the right story. Then I was made redundant and decided to walk Via Francigena. I wondered if this might be the right story to tell and I carried that dream with me as I walked. By the time I arrived in Rome, I knew this was the story I needed to write. It just felt right and writing it was a way that I could serve others by shining my spirit brightly and sharing my own humanness, strength and vulnerability.

I also knew that returning home gave me the opportunity to prepare to walk towards my next adventure, which was walking from Rome to Jerusalem. This was something I had never thought of until I met Peter and Paulius. They both spoke of walking to Jerusalem as their next pilgrimage, and my instant gut reaction was "Yeah, I want to do that too". It would be a longer and more arduous journey without the way-marking, guidebook and pilgrim accommodation to support it, but my spirit felt excited by this challenge of walking through new landscapes to the holy city of Jerusalem. My decision to walk was made as soon as the idea was spoken.

Not long after I returned to Melbourne, I started to doubt my realisations and callings. In a landscape that still values knowledge and the material rather than who we are in any given moment, my dream of serving others by shining my spirit brightly and living authentically didn't seem to make sense and it began to disappear as my mind filled with the static of confusion and doubt. I wasn't sure how to get started as a life coach and teacher, and the part of me that was scared to step into this work that required me to act from my heart more than my head told me over and over that I'm not qualified. Not even the intensive three-month, real-life experiential course of finding my way along a 2000 kilometre pilgrimage route was enough as far as my fear was concerned. I needed to work to earn money and pay my way. I didn't have enough savings behind me to allow enough time to get a coaching practice up and running to support myself, so I started looking for a job. I spent days trawling advertisements and coming up blank. I didn't fit the boxes anymore and I realised I didn't really want to fit them either.

For a while, I was stressed, anxious and joyless. It felt like part of me was going to die, but sometimes our challenges are just the universe showing us another way. I dug deep and reconnected to my faith that everything works out okay when I follow the calling of my heart. I reminded myself of the purpose I had chosen for my life, sometimes stating it like a mantra to give it more power, and I prioritised the actions I needed to take to live my dreams and purpose. This removed a lot of the pressure and expectation I had put on myself to do it all now. My first priority was to work and earn money to live on and save so I could walk from Rome to Jerusalem. It took a couple of months, but I secured a twelve-month contract position in financial planning at a global business only a twenty-minute drive from my home. I worked with people I really liked in an office where I could see the sky and grass and trees and still feel connected to nature. I started writing this book about my Via Francigena journey, and I completed courses to learn about setting up a business and attracting clients. I created my own website and started writing for other popular blogs, to share and teach what I had learned about following dreams, moving through fear and living with wonder, all the while building what I hoped was a launch pad into life coaching once I returned from Jerusalem. And as I did all of this, I dreamed into the possibilities of a pilgrimage from Rome to Jerusalem, speculating about which way I would walk and how long it might take me to complete the journey.

My life didn't end up looking quite the way I thought it should have post-pilgrimage. I expected to walk away from financial planning permanently and immediately launch into a coaching career. I put a lot of pressure on myself and I felt really stressed, but instead of getting caught in those feelings, I started taking all the steps I needed to live my dreams, and in doing so I began to live my purpose because it fuelled all of my actions. I also discovered that it was possible to fulfil my sense of purpose within a corporate workplace. I could see how my presence and the sharing of my stories and experiences inspired those around me. I also had the opportunity to teach about change and bringing others on that journey. By returning to corporate life, I realised that purpose is not just about a job or career. Purpose is how we live. The problem is that we so often think it is about *what* we are doing rather than *who* we are being.

As for that next pilgrimage from Rome to Jerusalem, I dreamed it, I mapped it out, I planned my life around it, and I turned up to the starting line, even though I was still recovering from a badly sprained ankle and a hip injury. Perhaps through divine intervention, my lower back seized just after I arrived at my friend's place in London, and I didn't end up walking. Instead I spent months healing and learning how to be and move in my body in a new and different way. During this time, I realised that I didn't need to walk from Rome to Jerusalem to prove anything to myself or to launch my coaching practice. What I needed was to learn some practical skills that would enable me to help others. So I enrolled to study holistic counselling and started walking directly down the path of my heart's calling.

Sometimes, the way to serve our spirits and the spirits of others is to walk the path less travelled. Whether we walk alone or with others, we make our own paths in life by making choices and taking steps that lead us in the directions of our dreams, even when the steps are muddy and difficult. The unknown path can be scary and we might want to cling to what we believe is the safety of what we know, but there is no lasting joy in safety. We have this one precious life to live, to sing our songs, to write our poems, to dance and walk our own way, and to offer our own special gifts to this world in whatever form they emerge. Often, we need to complete the first step before the next step becomes clear, but it all starts with just one step then the next step and then the next step that emerges after that. The question we must ask ourselves is when we will take that step, for if not now, then when?

End notes

1. Wikipedia contributors, "Canterbury Cathedral," *Wikipedia, The Free Encyclopedia,* https://en.wikipedia.org/wiki/Canterbury_Cathedral (accessed September 10, 2018)

2. Wikipedia contributors, "Via Francigena," Wikipedia, The Free Encyclopedia, https://en.wikipedia.org/wiki/Via_Francigena (accessed September 10, 2018)

3. Commonwealth War Graves Commission, "Sunken Road Cemetery, Boisleux-St.Marc," https://www.cwgc.org/find-a-cemetery/cemetery/28902/sunken-road-cemetery,-boisleux-st.-marc/ (accessed September 10, 2018)

4. Wikipedia contributors, "Péronne, Somme," Wikipedia, The Free Encyclopedia, https://en.wikipedia.org/wiki/Péronne,_Somme (accessed September 10, 2018)

5. Wikipedia contributors, "Certosa di Pavia," Wikipedia, The Free Encyclopedia, https://en.wikipedia.org/wiki/Certosa_di_Pavia (accessed September 10, 2018)

6. Wikipedia contributors, "Keys of Heaven," Wikipedia, The Free Encyclopedia, https://en.wikipedia.org/wiki/Keys_of_Heaven (accessed September 10, 2018)

7. Wikipedia contributors, "Piacenza," Wikipedia, The Free Encyclopedia, https://en.wikipedia.org/wiki/Piacenza (accessed September 10, 2018)

8. Wikipedia contributors, " Rocca di Federico II," Wikipedia, The Free Encyclopedia, https://it.wikipedia.org/wiki/Rocca_di_Federico_II (accessed September 10, 2018)

9. Wikipedia contributors, "San Gimignano," Wikipedia, The Free Encyclopedia, https://en.wikipedia.org/wiki/San_Gimignano#Towers (accessed September 10, 2018)

10. Wikipedia contributors, "Viterbo Papacy," Wikipedia, The Free Encyclopedia https://en.wikipedia.org/wiki/Viterbo_Papacy (accessed September 10, 2018)

Acknowledgments

I would like to express my deepest gratitude to my big, beautiful family for your never-ending love, support, encouragement and belief in me. A special thank you to Dad and Carole, Julie, Bruce, Daniel and Andrew, and Andrea and Chris. You stored my belongings, tracked my journey for safety and put a roof over my head when I returned (and shared your bathroom with me.)

To Mum, I live because you lived and I have become who I am because of everything we went through. You are always a part of my journey.

To Dad, thank you for being willing to have the hard conversations and listen, and for your unconditional love always. Thank you also for being my proof-reader.

Myree, my eternal love and gratitude for all the beautiful healing and transformation you have facilitated that has enriched and changed my life.

Jacques, your kindness, generosity and support transcended language barriers.

Peter and Paulius, thank you for sharing the journey into Rome with me as my personal apostles, for your support, kindness and instant friendship, and for sparking my desire to keep walking to Jerusalem, although I never made it there it changed the direction of my life.

For my beautiful friends, Kelli, Danny, Heather, Stephen,

Tracy, Sophie, Ina, Viv, Kate, Ursula and Peta, you opened your homes to me, you fed my belly, heart and soul, you believed in me and encouraged me.

Dijana, thank you for creating the map of my journey for this book, for all the time you dedicated to getting it just right, and for your friendship always.

Holly, thank you for inspiring me with your big, bold goal.

Joey, thank you for your friendship and your teachings that resonated, inspired me to walk and helped me keep going when things got tough.

My editors, Nicola O'Shea, and Caitilin at the Artful Words, thank you for your expertise, your kind and supportive feedback and guidance, and for helping me go deeper and make my story shine.

Donna Klajman, I'm so grateful we reconnected just as I was preparing to send this book out into the world. Your energy and passion for copywriting is infectious. Thank you for your generosity in time and spirit.

To the pilgrims that I connected with through the Via Francigena Facebook group, Yahoo Forum, blogs and books I have read, your feet that walked before me really did bless my own steps. Thank you for sharing your stories and for your support and guidance.

For my beloved Enrico, although we met after this book was written, your love, support and belief in me has helped me to soar, and to finally release this book into the world. Thank you. I love you.

About the author

Kym Wilson is a writer and holistic counsellor and coach. She helps people tap into their own intuition and wisdom so that they can courageously follow their soul's callings. Her work focuses on deep listening to the call within, navigating the barriers to change and cultivating the courage to step over edges into the wild unknown.

Kym draws upon all areas of her life, including her leadership and management experience from over 15 years in the Financial Planning industry, her own awakening and healing experience, along with her natural gifts of intuition, insight and empathy. She has completed a Bachelor of Commerce and a Diploma in Holistic Counselling.

Following the call to freedom and her passion for scuba diving, Kym travelled intuitively and lived between Melbourne and Thailand for several years. She trained as a divemaster and open water scuba instructor, blogged extensively and eventually discovered then walked the Via Francigena pilgrimage route. She currently lives in Melbourne, Australia.

Whether you cross paths in person or online, her sincere wish is that she touches your heart in some way, and leaves you feeling encouraged and inspired to live boldly.

www.kymwilson.com.au

Something extra

For a behind the scenes peak at my journey, including a video I filmed while walking the Via Francigena, and my favourite photos taken during my journey, go to:

www.kymwilson.com.au/thepathbonus

Made in the USA
Las Vegas, NV
05 November 2021